Grandparents

Grandparents

A New Look
at the
Supporting
Generation

Ursula Adler Falk and Gerhard Falk

Prometheus Books

59 John Glenn Drive
Amherst, New York 14228-2197

Published 2002 by Prometheus Books

Inquiries should be addressed to
Prometheus Books
59 John Glenn Drive
Amherst, New York 14228–2197
VOICE: 716–691–0133, ext. 207
FAX: 716–564–2711
WWW.PROMETHEUSBOOKS.COM

06 05 04 03 02   5 4 3 2 1

Library of Congress Cataloging-in-Publication Data

Falk, Ursula A.
    Grandparents : a new look at the supporting generation / Ursula Falk and Gerhard Falk.
        p. cm.
    Includes bibliographical references and index.
    ISBN 1–57392–966–2 (alk. paper)
    1. Grandparents—United States. 2. Grandparenting—United States. 3. Grandparents—History. I. Falk, Gerhard, 1924- II. Title.

HQ759.9 F36 2002
306.874'5—dc21

                                                                2002068085

Printed in the United States of America on acid-free paper

To our five amazing grandchildren—
Sophia, Lisa, Joshua, Gabrielle, and Benjamin—
with our love.

Contents

Acknowledgment

With all our love and gratitude to our son, Clifford Falk, for his unstinting patience, his many hours of assisting us with the computer, and for proofreading our manuscript.

Preface

*G**randparents: A New Look at the Supporting Generation* was written to describe and discuss the status and role of grandparents: to dispel the stereotypes and to realistically awaken the reader to the persons behind the label. It is unique in its content and approach, since no comprehensive study has been made relating to this topic. Until this writing, grandparent books have been for children and have perpetuated the myth of the benign, benevolent, loving white-haired men and women who devote their lives to young human beings: catering to them, tending to their emotions, and healing their hurts. In these books, grandparents are relegated to the status of pets, who have no needs of their own but exist to lend warmth and affection to their owners.

In contrast, this book begins with a brief history and an extensively researched review of relations between the genders as practiced in innumerable societies over the centuries. We discuss today's grandparents in the context of social change and the social forces that have created this change; we discuss longevity and life expectancy, including that which can be expected in the future. Grandmothers and grandfathers are described in separate chapters: their differences, their similarities, their roles, their characteristics, and their uniqueness. Grandparents who are in loco parentis—who step in to raise their grandchildren out of necessity—are described in detail, as are the background for these situations, the emotional forces that cause this need, and the impact—both problematic and beneficial—these forces have on children who are brought up by grandparents. Also included in this book is a discussion of the manner in which literature and the media portray grandmothers and grandfathers, exposing many common myths. The end result: an enlightened view of the role of grandparents today.

The final chapter shows grandparents as the supporting generation. They are not takers—as the stereotypes portray them—but givers in multitudinous ways. They give of themselves by babysitting, by chauffeuring little ones and teenagers, by giving them haircuts, by helping with homework, even by taking over when parents are unwilling or unable to care for them. They may extend themselves with gifts and necessities as well as money when the occasion calls for it. They work to create a better life for the younger generation and ultimately leave them their earthly goods.

Introduction

This book outlines the historical view of grandparents and the ways that view has changed during the last century. The focus is mainly on the United States, although the changes described here pertain to other industrialized nations as well.

Principally, these changes have come about as traditional farm families declined in number and importance. The rise of big government, the promotion of corporate interests, and the advent of the postindustrial age reduced the importance of grandparents and the elderly during the first part of the twentieth century. Today, however, those who are grandparents have attained a good deal of financial independence and education, so a second change in the status of grandparents has occurred during the past twenty years.

This second change is in part the product of increased longevity and a decline in fertility, all related to scientific advances. New grandparent-grandchild relationships are now evolving that reveal a more emotional and sentimental link between the generations than was in evidence when grandparents died at a much younger age. There are also many more grandchildren now who live with their grandparents than at any other time in history. This is a consequence of divorce, AIDS, and drug abuse.

Grandparents who must raise their grandchildren in the absence of the children's parents often sacrifice their own needs for those of their grandchildren. These grandparents face both financial and emotional problems, although many are happy to have their grandchildren in their home. The problems associated with raising grandchildren affect African Americans disproportionately.

All grandparents are, therefore, not the same. Ethnicity has a major impact on the status and role of grandparents. In this book we review how ethnicity affects grandparents among the Amish, Jews, and Mormons, who all incorporate a religious affinity within their culture. In addition, we show that marginal groups in American society, such as the Chinese and other Asian Americans, elevate grandparents to a higher social standing than is common in American society generally. We show how the current "postmodern" culture threatens to undermine the status of grandparents because of high mobility and the atomization of the American family by means of electronics, divorce, separation, and a low birthrate.

The media are also instrumental in affecting the status and role of grandparents in Western culture. Stereotypes of all kinds abound in the media, and grandparents are particularly affected by these messages. In researching this book, we reviewed children's literature as well as movies, television broadcasts, advertisements, short stories, novels, and humor pertaining to the grandparent role, and we found that with few exceptions, all of these media view grandparents in a negative light. This means that the representation of elderly persons in prime-time television advertising and in other media generally show disrespect for the elderly. The old are generally portrayed as incompetent, often demented, argumentative, and complaining.

Grandchildren, however, generally view their grandparents as more than merely "old people." This has come about not only because many grandparents are well educated and articulate, but also because the Kondratieff Wave (discussed in detail in chapter 8) has given these two generations common ground and common experiences.

Finally, we show that grandparents are of great help to grandchildren and to their own children; the belief that grandparents are a burden on fewer and fewer young people is negated by the reciprocal help derived by the younger generations from the generation of their grandparents.

In sum, this book makes a unique contribution to our understanding of the status and role of grandparents today, a role that will not disappear but—in altered circumstances—will always be with us.

1

Grandparents Then and Now

A Brief History

THE STATUS AND ROLE OF GRANDPARENTS

Any understanding of the status and role of grandparents in a historical context must rely on a review of the relations between the genders as practiced in innumerable societies throughout human history. It is therefore necessary to briefly examine these gender relations. Such a study must come to the inevitable conclusion that male ascendance and female submission to masculine demands were—and are—the most common method of maintaining gender relations throughout the world. We will see, however, that during the past fifty years, Americans and some Europeans have accorded women a near-equal standing with men in family life, in the economy, and in other social institutions. This has led to a considerable change in the status and role of grandparents as well, since those who are now seniors are called upon to play a role that is in concordance with these changes.

In 1929 the British anthropologist A. R. Radcliffe-Brown published a study of the Australian form of totemism. Citing the French sociologist Émile Durkheim, Radcliffe-Brown writes: "There exists a ritual relation whenever a society imposes on its members a certain attitude towards an object (person) which attitude involves some measure of respect expressed in a traditional mode of behavio(u)r with reference to that object (person)."[1]

One example of such an attitude is the manner in which most people deal with such national symbols as a flag. Another example is the manner in which those belonging to a religious group approach an object or person having a religious significance for them. A third example is the manner in which traditions in America and elsewhere deal with the old—in particular, parents and grandparents. Such a ritual attitude exists in all societies.

Durkheim was influential in teaching that a social group—such as a family, a clan, or a nation—can possess permanence or solidarity only if its members view that group with a positive sentiment of attachment. Durkheim says that "all authority is the daughter of opinion."[2] That opinion includes the commonly held view that earlier generations, particularly living grandparents, transmit family traditions, modes of expression, and family rituals that we ourselves did not invent and that are not our own work. It appears to people everywhere that these traditions, expressions, and rituals are sacred and are of great emotional importance, because they serve to identify who we are and whence we came. This is true of those who participate in religious activities as well as those who have no interest in religion. Examples of the former are easily found amid the immense number of religious rituals known in all human societies. Yet those who have no religion also participate in rituals and ceremonies of a sacred nature. Patriotic assemblies are eminently ritualistic and include flag-raising and flag-lowering ceremonies; patriotic parades on "sacred days" such as Independence Day; the use of patriotic songs; and the manner in which elected officials are addressed, such as "Your Honor," "Governor," or "Mr. President." All of this indicates that respect and an attitude of deference can be directed toward people as well as objects. Surely the manner in which the ancient Roman high priest, or *Pontifex Maximus*, was approached is only one example of how honor and respect can be conferred upon a person through the belief of others. That tradition has, of course, continued to this day as the Roman Catholic pope, still called *Pontifex Maximus*, continues in that ancient tradition. It is noteworthy that the head of the Catholic Church is called pope or *Papa*, meaning father. This, despite the fact that priests in that religion are not allowed to marry or become biological fathers. Evidently, the title "Father" evokes modalities of respect and social honor, which church officials have adopted to their benefit and the edification of their followers. The reason for this justified assumption is that the old, grandfathers and grandmothers in particular, have traditionally furnished their descendants with important attributes not available elsewhere.

In preindustrial societies universal endorsement of traditional norms and customs was assumed by all individual members of any group and were based on "the power of the collective standards of conduct."[3] In Rome and in other ancient societies, these standards of conduct were embedded in the families, which traced themselves to common ancestors. They were united not only by reason of genetics but also by common worship of household gods, whose chief "priest" was the paterfamilias. The father— and therefore the grandfather or the oldest male in such a household—was viewed as the absolute ruler of the Roman family. He alone had rights before the law. Only the oldest male could buy and sell property or make contracts. The paterfamilias had the power of life and death over his wife and children and could even sell them into slavery. Wives and children, no matter how old, were under the control of the father and were considered *mancipia*, "taken in hand." The whole family remained so unless and until the father or grandfather *emancipated* them, that is, let them "out of hand." The rights of the oldest male, then, lasted until his death, although these rights were generally mitigated by the love and affection that encompassed the ancient Roman family as much as it does modern families.

Evidently, then, this Roman patriarchy prevented women from having any privileges other than those voluntarily allowed them by their fathers, brothers, husbands, or sons. At all stages of their lives, Roman women were under the supervision of the men in their family. Women, including grandmothers, had no legal rights. No woman could appear in court, even as a witness. Widows could not claim any right to their husbands' estates, although women could inherit a limited amount of money. While the Greeks confined women to a women's quarter in the house called *gynaceum* or gymnasium, Roman women were allowed to eat with their husbands and other male members of the household. Thus, the Roman family consisted of the dominant grandfather, the subservient grandmother, their married children, and their grandchildren who were "an assembly of owned persons and things subject to the oldest male."[4]

Likewise, the ancient Hebrew family and its later manifestation, the medieval Jewish family, was also patriarchal. A brief excursion through the Torah or the Five Books of Moses reveals the dominance of the most senior man in the Hebrew family. First we find, in Exod. 21:7–11, an indication that men alone decided the fate of women. The personal property of women was managed by their husbands. Marriages were arranged by the fathers of the prospective spouses, a practice continued in Jewish families well into the twentieth century, as portrayed in *Fiddler on the Roof*. In *Life Is with People*, a detailed anthropology of the Eastern European Jewish community, Elizabeth Herzog and Mark Zborowski portray the lives of these Jews until the Second World War. Here, we again see the total dominance of men over their women. Because biblical law did not take women's wishes into consideration, it is no surprise that later Jewish custom also ignored the wishes of women. In medieval Europe, Jewish marriages were arranged by fathers, and "few girls were indelicate or impudent enough to express their own fancies or preference."[5] In fact, a father could give his daughter in marriage as early as age six, although such child marriages were not consummated until maturity. Marriage among the medieval Jews was patriarchal and patrilineal—although matrilocal. This meant that, in most cases, newlywed couples lived in the home of the bride's parents. There, "the authority of the oldest father (grandfather) in the home was almost as absolute as it was in republican Rome. He (the father and grandfather) could excommunicate his children and beat his wife. Each morning Jewish men assembled for prayer and thanked God that they were not born as women." In the medieval synagogue (Greek = Assembly) women occupied a separate space in the gallery or behind men, segregated by a curtain. Such arrangements can still be seen in orthodox American synagogues today. While husbands among the medieval Jews were the sole heirs of their wives, women could not inherit from their husbands. Instead, their sons inherited their fathers' property and were charged with supporting their mothers from then on. Daughters inherited only in the absence of sons. Therefore they had to depend on their own husbands or brotherly affection.

Because scholarship within the confines of religious teachings was the most prestigious work a man could do, the most learned men in the Jewish community were generally the oldest men, that is, grandfathers. Women received no formal education among the medieval Jews, a practice that continued well into the twentieth century in Europe. Consequently, fathers and grandfathers were revered not only as heads of families but also as scholars. That reverence was so great that a son stood in his father's presence until asked to sit. Because boys were circumcised and dedicated to the service of God through the covenant with Abraham, every family strove to have at least one rabbi in the family.[6]

This wish to dedicate at least one boy to the rabbinate was enhanced by the otherworldly orientation of the Eastern European Jewish family. This otherworldly orientation was necessitated by the brutal conditions under which the Jewish communities of Europe had to exist in Christian Europe. Despised as "Christ killers," Jews survived by drawing a sharp distinction between the real world and their own religion-inspired world, which outsiders could not enter and where the rules of the cruel Christian world did not exist. In this exclusive Jewish world, male Jewish scholars were so honored that a woman would work to support an ever-studying husband. That custom still exists among some American Jews living in Hasidic enclaves in New York City and elsewhere.[7] In sum, these arrangements favored men and permitted the oldest man in any family a level of ascendancy similar to that found in almost all human cultures all over the world.[8]

As in the Roman family, ancient, medieval, and early-twentieth-century Jewish families did not permit women to compete with men for social honors or income. It was only with the immigration to America beginning in the late nineteenth century that these customs changed dramatically in both Europe and the United States. It is important to note, however, that when the European Jewish community was slaughtered by its Christian neighbors in the early 1940s, many families still adhered to those patriarchal mores.

Hindu families, although far removed from these Roman and Jewish models, nevertheless exhibit the same patriarchal forms. "The duty of a chaste and faithful wife who is religiously devoted to her husband is to serve him as she would a god."[9] Most extreme was the custom of *sati*, which demanded that a faithful wife burn herself to death on her deceased husband's funeral pyre. This custom was derived from an earlier practice of cremating widows, which was continued into the nineteenth century in the province of Bengal.

Everyday life among the people of India has historically been marked by avoidance and separation of the sexes. Both Hindu and Muslim women in India wore veils, a practice continued in Iran and Afghanistan today. This practice, known as *parda,* serves to protect women from the world of men, although the poor could not practice *parda*, as poor women have to work in physical farm labor alongside men. In all Hindu families, however, girls are taught the values of submission that will make them docile daughters and daughters-in-law and good wives. Sons, in contrast, are taught the patriarchal traditions so common everywhere. "The Hindu family was (and is) typically patriarchal with the father full master of his wife, his children and his slaves." Woman is considered an inferior being. Hindu law requires that, throughout her life, a Hindu woman should obey her father, her husband, and finally her son. Wives in traditional Hindu society address their husbands as "master," "lord," and even "my god." In public, Hindu wives walk some distance behind their husbands. Women are required to prepare all meals for their husbands and sons, who eat first. The women then eat the leftovers.

Like women in Europe and America before the twentieth century, Indian women received an education only if they were of the highest social class. Only men studied the *Vedas*, the Hindu scriptures. Women's earnings became the property of their husbands, who could divorce their wives— although women could never divorce their husbands. Some reverence was nevertheless shown mothers and grandmothers, as expressed in the code of Manu, which holds that "the mother exceeds a thousand fathers in the right to reverence." Despite this, widows among the Hindus even today remain unmarried, in the care of their children. Again, we find that this custom is not practiced among the poor, who need to remarry and work to survive.[10]

Muslim women were and still are generally as impotent as others already discussed. According to the Qur'an, the Muslim scriptures, woman is subordinate to man. Muslims are taught that God created woman from a fragment of man's body, a story similar to the biblical legend of Adam and Eve. This legend holds that women were created to serve men, a view entirely in accord with Muslim religious law. Female disadvantages among Muslims can be seen in many ways. For example, two female witnesses are required in a court of law, although only one male witness suffices. According to Muslim law, a woman can neither initiate a marriage nor present a gift to her husband's family. A man, according to Muslim religious law, can divorce a woman by simply repudiating her, but a woman cannot divorce a man. Polygamy was and still is practiced in Islam. This does not mean, however, that all Muslim men have several wives, as such a practice is very expensive and therefore only feasible for the rich. Nevertheless, polygamy implies the reduction of female status to that of a sycophant.[11]

Education in Muslim societies has historically been limited to males. Today, this practice varies between various cultures. Thus, in Afghanistan and Iran, women are provided no education beyond what is needed to perform some religious duties. Marriages in those and other Muslim countries are arranged by fathers. Women are held in "sacred subjection" in these marriages, while their value is determined by their fertility. The opinion Muslim men generally hold with regard to women is illustrated by the proverb: "Consult women and do the contrary of what they advise." Because the Muslim family was and still is usually a clan, the oldest male holds the greatest prestige and power, as already seen in the cultures previously discussed.[12]

The Japanese family furnishes us with yet another example of the power of the oldest male—usually the grandfather—over his family. According to the Meiji Civil Code, the head of each Japanese family was the oldest male, who had authority over all its members. His consent was required for the marriage of any men under the age of thirty and for women under the age of twenty-five. (The age of consent was younger for women because women were thought to mature earlier than men.) The male head of the household could also secure the annulment of a marriage. Fathers had final authority over their children, an authority in which mothers and wives did not share. Even today, wives in Japan have no right to demand a divorce. Furthermore, the property of a woman was to be administered by her husband. This means that a Japanese woman was (and is) entirely subject to decisions made by her husband.

In 1948 the government of Japan adopted a new civil code, which granted women more rights than were previously allowed. In practice, however, this has led to few improvements in the status of Japanese women.[13]

If we were to list the power relations between the genders in all the cultures of the world, we would find that only in the twentieth century— and only in America and some Western European countries—have these relations changed somewhat. Because we seek to discuss American grandparents, we shall focus next on the history of gender relations in the United States.

THE HISTORY OF GENDER RELATIONS
IN THE UNITED STATES

Because New England was first settled by Puritans with most decided prejudices concerning human relations, it is not surprising that gender relations in the New England colonies resembled those of England, whence the Puritans had come. We have already established, however, that all societies organize gender relations on the basis of senior male dominance, so that any population arriving in this hemisphere would have lived by a gender code similar to that practiced by the English settlers of Massachusetts. This has proved to be true throughout the nation's history, as immigrants from all over the world have come here. Whether we look at the Germans who came to Pennsylvania in the early eighteenth century or the Vietnamese who are arriving at the beginning of the twenty-first century, all bring with them families dominated by old men. Yet a look at the American family today reveals no such pattern. On the contrary, the present-day American family is largely a nuclear family consisting of a father, a mother, and their children. Furthermore, the present American family is frequently headed by a single female, and in a few cases by a single male, and divorce and desertion have become so common in America that paternal authority as it was once known even in this country has been greatly reduced, if not obliterated altogether.

The changes in gender and age relations that have produced the current American family came about gradually. In the seventeenth century colonies of New England, women were generally reduced to breeding boxes for enormous families, often including more than ten children. Old women no longer capable of producing children were eliminated from active participation in communal affairs by accusations of witchcraft. It was, of course, not necessary to accuse everyone. It sufficed that a few of those so accused were drowned or hanged to convince other women to keep quiet and express no views or opinions.

Disdain for the old and fear of aging are by no means new feelings, despite the authority the old imposed on the young in earlier centuries. This display of authority by the old over the young was possible because old men controlled the land, which was the only material resource available to the vast majority of Americans before the First World War.

In all nonindustrial societies, ownership of land is a privilege that comes with age. In such societies, old men have the power to transfer land and livestock. Young men acquire their wealth from their fathers or grandfathers—who may retain control into their old age and even until death. The young are therefore dependent on the old for their livelihood. The old, in such societies, are also capable of giving lavishly to charities of all kinds, which the young cannot do. This, in turn, enhances the power and prestige of the old in the community. Sons, daughters, and in-laws are also a source of labor in agricultural clans. Old men in agricultural societies are also the beneficiaries of human resources in that they can command the loyalty of many adult children and grandchildren. Such large families and their friends and associates in turn provide the old men with political power. In preindustrial societies, old age is held in esteem ipso facto, so old men usually have access to roles that bring them respect and social honor. All this accrues to the benefit of grandfathers more than it does to grandmothers. The old men can therefore assume leadership roles in their community based mainly on knowledge and experience that are available to the old by virtue of longevity alone.[14]

It is, of course, true that the word "old" is relative: Someone fifty years old was indeed "old" as late as 1890, when only 60 percent of Americans were expected to live that long. A century earlier hardly anyone lived past age sixty, so the "old" were few from the viewpoint of a twenty-first-century American. But whatever definition may attach to the word "old," that label has for centuries aroused hostility. The accusation of witchcraft was, in this regard, therefore an expression of the hostility—or at least ambivalence—felt by the young toward the old. The source of that hostility was, first, the resentment the young felt at the domination by the old. In patriarchal societies the young find their subordination to the old and powerful both grating and disgusting. That subordination arouses anger, and accusations such as those of witchcraft serve to relieve this tension—even though they were directed at old women more than at old men.

A more important source of hostility toward old women was the obligation of distant relatives to support old women financially at a time when women could not work outside the home and could not support themselves. In the seventeenth and eighteenth centuries—and even in this century—there were those who resented the obligation to support others, particularly the old. Accusations of witchcraft relieved the need to continue such support. This was most important before the rise of the nuclear family when "kin" were obliged to do for distant relatives what government programs would do today.[15]

The anthropologist Philip Mayer notes that social pressure demands that the young feel toward the old what they cannot feel, which leads to such accusations. Mayer writes: "The demand for a positive sentiment—and the inability to provide it—are equally essential to the picture of witches and their accusers. Painful tension arises because one individual cannot feel towards another as society expects him to feel. . . . If, in fact, one cannot get on well with him or her, the situation may become tense."[16]

Because expressions of hostility or physical violence against the old are considered an offense everywhere, witchcraft accusations served the purpose of expressing hostility—or even killing the old—by placing the deed into the hands of the community and thus avoiding personal responsibility.

Witchcraft accusations may be passé in twenty-first-century America, but intergenerational hostility is not. Nevertheless, as the kinship family declined, accusations of witchcraft also declined, since the need to care for distant relatives diminished and is almost unknown today.

The "old" population of the United States has, of course, grown considerably since witchcraft lost its appeal in the eighteenth century. Thus, in 1900, only 4 percent of the population—or 3 million Americans—were over sixty-five years old. In 1940 that number had grown to 6.8 percent, and it was 9.2 percent in 1960. In 1980 more than 11 percent of Americans were over sixty-five years old. Currently, 13 percent of Americans are past the traditional retirement age.[17]

As longevity increased, kinship decreased. The evidence for the decline in kinship may be seen in several ways. For example, the belief that relatives are responsible for the crimes of a member of their "clan" is unheard of in America today. Yet the famous feud between the Hatfields and the McCoys is legendary in Kentucky. During the second half of the nineteenth century, collective kin responsibility satisfied the vendetta mentality, which was satisfied with the killing of the criminal's brother or father, uncle or nephew. Yet by the beginning of the twentieth century that custom had died out.[18]

The decline in kinship can also be seen in the decline in nepotism practiced in the recruitment and advancement of American political officeholders. However, money came to be substituted for kinship as the country entered the nineteenth century. For example, the Revolutionary War and the Civil War were first fought by volunteers who were related to one another and who recruited one another from among brothers and cousins. It was only at the end of the Civil War that a draft was instituted by the Union government. Yet even then, a draftee could pay someone to take his place if he did not wish to fight. This had become quite impossible by World War II, when the military relied entirely on the draft to build a fighting force of 13 million.[19]

A third indication of the decline of kinship in American society has been an increasing government responsibility for the support of the unemployed, the poor, the old, the disabled, and dependent children. The Social Security Act and its later amendments testifies to the decline in kinship as Americans moved away from home, away from their families, and into the nuclear family. Prior to the First World War, the majority of Americans were still living on farms. After the war America became an industrial country and the farm population became smaller and smaller. Now, only 1.8 percent of all Americans live on farms, so the earlier farming clans hardly exist here any more.

A fourth area in which the decline of kinship can be seen is in education. There was a time when the extended family taught a child all he needed to know on the farm. Indeed, there were one-room schoolhouses that taught "readin', writin' and 'rithmetic." With the increasing complexity of industrial life, however, extended schooling became mandatory in all states by the end of the First World War, and the extended family no longer participated in the education of children except to back up teachers.

As industrialization progressed, more and more functions of the family became the responsibility of the state, supported by taxes. All this made the family less important and in particular reduced the need for extended family members such as grandparents. The immense mobility of the American family gave kinship its final blow, as millions of children now live far away from their grandparents, whom they see only on special occasions.

It would seem, therefore, that grandparents have lost their function and are no more than ceremonial objects to be trotted out on Christmas, Easter, or other holidays for picture-taking occasions.

Until the 1950s that was indeed the case. However, after the 1950s things changed so dramatically in American social life that the role of grandparents also changed from that of occasional visitor to that of backup parent to the millions of children born to single mothers each year.

These developments came gradually and were at first accompanied by the maintenance of the patriarchy that had existed in this country since colonial times. Since loyalty to the clan or kin was declining, loyalty to the state and the immediate family took its place. This was well understood by Wilhelm Reich, a psychoanalyst and student of Freud, who wrote about the European family: "[I]n the figure of the father the (authoritarian) state has its representative in every family so that the family becomes the most important instrument of power."[20] This was true in the United States as well, although the U.S. government is based on a democracy. An examination of the American family through the first half of the twentieth century will reveal this trend.[21]

THE NUCLEAR FAMILY

The nuclear family is one in which the married couple resides with their children. Such families are as much the product of economic conditions as were the extended families of earlier years. In Western civilization, then, the nuclear family owes its existence to industrialization. The family was no longer an economic unit once paid labor came to dominate the economic scene in this country. Domestic production was no longer featured after the First World War; instead, cash became the dominant source of income for American families, who depended thereafter on the family wage earner for support. That wage earner was almost always a man, generally the father of the children in the house, whose wife stayed home and took care of household chores and children. In fact, the status of men in these arrangements depended on having a wife who could stay home because he earned enough to support everyone in the household. This, then, kept women dependent on men for their survival even as the workplace shifted from the home to factories and offices.[22]

The nuclear family is, of course, well adapted to the pressures of industrialism. This is so because industrialism demands horizontal and physical mobility so that a workforce is available wherever new factories or businesses are built. This tells us that younger people in an industrial society are likely to leave the parental community and move to wherever economic opportunities are available. Because of this, the nuclear family cuts its ties to the extended family network, leaving the old behind. This trend began with laboring families in earlier decades, but is very common among business and professional groups today.

Industrial societies also permit workers to attain higher social class positions than can be achieved by the traditional extended family. Many of those who move from their family community to other parts of the country do so because they can gain social honor and prestige by making such a move. Such moves isolate the nuclear family and make it dependent on others with similar ambitions and backgrounds. Those who move a great deal for the sake of improving their social class position see very little of their parental families, who become the "old folks" for their mobile children in the next generation. Hence, the position of grandparents in the highly mobile twenty-first-century American society is indeed ephemeral and tenuous.

It is evident that inheritance in the nuclear family is no longer dependent on land. Since this country has only about 5 million farmers, inheritance no longer depends on the oldest male landowner, but on the largesse of both parents. Inheritance is now passed down through both sides of the family. Therefore, women as well as men preside over wealth, which they may distribute to the next generation as they see fit. This is particularly true of those women who are now employed in business, industry, and the professions, who no longer depend on support from male providers.[23]

The position of grandparents in this new family scenario is best understood if we consider the changes in household size throughout American history. In 1790, when the first census was taken, the American household had an average of 5.8 members, with many households much larger than that. These households almost always included grandparents, although life expectancy was quite short. In 1890 the average household size in the United States had fallen to 4.9, and in 1990 it was only 2.6 persons. These figures should not, however, be confused with family size, because many households include people who are not related. Hence, the average family size in 2000 was 3.19, reflecting the fact that the vast majority of married American couples now have only one or two children.[24]

The second reason for the decline in household size in America is the sharp decline of households that include aging parents living with grown children and their families. In 1900, 60 percent of aging parents lived with their grown children. Now, only 10 percent of aging parents live with their grown children. There are a number of reasons for this development. One of these is the self-centered attitude the drive for money, power, and prestige has created among many people, who see old people as a burden hindering their ambitions. Yet the same increase in wealth that leads some to cast off their elders has also made these same elders more independent of their grown children. There was a time when "old" and "poor" were nearly synonymous. As late as 1970, 24.6 percent of the elderly were living in poverty. In 1994 that rate had fallen to 11.7 percent, and in 1999 it was 9.7 percent.[25]

Third, as the population of the United States has aged, nursing homes have proliferated, separating the old from the families of their adult children. The use of nursing homes to house the old has increased in part because of the immense increase in life expectancy in this country during the past century. Thus, in 1900 life expectancy for men was only forty-eight years at birth and twenty-seven years at age forty. So a forty-year-old American man was likely to live only to age sixty-seven at that time. A forty-year-old woman in 1900 could expect to live only to age sixty-nine. Now, the life expectancy of a forty-year-old man is seventy-six, while a forty-year-old woman may expect to reach age eighty-one. To meet the needs of an increasing elderly population, there are twenty-one thousand nursing homes in the United States today. These nursing homes house 1.8 million people, mostly women, including seventy-two thousand people who have reached the age of one hundred.[26]

A fourth reason for the decline in family size is the ever-increasing divorce rate. Divorce not only affects those directly involved, but it also impacts the parents of the divorced, who thereafter have to contend with difficulties surrounding their grandchildren and the pain contentious divorced couples sometimes impose on them.

In many cases, this affects the rights of grandparents, who are often refused visitation of their grandchildren by one of the divorced parents, who include the grandparents in their antagonism for the erstwhile spouse. The two areas of concern to grandparents in these situations are visitation and custody.

These issues have become more important as the divorce rate in the United States has reached the 50 percent mark, meaning that there is one divorce for every two marriages on any one day in this country. This does not as yet mean that one-half of all people who were ever married are now divorced, because the divorce rate was so much lower prior to 1980. But this high rate of divorce affects grandparents, because there are now many senior citizens who are divorced and are therefore living alone. Since 1970 the proportion of men over sixty-five who are living alone has doubled from 11 percent to 22 percent. The number of women over sixty-five who are living alone has increased from 36 percent in 1970 to 52 percent in 1999. Hence, 2.2 million men and nearly 10 million women over the age of sixty-five now live alone in this country. No better evidence for the isolation of the old from their families can be exhibited than the condition of these 12 million.

For those who are now more than seventy years old, the most important events in their lives were the Great Depression of 1929 to 1940 and the Second World War, which followed directly thereafter. The consequences of these important, defining events in their lives left them with attitudes that even a lifetime cannot erase. Even those who were children during the depression fear suffering such great losses to this day. Many have accumulated real estate in the belief that if such a depression should come again they will be able to live off the land. It was also a mark of the depression that the millions who lost their jobs blamed themselves for this loss, viewing themselves as "failures." That belief was the product of the Puritan ethic that still dominated public opinion in the 1930s and is by no means dead in the twenty-first century. Even today, those who view themselves as "losers" in American life believe that they are guilty and that it is their fault. Those who remember the 1930s also remember that all predictions concerning the economy by the bankers and government officials of the time proved false and unreliable, and that these moneyed icons of American society "hadn't the foggiest notion."[27]

There are, of course, more survivors of the Second World War alive today than there are survivors of the Great Depression. For them, the battles of that war—the horror of death, dismemberment, and seemingly endless frontline misery—left indelible marks on their lives. Chronicled in thousands of books, movies, and television dramas, and shown almost every day on the History Channel, these events are kept alive not only by the veterans of that era but by a seemingly unending public interest in that great war. There are still grandfathers today who can tell their grandchildren and great-grandchildren about the attack on Pearl Harbor by the Japanese in 1941. There are even now veterans of the American defeat at Corregidor in the Philippines and the North African campaign against the German Afrika Corps. There are veterans among today's grandfathers who remember the Atlantic convoys to Russia and the fighting in the Pacific islands. There are grandfathers who cannot forget the landing in Sicily and the final fight for the liberation of Europe, and the atomic bombing of Japan. In fact, many grandfathers today can tell stories such as will never be experienced again by any generation, if we can keep the peace.

One of the consequences of the Second World War was the great increase in educational opportunities for the generation who fought it. These are mostly men who were born between 1920 and 1925 and who were drafted into the service between 1941 and 1945. Those who entered an institution of higher education directly after the Second World War because of the Servicemen's Readjustment Act, also known as the "G.I. Bill of Rights," increased the number of college graduates dramatically. In 1940, when the census reported a population of 131,669,275 in the United States, American colleges conferred 105,000 bachelor's degrees on men and 95,000 bachelor's degrees on women. In 1949–1950, 210,000 men and 100,000 women attained such degrees. This meant that there was a 100 percent increase in the number of men attaining a college education between 1940 and 1949. The census of 1950 revealed that there were then 150,697,361 Americans. This constituted a population increase of 13 percent, far less than the increase in the college educated. For both men and women, the increase in numbers attaining a higher education has continued since then, although by 2000 the number of degrees attained by men has held steady at about 530,000 for the past twenty years, while more than 650,000 women now earn bachelor's degrees every year. In any event, when we consider that in 1920 only about 30,000 men and 20,000 women earned college degrees—at a time when the population of the United States was 105,710,620—it is evident that the generation who are now grandparents are better educated than any other generation of American grandparents before them.[28]

AGEISM AND CHANGING ATTITUDES

Societies around the world vary with respect to their treatment of grandparents. As we have already seen, in many societies now and in earlier years, grandparents were promoted to positions of leadership on the grounds of age alone. Retirement at a specific age is unknown in most societies outside the industrialized world. In this country, as we know, the elderly had a good deal of prestige in colonial America, where people wore powdered white wigs to look older. Since only 2 percent of Americans lived to the age of sixty-five at the first census in 1790, old age was viewed as a special gift from God, and hence greatly honored as a sign of "election."[29]

A mandatory retirement age was utterly unknown in early America and was most uncommon until the end of the nineteenth century. It was the great increase in the number of older people that led to mandatory retirement from industrial employment. Unlike farm employment, which was a family enterprise, industrial employment rejected the old—who were, in fact, the farm owners and family leaders in an earlier agricultural age. Hence, as longevity increased, grandparents became more common in families, and as grandparents were isolated from the daily life of the family and were often poorer than their children, they became the targets of ageism.

Ageism has a number of dimensions. One of these indicators is the manner in which grandparents are often addressed. Such endearments as "little old lady," "old hag," or "old mare" imply that the grandparent is devalued and is viewed as having no characteristics other than age. Such ageism targets women more than men because older women are generally poorer than their male counterparts. We have seen that large numbers of men entered colleges directly after the Second World War, but women went to college in increasing numbers much later than men. Therefore, in the present generation of grandparents, grandfathers have a good deal more money and more adequate pensions than do grandmothers. A brief overview of occupations indicates at once that women in this country were, and still are, located predominantly in the lower-paying occupations. For example, 99 percent of child care workers and 99 percent of secretaries are women. Women comprise 97 percent of dental assistants, early childhood teachers, receptionists, and private household workers. Ninety-seven percent of typists, teaching assistants, and licensed practical nurses are also women. Obviously, women earn a good deal less than men; hence, grandmothers are generally poorer than grandfathers. In fact, during the 1990s the median income for American men was $31,000, while the median income for women was only $22,000—71 percent of that of men.[30]

In 2001 only fifty of the approximately twenty-five hundred best-paid corporate officers in the United States were women. These women earned an average of only about $248,000 per year while men in the same positions earned millions.

In that same year, 77 percent of physicians were male, and 75 percent of lawyers and college professors were men. Dentists were overwhelmingly male—81 percent—and 88 percent of scientists, such as physicists and geologists, were men. Fully 88 percent of the highest-paid chief executive officers of American corporations are men.

In short, even now, years after gender equality first became a major economic issue in the United States, women lag far behind men in holding lucrative occupations.

Because the elderly are believed to be helpless and, in fact, generally imbeciles, the old are frequently associated with children in American perception. Hence, Grandpa is portrayed in television commercials as playing with grandchildren—or advertising lemonade that, the grandfather claims, tastes as good now as it did when he was young.

There are some grandparents who are indeed possessed of considerable productivity and talent. These are a small minority, because creative achievement is also rare among middle-aged and young people. Productivity and true inventiveness are rare at any age, yet whenever an old person turns out to be an achiever of great competence, the media present that person as a "miracle," an "unbelievable" exception. It is ageism and the negative stereotypes it produces that lead to great astonishment just because Grandpa wrote another book and Grandma works as a doctor in private practice twelve hours a day. So entrenched is ageism that the old who continue to work are endlessly harassed and asked, "When are you going to retire?" In short, there are many who cannot tolerate the sight of an older person working, supporting himself, and showing no sign of weakness and/or illness.

It is now anticipated that between 2010 and 2030 the growth rate of the elderly population in the United States will be 2.8 percent. During that period, the "baby boom" generation will reach sixty-five years. This means that while there were 3.1 million "old" Americans in 1900, there were 33.9 million in 1996, and there will be 69.4 million "old" Americans in 2030. If all of these people were to retire promptly at sixty-five, the cost of such retirement would be so great that those working could hardly support the pension payments, including Social Security, that such a financial outlay would require. It is for that reason that Congress raised the minimum age for collection of old-age benefits under Social Security to age sixty-seven beginning in 2000.[31]

Proof that the status of grandparents in America is culturally influenced—not the product of physical disability or mental degeneration—is the position of Japanese grandparents, who live in an entirely different culture. In Japanese culture, the relatively high status of Japanese grandparents is maintained by a tradition of respect for the aged. The origin of this tradition lies in the vertical social structure of Japan coupled with filial piety. These twin pillars of honor require that all young people respect all older people, and that children, whatever their age, honor their own parents and grandparents. These mores of interaction are, in turn, a reflection of the entire Japanese social structure, which is not based on the principle of equality but on the view that there is a hierarchy of superiors and inferiors in any interpersonal relationship. The Japanese therefore maintain a strict ranking between parents and children, between teachers and students, between friends and colleagues. That ranking is almost always based on seniority. All of this is further augmented and solidified by ancestor worship in the Confucian tradition, to the effect that the happiness of the living depends on the respect they show the dead. It should be noted, however, that at the end of the twentieth century, Japan has seen some major changes, which threaten to undermine these traditions in the same fashion as the changes seen in the United States following the American Revolution and most assuredly after 1830. From then on, the status of the grandparent generation declined. The idea of equality became a major force in America after the election of Andrew Jackson to the presidency in 1828, at which time the concept of equality called into question the hierarchies of sex, race, and age. Consequently, the position of the old was totally reversed in this country. Preferential seating was abolished, mandatory retirement ages appeared, youthful fashions were preferred, and eldest sons lost their inheritance advantages.[32]

Over the past hundred years, attitudes toward grandparents have changed dramatically. Grandparents are no longer revered or valued as they were in colonial times. Economic dislocation, mainly during the Great Depression, led to the atomization of the family, as the money grandparents had saved vanished and with it the independence grandparents had hoped to maintain during their retirement.

The concept of liberty also changed in America in the twentieth century. This concept reduced the authority of grandparents by destroying the communal ties of grandparents to their families, towns, and religious affiliations. The growth of individualism loosened the obligations between age groups and fostered "a spirit of social atomism."[33]

In America, individuals are rewarded on the basis of their economic utility. Therefore, the limited access of grandparents to employment is particularly important in reducing the social prestige of grandparents in an "achieving society."[34]

SUMMARY

Respect for elders is universal in human culture and is derived from religious and other traditional sources. Almost all societies around the world are and have historically been patriarchal and hierarchal. This was true in ancient Rome, Israel, Greece, and India and was taught in Jewish, Christian, Muslim, and Hindu societies.

In North America during the ascendancy of the Puritans of the seventeenth century similar beliefs were enforced. Then, and for centuries thereafter, land was the only wealth, and inheritance was passed through the eldest males in each family. Knowledge came from experience, not from school. However, the traditional kinship family declined with the advent of technology, as can be seen in the end of blood feuds, the decline of nepotism, the rise in government responsibility, the transfer of education responsibilities to government, and the high mobility of American families. As the nuclear family relinquished the land, wages paid in cash became the source of wealth and high mobility cut the ties between generations. The old, who were left behind in the rush for success, were at first left poor and relatively helpless. They also became the targets of ageism.

It was the Second World War and the resulting increase in the number of people earning college degrees that led to an increase in income for many in the older generation, whose numbers have increased steadily over the past one hundred years. Ageism has now become commonplace in the United States as the lives of present-day grandparents in America have been changed immensely. The present condition of American grandparents will therefore be the topic of our next chapter.

2

Grandparents Today

Social Forces and Social Change

LONGEVITY AND THE CHARACTERISTICS OF GRANDPARENTS

The number of grandparents in America is determined by at least two demographic conditions: longevity and fertility. While longevity has increased in the past century, fertility has decreased. But the increase in life expectancy of the American population is not homogeneous. Important gender and race differences in longevity and fertility have existed in this country throughout our history, and still exist today. Historically, life expectancy in the United States has favored women and whites. For example, in 1950 a white male child could expect to live 66.5 years, and a white female newborn could expect to live 72.2 years. A black male child born in 1950 could expect to live only 58.9 years, and a black female child could expect to live 62.7 years. In 1997 a white male could expect to live until he was 74.3 years old, while a black male could expect to live only 67.3 years. Because women live longer than men, a sixty-year-old woman in 2000 could expect to reach age eighty-five, while a seventy-year-old man could expect to live only twelve more years. At present, life expectancy at birth is approximately seventy-seven years for both sexes and all races. For women, life expectancy is nearing eighty, although it is somewhat less for black women than for white women. Those who are fifty years old can expect to live another twenty-nine to thirty years, while those aged seventy can now expect to live another fourteen years, regardless of gender.

Compared to earlier years in American experience, these life expectancies are indeed considerable. In 1970 overall life expectancy was only 70.8 years; in 1960 it was 69.7 years; in 1950, 68.2 years; and in 1940, 62.9 years. This means that life expectancy increased by 18 percent in the past sixty years.[1]

Consequently, a large number of Americans reach an age at which they can look forward to becoming grandparents, their fertility and that of their children permitting. Accordingly, the number of children born to American mothers has a vital impact on one's chances of becoming a grandparent. That number reached a little more than 4 million annual births in 1990, then declined to 3,915,000 in 1991 and beyond. Because of this fertility and longevity, most of today's grandchildren have all or most of their grandparents alive during a good part of their childhood and adolescence, and many will have grandparents well into their adult years. Currently, more than one-third of all children have all of their grandparents living until they are ten years old, and three-quarters of all Americans have at least one grandparent alive when they themselves are thirty years old.[2]

The baby boom of the 1950s led to the birth of twenty-four to twenty-five children for every thousand in the population. That meant that very few older adults with grown-up children did not have grandchildren. However, the current decline in the birthrate is such that for every thousand in the population, there were only 14.6 children born in 1998 and in each of the previous five years. Therefore, a much larger number of senior citizens will be without grandchildren in the generation to reach old age after 2010. Furthermore, the increase in longevity at the beginning of the new century as compared to the beginning of the previous century is minimized by the considerable reduction of births per woman. This can best be understood by comparing the fertility of "high parity" women—those with five or more children—who were born in 1889 and those who were born in 1914. Considering that female reproductive capacity generally ends at age forty-four, we find that 18.1 percent of mothers born in 1889 had five to seven children. Of those mothers born in 1914, who became forty-four years old in 1958, only 11 percent had five to seven children. Thereafter, the number of women who had five or more children became negligible in America. Therefore, the younger children of mothers born in the nineteenth century seldom knew their grandparents, whose life expectancy in 1900 was only 48.2 years for men and 51 years for women. It was somewhat less than that for Americans of African descent. The interval between the birth of the first and last children in most American families in 2001 is much smaller than it was one hundred years ago.[3]

Evidently, age differences between grandmothers and grandfathers favor women, because women live longer than men. In the past, therefore, many more children knew their grandmothers longer than their grandfathers. More recently these age differences have lessened, so that today's grandchildren are less likely to have grandfathers who are much older than their grandmothers.

In sum, these facts mean that today's grandparents will spend several years as grandparents, and that they will share these years with other grandparents—their own spouses and the parents of their sons- and daughters-in-law. As life expectancy increases and fertility declines, families have become more vertical than in past years, when families were very much horizontal—with large numbers of children in each family, many people had numerous cousins in addition to siblings, but few knew their grandparents or great-grandparents.[4]

As the life expectancy of grandparents has increased, many people now become grandparents while they are still working and participating in the numerous activities of midlife. In earlier years, women often became widows before their last grandchild was born. Now, large numbers of Americans live long enough to spend many years in the so-called empty-nest period of their lives, so a grandparent generally experiences the death of her partner long after they have become grandparents. Furthermore, numerous grandmothers are now divorcées since the divorce rate in the United States has been approximately 50 percent since 1985, when there were 2,413,000 couples married while 1,190,00 divorced. Likewise, in 1998 the rate of marriage in the United States was 8.3 per thousand, while the divorce rate was 4.2 per thousand. Compared to 1920—when there were 12 marriages per thousand population in this country but only 1.6 divorces per thousand—the increase in divorce is indeed phenomenal. There are, therefore, a good number of grandparents whose role has been disrupted by divorce, either because they can no longer visit with their grandchildren or because they themselves have become responsible for raising their grandchildren in loco parentis.[5]

Grandmothers in the new century are far more likely to work than to stay home and wait for the visits of their grandchildren. Traditionally, until the 1960s grandmothers were busy in the kitchen, always ready to dish out food, and the common image of traditional grandmothers was one that lent itself to the assumption that she was a perpetual cook, baker, and "food pusher." Now, that picture has changed as the increase in labor force participation has ensured that many middle-aged and older women are employed. This means that few grandmothers are now available to care for grandchildren during the day—or even at night.

In 1960 only 38 percent of women worked outside the home. In 2001, 60 percent of women were gainfully employed. This increase means that in 1998, 46 percent of the American labor force was female—up from 33 percent in 1960. The occupations of working American women have also changed a great deal, so many women simply cannot find the time or energy to spend on young grandchildren. For example, in 1998, 27 percent of all American physicians, 29 percent of all lawyers, and 51 percent of all editors and journalists were women. In 1970 only 13 percent of physicians, 7 percent of lawyers, and 45 percent of journalists were female. Even such traditionally male occupations as airline pilot now accommodate 3.4 percent women within their ranks. Obviously, then, Grandma may be flying a plane, treating a patient, or arguing a case in court instead of dealing with grandchildren—or any children, for that matter.

Yet older grandchildren have a better chance of meeting and living with grandmothers and grandfathers. This is true because pensions and retirement benefits are more available now than ever before. The implementation of the Social Security Act in 1937, the development of pension plans, and the increased incidence of retirement benefits have all led to a decline in retirement age, so that many men and women retire while they still have many years of life to devote to family instead of business. Unlike in earlier centuries, grandparents are not now ill and frail, nor do very many die while they are still in the labor force. Instead, large numbers of men now spend a decade as retirees and grandfathers.[6]

This contrasts with the retirement conditions prevalent in the first half of the twentieth century and before, when many men did not retire at all, but died while still working. Others did retire but lived only a short time thereafter, usually poor, frail, and ill.

Most American working women also retire in their midsixties. Unlike earlier generations, these women generally have earned their own pensions and Social Security benefits because they were employed in gainful occupations outside the home. So grandmothers of older children are unlikely to be in the labor force, although few have spent their lives working exclusively at household tasks.

One consequence of the increase in longevity in this country is *upward household extension*: the inclusion of grandparents in the households of their adult children. Such arrangements may benefit grandparents who can no longer maintain households of their own. It may also be of benefit to adult children who need to work but also need supervision in their home of young children and grandchildren living there. There is also an arrangement in some families that we may call *downward household extension*. This occurs when adult children move into their parents' homes, bringing their own children with them. Despite the possible benefits, there has been a considerable decline in extended households since the middle of the twentieth century. This decline is particularly evident in two-parent families. Single-parent families, however, are more likely to live with grandparents. The proportion of grandchildren living with single parents and grandparents increased from 3.1 percent of all children in 1940 to 5.7 percent in 1990. The increase in children living in grandparents' households is much greater among blacks than among whites. Hence, in 1993 only 3.7 percent of white children, but 12.1 percent of black children lived in the household of a grandparent.[7]

The characteristics of grandparents at the beginning of the twenty-first century may be summarized and include these features:

(1) Most Americans will experience being grandparents.

(2) Typically, grandparenthood now begins in middle age. Women and minorities tend to become grandparents sooner than men and whites.

(3) Grandparents usually survive past the adolescence of their grandchildren, so most grandchildren have several living grandparents when they reach age eighteen.

(4) The chances of having a surviving maternal grandmother are better than having a surviving paternal grandfather because of gender differences in life expectancy and because of age differences between spouses.

(5) During the twenty-first century, the majority of Americans will have at least one living great-grandparent, or four living generations.

(6) Few grandparents will have young dependent children living in their households.

(7) Only a minority of grandparents with young grandchildren are widows, as widowhood now tends to follow rather than precede becoming a grandparent.

(8) Between 20 percent and 25 percent of grandparents are now step-grandparents because of divorce—their own or their children's.

(9) The majority of grandparents with young grandchildren are now employed, while the majority with older grandchildren are not employed.

A recent study of grandparents included in the National Survey of Families and Households revealed that among those Americans with children forty years old or older, close to 95 percent are grandparents. On average, grandparents had five grandchildren. Furthermore, over 80 percent of American families now have three living generations, and 16 percent have four or more generations. There are also ethnic differences among American grandparents. More than one-half of black women under age fifty-five are grandmothers, while only one-third of white women under age fifty-five are grandmothers. There are also a number of families, mostly black, who include among grandchildren so-called fictive grandchildren, who are not biologically related but who live permanently in the households of older Americans.

The National Survey of Families and Households again showed that maternal grandmothers had a better chance of living into their grandchildren's adolescent years than paternal grandmothers. These are followed by maternal grandfathers and finally paternal grandfathers, who have the least chance of survival.[8]

PROXIMITY, EMOTIONAL TIES, AND AFFECTION

Because survival of grandparents into the adolescence, young adulthood, and even middle age of their grandchildren is so common in this century, long-term relationships between grandchildren and grandparents are now common. Therefore, practical support for each other and emotional relationships are significant in the lives of both groups now and will become ever more important as the century progresses.

This has become the rule, rather than the exception, as more than half the population sixty-five years of age or older has at least one grandchild who has reached adulthood. By contrast, it is significant that in 1900 fewer than half of adolescents had two or more living grandparents, while now, 90 percent of grandchildren reach adulthood in families including two or more grandparents.[9]

Young adults who are establishing their careers and starting their own families generally distance themselves somewhat from their grandparents until these twin goals have been achieved. Over a lifetime, then, involvement with grandparents ebbs and flows, as newly married couples have children of their own and grandparents become great-grandparents, which is no longer uncommon. The relationships between grandchildren and grandparents is also greatly influenced by gender. Researchers have found that ties between grandmothers and granddaughters are the strongest and can span several generations.[10]

This was not always the case. Sociologists Andrew Cherlin and Frank Furstenberg interviewed grandparents in the 1980s concerning their experiences with their own grandparents. They found that bonds of sentiment and friendship between grandparents and grandchildren are a recent development in American culture and that those who have become grandparents during the last twenty years of the twentieth century had a more distant relationship with their own grandparents than is common now. Cherlin and Furstenberg report that grandparents of the past were "respected, admired figures" who nevertheless maintained an emotional distance from their grandchildren. According to the Norwegian sociologist Gunhild Hagestad, as quoted by Cherlin and Furstenberg, "Seldom, if ever, was the 1880s grandmother described as dealing with the nitty-gritty aspects of everyday family life. The frail figure by the fire was not withdrawn from everyday living, but was above it. She had a place on a pedestal and she had earned it."[11]

Today, parents and grandparents usually report greater closeness to the next generation than does the younger generation. The reason for this is evidently that the old seek to emphasize continuity, while the young seek to establish autonomy. Once that autonomy has been achieved—by establishing themselves in their chosen occupations and founding their own families—members of the younger generation reestablish their relationships with their grandparents. This is particularly true when grandchildren have children of their own, whom they then seek to introduce to the great-grandparents.

Because the number of grandchildren decreased the last fifty years of the twentieth century while longevity increased, the number of grandchildren among whom grandparents divide their attention has also declined. The increased attention grandparents can focus on one or two grandchildren tends to strengthen the ties between the generations.

There are, of course, some relatively new structural obstacles to grandparent-grandchild relationships. The principal structural obstacle in the way of such closeness is distance. Sociologist Terry Mills has found that "affectual solidarity" is significantly associated with geographic proximity. Says Mills: "As the distance from grandparents increases, the feelings of closeness and affect for either grandparent decreases." This means that because large numbers of children and grandchildren live at considerable distances from each other, distance itself defeats reciprocal relationships between relatives.

As grandparents age and become ill and frail, the support of middle-aged grandchildren becomes increasingly important to them. Such support depends, in turn, on the economic, emotional, and structural conditions inherent in each generation.[12]

A recent study by Mills on the effects of adolescent-to-adult role transition by grandchildren on family solidarity with their grandparents found that grandchildren's adult role transitions were stronger predictors of intergenerational solidarity with grandfathers than with grandmothers. This finding differs from the results of earlier research, which showed that grandchildren in their younger years are more attached to grandmothers than to grandfathers. This is particularly true of granddaughters, whose occupational standing, financial condition, and education in the current generation makes them more like their grandfathers than their grandmothers, who seldom worked outside the home and often did so only sporadically. Getting a job and attaining a career by staying in the labor force increases affection for grandfathers far more than for grandmothers. However, parenthood led to greater feelings of solidarity with grandmothers than with grandfathers.

The same study by Mills concluded that divorce by grandchildren led to a decline of feelings of closeness with grandparents of both sexes.[13]

It is common for middle-aged parents to evaluate their own success in raising their children by attributing the successes and failures of their children to themselves. Grandchildren who are considered a great success or a failure therefore have an impact on their grandparents' well-being. Few have escaped the grandparent who "swells with pride" at the achievements of his grandchildren, whose pictures he exhibits to any and all, willing or not. Such attitudes must therefore also include shame and disappointment at grandchildren who are perceived to be doing poorly. Furthermore, grandparents can become as annoyed with a grandchild who "misbehaves" as parents are.

We have already seen that grandchildren who live nearby and are seen regularly by their grandparents are emotionally more salient to them than grandchildren who live at a distance. Furthermore, grandparents favor some of their grandchildren over others, particularly if one or more grandchildren worry them and appear to be irritating and annoying. Therefore, emotional reactions to their grandchildren influence the well-being of grandparents. Of course, all personal investment in emotionally meaningful relationships affect the well-being of all of us. It is important to note here that grandparents and grandchildren of different ethnic backgrounds will, of course, interpret success or failure, emotional salience, and other features of their relationship in the light of the culture in which they were reared.[14]

American culture is ageist. That means that we deprecate the old and that the status of grandparent, which indicates old age, is not always welcome among those who occupy it by virtue of time and biology. In 1964 social work professors Bernice Neugarten and Katherine Weinstein conducted a study of grandparents that yielded some surprising results. Contrary to popular stereotypes and media depictions about grandparents being "central figures in family portraits" both literally and symbolically, many grandparents in the Neugarten study were not at all happy about their grandparent status. In fact, the Neugarten study showed that one respondent in three derived no real satisfaction from being a grandparent and made "open reference to their discomfort, their disappointment or their lack of positive reward."[15]

The reasons given by grandparents for their unhappiness with that status was first that being a grandparent defeated their youthful image. In short, the grandparents were ageists themselves. The second reason for unhappiness with the grandparent status was that many grandparents engaged in conflict with their children over the manner in which the grandchildren were being raised. There were also some less defined reasons for unhappiness with the grandparent status. In 1999 psychologist Candida Peterson restudied the Neugarten and Weinstein results in Australia and found that now, a half century later, the rate of dissatisfaction among Australian grandparents was only 8 percent. The largest number of grandparents interviewed in both the old Neugarten study and the more recent study in Australia were happy about their grandparent status. "Sharing love and affection" and comments about biological renewal were the most frequent reasons given by grandparents included in either study. The most important reason for satisfaction with the grandparent role, however, was frequency of contact with grandchildren.[16]

At least one measure of the satisfaction grandparents derive from grandchildren is the amount of money they spend on their grandchildren. Since this generation of grandparents has more money than any of their predecessors, these grandparents can and do spend an average of $505 per year on their grandchildren. That is a 58 percent increase since 1992, when grandparents spent an average of $320 on their grandchildren. There are now approximately 80 million baby boomer Americans about to become grandparents, and 60 million of these are already grandparents. It is estimated that these 80 million constitute a $30-billion grandparent "market" even if they don't spend one dime more on their grandchildren than their own grandparents did on them.

The affluence of the grandparents of this generation, as compared to the usual poverty of the old in earlier generations, is illustrated by the spending habits of the old at the beginning of the new century. Travel, computers, financial services, entertainment, food, and clothes are all being sold in ever-increasing numbers to the old—or "elderly," as the euphemism would have it. No doubt by 2010, when the majority of the baby boomers reach age sixty-four, that market will grow to over $40 billion annually. The 80 million seniors represent less than one-third of the American population but control more than 78 percent of America's household wealth. In 1998 the aggregate income of the old in America was $994 billion. As the generation preceding the baby boomers dies, the baby boomers will inherit $10 trillion, so the spending power of America's wealthiest age bracket will indeed become phenomenal.

The sale of toys, games, and clothing for grandchildren reveals the purchasing power of grandparents most succinctly. In 1997 those aged between forty-five and fifty-four spent $930 million on these items.

Those aged between fifty-five and sixty-four spent $346 million, and those aged sixty-five and older spent another $207 million. Clearly, the old are a major economic force today, and their young grandchildren are the catalyst for much of their spending.[17]

Not only are the old now spending a great deal of money on their progeny, but they also function more and more as caregivers. This is indeed a recent development, since traditionally the old were the target of home care by younger people. Spouses, siblings, children, and more and more grandchildren now depend in part or altogether on their older relatives. At present, about 4 million, or 5.6 percent, of all American children live in households maintained by one or more of their grandparents.[18]

GRANDMOTHERS AS CAREGIVERS

The incidence of households including grandchildren has increased since 1970. In that year approximately 2.2 million, or 3.2 percent, of children under the age of eighteen lived in a household headed by a grandparent. Ten years later, these numbers had risen to 2.3 million, or 3.6 percent, of all American children. Then, in 1997, approximately 3.9 million, or 5.5 percent, of all American children lived with grandparents or other relatives. These changes represent a 72 percent increase over thirty years in the number of children living in a grandparent-headed household.[19]

In addition to those grandparents who have a grandchild living with them, there are also numerous grandparents who provide lesser levels of care for grandchildren. There are those who accommodate a child on overnight visits and those who provide care for children while the parents work full-time. Those who do so are generally motivated by a wish to avoid having the child enrolled in a day care facility or sitter's home. Many grandparents want to be of financial assistance to their children and take in their grandchildren for that reason. Other grandparents live with their adult children and therefore provide ipso facto part-time care, often either because an unmarried mother had a child or because the parents are divorced.[20]

Grandparents rarely choose to become full-time caregivers for their grandchildren. Usually grandparents take over when the circumstances of the grandchildren's lives are such that no other option is possible or the state requires an out-of-home placement in an institution or foster care unless the grandparents accommodate the child. It is common to hear grandparents say that they enjoy the limited role they play in the lives of their grandchildren in that they, the grandparents, can always retreat to their own homes and enjoy the freedom from child raising that their advanced years permit them.[21]

There are, then, a number of events that precipitate the introduction of children into the household of grandparents. The first of these is usually trauma in the life of the child's family, such as alcoholism, physical violence, abuse, or the death of a parent. Second, such events lead to a perception by the grandparents that it is now their responsibility to care for the grandchildren involved. This perception depends largely on whether or not the grandparents view grandchildren as having behavior problems and whether or not the grandparents can tolerate the changes in their own lifestyle precipitated by the introduction of grandchildren into their home. Third, grandparents will be influenced by the resources available to them in making a decision to raise their grandchildren. Such resources include the ability to pay for the cost of raising children, the educational background of the grandparents, and the community support available to them.

Psychologists Bonita Bowers and Barbara Myers conducted a study of the consequences of various levels of caregiving for grandmothers who have grandchildren living with them. This study reveals that the grandchild's behavior has the most important impact on a grandmother's feelings of burden, stress, and/or satisfaction. Since grandchildren usually come into the care of their grandparents because of parental difficulties, it is no surprise that children raised in the homes of grandparents have more behavior problems than children who are raised in their parents' homes. Evidently, the difficulties encountered by grandmothers in raising grandchildren are made worse among the poor and among those who receive little or no support from the parents of the children they are accommodating.[22]

Since 1990 approximately one-third of American children have been born to single mothers. This trend is even more pronounced in the African American community than in the white community, although the number of children of both races who live in these circumstances has more than doubled since 1970. In an effort to reduce the cost of this development for the taxpayer, and with a view to maintaining some sense of responsibility on the part of adolescents, Congress passed the Personal Responsibility and Work Opportunity Reconciliation Act in 1996. This federal law is the most recent amendment to the Aid to Families with Dependent Children Act, now renamed the Temporary Aid to Needy Families law. This law requires unmarried mothers under the age of eighteen to live at home, under the supervision of their parents or other responsible adults, in order to receive financial assistance. The purpose here is to avoid financing independent households headed by young unmarried mothers. Proponents of this measure believe that this law will reduce repeat pregnancies, improve high school graduation rates for unmarried mothers, and reduce both poverty and premature marriages. The mothers of such unmarried girls are, of course, the grandmothers of the new arrivals. While this effort by Congress may have appeared to solve the problem of illegitimacy, the consequences of the Personal Responsibility Act have been quite damaging to many grandparents raising grandchildren.

Sociologist Ariel Kalil and his colleagues at the University of Michigan Poverty Center have investigated the mental health outcomes associated with the coresidence of grandmothers on the adolescent mothers involved. This investigation is important because under the Temporary Aid to Needy Families law, states are allowed to exempt minor mothers from the coresidency requirement if such arrangements are deemed detrimental to the physical or mental health and well-being of the mother or her child.[23]

The results of this study could have been anticipated. Obviously, the emotional well-being of the coresidence of mothers, grandmothers, and young children was very much affected by the ability of the new mother and grandmother to live together in harmony. Tension, recriminations, poverty, and other forms of stress made such coresidence impossible, while harmony and nonjudgmental acceptance made such coresidence feasible. Surely the findings of Kalil et al. demonstrate that the mere passing of a law requiring young mothers to live at home does not solve all problems, nor does it lead to inevitable success. The law as it is now written describes specific physical dangers as cause for exemption from the living requirements mandated. The law does not include the outcomes of conflict between adolescent mothers and their mothers. Therefore, group homes and independent-living programs for adolescent mothers may be a better alternative for some young mothers than living at home.

It is significant that the law does not mention the support an adolescent mother should receive from the father of her child, although such support would be the most important means of dealing with the emotional outcome of early motherhood.[24]

In view of the legal and emotional aspects of support of grandchildren by their grandparents, it is useful to investigate the nature of grandmothers who are supportive of grandchildren versus that of those who are not supportive. The support of grandmothers is considered more important in this connection than the support of grandfathers, because the traditional role played by grandmothers concerning their own daughters and their grandchildren is still dominant at the beginning of the twenty-first century.

In the late 1980s and the 1990s, just under one-half of all American grandmothers provided care for at least one of their grandchildren on a regular basis. It is likely that the percentage is even higher among those grandmothers who have grandchildren under the age of twelve. There are some sociodemographic characteristics that are associated with caregiving. Grandmothers who are between sixty and seventy years old, those who have younger adult children, those who live with their husbands, those who are highly educated, and those who are in good health are more likely to give care to their grandchildren than other grandmothers. Of course, living in the same household as their grandchildren more than doubles the likelihood that grandmothers will give care to their grandchildren.

A study by Nazli Baydar and Jeanne Brooks-Gunn, professors of child research and education at the University of Washington at Seattle, identified four groups of grandmothers with respect to whether or not they provide care to their grandchildren. Baydar and Brooks-Gunn labeled the first group of grandmothers "homemakers." These constituted 19 percent of the sample studied. Their characteristics were that none of these "homemaker" grandmothers worked outside the home, all of them provided care to their grandchildren on a regular basis, and they were the most likely among the four groups to live with someone needing care on a regular basis. These were also the grandmothers who spent the most hours doing household chores. "Homemaker" grandmothers in the Baydar and Brooks-Gunn study were relatively young, with only about a third older than sixty-five. They were the group most likely to have four or more adult children who were mostly younger than forty years old. None of these grandmothers lived alone, and over 80 percent lived with their husbands. One-fifth of the "homemaker" grandmothers lived with their children. Although almost one-half of these grandmothers were high school graduates, few had any higher education.

The second group of grandmothers studied by Baydar and Brooks-Gunn were labeled "young-and-connected" by the researchers. These grandmothers constituted 23 percent of those included in the study. Almost one-half of the "young-and-connected" grandmothers were under fifty-five years old. One-quarter of them had some higher education, and all of them had lucrative employment. Nevertheless, 83 percent of these grandmothers provided care to their grandchildren on a regular basis, and three-quarters said that they participated in a social or community organization at least several times a year. These grandmothers also had relatively young adult children who were mostly younger than thirty years old. These grandmothers were generally healthy. The majority—58 percent—lived with their husbands, but evidently a large minority did not. Twenty percent lived with their grandchildren.

Baydar and Brooks-Gunn labeled a third group of grandmothers associated with their study as "remote." They constituted 32 percent of the sample studied. All of these grandmothers lived with their husbands and very few lived with their grandchildren. None of these grandmothers provided care to their grandchildren on a regular basis, and more than one-quarter were employed.

The fourth group of grandmothers were labeled "frail" grandmothers by Baydar and Brooks-Gunn. They constituted 26 percent of all grandmothers in this study. They were characterized by low levels of mental and physical health, had few adult children, and were usually living alone. Three-quarters of these "frail" grandmothers were sixty-five years old and one-fifth had only one adult child. These adult children were generally older than forty years. None of the "frail" grandmothers lived with their husbands, one-third did not attend high school, and more than half did not finish high school. Only 18 percent of these grandmothers provided care for their grandchildren on a regular basis, largely because a high percentage were in poor health.

The principal result of the Baydar and Brooks-Gunn study is that the role of grandmother has not become remote and detached in present-day America, but that a large number of grandmothers are actively contributing to the care of their grandchildren despite their many other responsibilities. This is of great importance because so many mothers with young children are employed. Certainly the help given by grandmothers is most important to poor mothers, for whom the biggest obstacle to employment is expensive child care.[25]

A number of conditions continue to promote the trend for grandparents to assume a parental role when their child is deemed an unfit parent. The most important and frequent of these conditions is nonmarital childbearing. Others are an increase in substance abuse, mental and emotional problems, incarceration, and divorce.

IN LOCO PARENTIS— GRANDPARENTS RAISING GRANDCHILDREN

Because one-third of all children are born to single mothers and because one-half of couples who married in the past twenty years are now divorced, there is an ever-growing number of children in this country who are raised by their grandparents. Therefore, the role of grandparents as caregivers is becoming more and more important. This role faces problems seldom anticipated by those who must play it. One of these problems is that the role of grandparent caregiver is time disordered. This means that grandparents are mostly aging people who need to cope with their own decline and disabilities when they are suddenly confronted with the needs of a child. Another obstacle to successfully rearing a grandchild is the financial burden grandparents face on a retirement income if they add a grandchild to their household. Therefore, the intervention of social service agencies can be of great help to such grandparents, particularly if such agencies succeed in introducing grandparents raising grandchildren to other grandparents in the same situation.[26]

Raising a second family at an advanced age is almost always an exhausting experience. The myriad tasks necessary to raise children are emotionally draining and stressful. Consequently, grandparent support groups are of great help for grandparents who have once again become responsible for children. The purpose of such support groups is to lessen the isolation experienced by many grandparents and to provide physical and emotional respite for them. These needs are driven by the fact that the parents of the grandchildren—the grandparents' own children—have been unable or unwilling to meet their own responsibilities. Grandparents may have to confront their children's substance abuse, handle housing problems, and deal with numerous mental and emotional health issues and high crime rates in their neighborhoods.

Georgia State University (GSU) in Atlanta has conducted an experimental effort to help grandparents who are suddenly responsible for their grandchildren. Social workers and nurses associated with the university have used a "strength-based" approach to such grandparents by first recognizing that all individuals have strengths that they may not recognize. Building on this insight, the team from GSU showed that adversity can increase rather than decrease one's resilience and strength. Finally, the team from GSU seeks to help grandparents to become highly motivated to find solutions to their problems. Such motivation is considered far more promising than imposing the opinions of social workers or nurses on the grandparents. The team from GSU has been successful in developing a partnership between itself and some fifty families it has approached and helped at any one time.[27]

There is indeed a significant need to develop a great deal of psychological and emotional strength while raising a grandchild. Older adults often view responsibility for a grandchild in their home as a burden. At an age when most Americans enjoy retirement—or at least feel relieved of the anxieties of the childrearing years—some grandparents are suddenly confronted with rearing children a second time, just as health problems and the loss of their spouses beset them. Nevertheless, a study by Robert Sands and Robin Goldberg-Glen, social work professors at the University of Pennsylvania, found that middle-aged grandparents were even more stressed when confronted with raising a grandchild than were older grandparents. The younger grandparents in the study were subject to a great deal of anxiety in the face of their new child-rearing responsibilities because they were generally still employed and had to deal with on-the-job stress as well as the stress of raising a grandchild. The stress felt by these grandparents manifests itself as depression—a sign of stress—and younger grandparents tend to be more depressed than older grandparents.

Because a lack of family cohesion is almost always the reason for placing grandchildren with grandparents in the first place, family therapy aimed at improving the quality of family relationships should be of great help to such families.[28]

The extent to which help may be needed in making the lives of grand-parents raising grandchildren easier varies with the ethnicity of the families involved. Because by far the majority of Americans are of European descent, the majority of grandparents raising grandchildren are of course also of European descent. However, the probability of living in a coresi-dence or custodial care household is higher for African Americans and the poor than it is for the wealthy and those of European American ethnicity. The probability of such coresidence is also higher for Hispanics. Like-wise, the probability of inner-city residents engaging in the raising of grandchildren is higher than that for suburban residents, because the poor and minorities are more likely to live in inner cities.

In fact, black grandmothers have historically been much more often involved in child rearing and in the maintenance of stability in their fam-ilies than have white grandmothers. This ethnic difference is mostly caused by higher rates of poverty and less job stability among minorities.

That difference is dramatized by comparing the overall percentage of children living with grandparents with that of black children who live in such arrangements. We have already seen that 5.5 percent of all American children, 82 percent of these of European descent, live with grandparents. Among black children 12.5 percent live with grandparents. In fact, throughout the twentieth century, African American children have been three to six times more likely than white children to not be living with either parent.[29]

At least one reason for this imbalance in fostering between the races has been the considerable spread of the human immunodeficiency virus (HIV) among African Americans, far in excess of their share in the Amer-ican population generally. It is no exaggeration to say that "HIV disease has had a devastating effect on black women of child bearing years age 25 to 44"[30]—and therefore on children. It has been estimated that three-fourths of HIV-infected women have children, and the majority of these mothers have sole responsibility for child care. In 2000 there were about 125,000 HIV-infected children and adolescents in this country. Further-more, many young mothers with HIV are dying, increasing the number of grandmother caretakers now and in the future.[31]

Investigation has shown that race, ethnicity, and social class have a considerable bearing on the manner in which grandparents are socialized into the role of caregivers for their grandchildren. The management of this role over time, the types of problems these grandparents are likely to meet, and the fashion in which the caregiver role impacts their other social relationships are all tied to the ethnic, class, and status condition of the grandparents. All this is illustrated in a study of Latino grandparents conducted by Denise Burnette, a professor of social work at Columbia University. According to this study, in 1999 Latinos were the fastest-growing minority in the United States. It is now estimated that the Latino population will grow 76 percent between 1995 and 2020, double the rate of non-Latino whites.[32]

Burnette found that Latino grandparents who need to raise their grandchildren have the advantage of being "embedded in large, dense, helping networks of nuclear and extended family life." Unlike so many European American families, who have little or no contact with any extended family members, Latinos are far more likely to participate in large family networks and to have frequent social contacts that provide them with help in child rearing and household chores. Having such contacts seems to help in maintaining the mental health of those who belong to such extended families. Nevertheless, these networks of relatives and friends cannot meet all the needs of grandparents raising grandchildren, particularly because so many of the Latino families studied by Burnette are very poor and therefore cannot deal with the financial costs of raising grandchildren. Burnette found that 81 percent of Latino custodial grandparents in her study suffered extreme poverty, as compared to 23 percent for custodial grandparents nationwide.[33]

A 1997 report by the American Association of Retired Persons concluded that the main issues faced by custodial grandparents in minority communities are economic pressures and physical and emotional problems. It is well established and common sense that impoverished people, and hence minorities, are more vulnerable to health problems than those with more money and more resources. This is illustrated by considering that 23 percent of custodial grandparents have poverty-level incomes, while only 14 percent of noncustodial grandparents nationwide live in poverty.[34]

Most custodial grandparents are in their midfifties. As their age advances, the health problems of these grandparents become more pronounced. These conditions are aggravated if the grandparents raise more than one grandchild, have financial difficulties, or lack social support.

Since women earn only about 75 percent of male earnings in this country, the preponderance of grandmothers raising grandchildren alone promotes yet more poverty-related difficulty.

A study focused on activities of daily living concluded that custodial grandparents were significantly more likely than noncustodial grandparents to report limitations in each of six areas of daily living. These activities included mobility inside the house, completing daily household tasks, climbing stairs, walking six blocks, doing heavy tasks, and working for pay. Such grandparents also suffer health limitations, both physical and psychological.[35]

Nationwide, two-thirds of grandparent-headed households include a member of the "linking generation," the parents of the grandchildren who are now the responsibility of the grandparents. Many of these parents are single mothers, some of whom are as young as fourteen. Therefore, grandparents must often do "double duty" as parent of an adolescent and her child. In these situations, the bulk of daily care falls on the grandparents, and that is almost always the grandmother.[36]

There are, of course, numerous social welfare agencies that can be and want to be of help to these grandmothers. Unfortunately, there is often ignorance of the availability of these social services in minority communities, where custodial care of grandchildren is particularly acute. This may well be related to the lack of education in the Latino community. Among those Latinos involved in the custodial care of grandchildren, only 27 percent have completed high school, while the national high school completion rate among grandparents caring for grandchildren is 56 percent. The overall national high school completion rate was 83 percent in 1998.[37]

This lack of education affects all the unmet needs of the Latino community, and especially those caring for grandchildren. Alone, the difference in income reveals that minorities earn less because their educational level is generally lower than that of whites. That lack of education translates into lower incomes, and hence into greater unmet needs. The evidence is that in 1997, adults who had not graduated from high school earned an average of $16,124 a year, while those with a high school education earned an average of $22,895, those with a bachelor's degree earned an average of $40,470, and those with advanced degrees earned an average of $63,000 a year.[38]

DIVORCE, SEPARATION, AND VISITATION RIGHTS

Although there are now a good number of grandparents who are raising their children's children, there are also many grandparents who find themselves in the opposite situation: grandparents whose adult children have been divorced or separated and whose ex-spouses have custody of the children of their erstwhile unions. Numerous grandparents have thus been unable to visit or even speak with their grandchildren, because the parent who has custody refuses to let the grandparents of the "ex" see or deal with the grandchildren at all.

The issue of grandparents' rights has become so prominent in the past few years that the Select Committee on Aging of the House of Representatives held hearings on grandparents' rights in October of 1991. At that time, in any state of the union, grandparents had no more right to see or deal with a grandchild than did a nonrelative. The right of access was controlled entirely by the grandchild's parents, who could issue or withdraw invitations as they saw fit. It was the unchallenged view in all of America that in the event of death or divorce the custodial parent had the right to prohibit visitation by grandparents.

The reasoning behind such laws was that any judicial enforcement of grandparents' visitation rights would undermine parental authority. It was further contended that the "best interests of a child" would be injured if the child became involved in the disputes that led to separation and divorce in the first place.

In the last few years there has been a reassessment of this attitude, so that a growing number of legislators, child psychologists, and sociologists have concluded that it could well be in the best interests of a child to continue a relationship with his or her grandparents even after a separation between parents, whatever the reason.[39] This argument has no standing in law; however, all states use the phrase "the best interests of the child" as a guide in making decisions involving children.

Therefore, every state now has legal provisions allowing grandparents visitation rights under certain circumstances. These circumstances generally involve the death of one of the child's parents or the dissolution of the marriage. A few states allow grandparents visitation rights in connection with any child custody action, but some states limit visitation rights to the parents of the noncustodial parent. Finally, there are states that specifically grant visitation rights to grandparents whose child is an incarcerated or mentally impaired parent, or when a grandchild is in a foster home.

Some states allow grandparents visitation rights when their grand-child was born outside of marriage, or in cases of adoption if the adoptive parent is a blood relative. In no state are visitation rights for grandparents automatic; in all states the court decides on a case-by-case basis whether or not visitation rights should be granted to grandparents.

An example of the statutes that list the criteria to be considered by a court in determining whether to grant grandparents access to a grandchild is the Vermont statute that provides that the court shall consider the best interests of the child as to the love, affection, and other emotional ties existing between the grandchild involved and the grandparents. The court must also consider the capacity and disposition of the parties involved to give the child love, affection, and guidance. In addition, the court needs to consider the moral fitness of the parties, the mental and physical health of the parties, and the reasonable preference of the child, if the court deems the child to be of sufficient age to express a preference. Further-more, the court must consider the willingness and ability of the petitioner to facilitate and encourage a close and continuing relationship between the child and the other parties, and any other factor the court considers to be relevant in a just determination regarding visitation or access.[40]

While Vermont has this extensive list of criteria applied by judges to any decision regarding custodial rights, Montana has no special criteria to that end, and merely directs that "the district court may grant a grandparent of a child reasonable visitation rights" (circumstances are not specified).[41]

In 1991 Congress passed the Uniform Child Custody Jurisdiction Act, which has been adopted by every state. Together with the Parental Kidnap-ping Prevention Act, already in force since 1980, this law requires that states give "full faith and credit" to child custody and visitation decrees issued by courts in other jurisdictions. The main purpose of these two acts is the prevention of multiple custody orders and visitation orders that con-flict with one another. Prior to the passage of the Uniform Child Custody Jurisdiction Act, it was possible for two different courts in two different states to give custody rights to two different contenders. Now, a person who obtains a custody or visitation order can expect to have that order enforced anywhere in the United States. This means, therefore, that custody or visitation rights granted a grandparent in one state would be enforceable in another state that had adopted the Uniform Act. Now there are as many lists of circumstances under which grandparents may petition a court to obtain visitation or custody rights as there are states. Each state has its own procedures, and no two states agree on the criteria grandparents must meet.[42]

Nevertheless, there are a great number of similarities between the states concerning third-party custodial and visitation rights. It needs to be recognized, however, that any third-party right to visit or give custody to grandchildren contradicts the constitutional right of parents to raise their own children.

It is, of course, traditional and conventional to hold that no one is in a better position than a parent to know what is best for a child. However, changes in the American family over the past thirty years have altered the traditional American family to such an extent that stepparents and grandparents increasingly have been left to raise children after the death, divorce, or abandonment of the children by natural parents. Earlier, such third parties had no protection against the return of natural parents who wanted their children back. This led states to pass laws permitting third parties to file custody actions pertaining to minor children in the courts.

California has a priority list that recognizes the rights of third parties and the rights of children concerning the custody issue. The California priority concerning custody is this: (1) both parents jointly or either parent, (2) the person or persons in whose home the child has been living in a stable environment, (3) any other persons deemed by the court to be suitable and able and willing to provide adequate and proper care and guidance for the child.[43]

Even as the laws concerning custody vary between the states, the laws concerning visitation are also very heterogeneous. All states have laws regarding visitation rights by grandparents. These laws may be distributed according to three categories: First there are those ten states that permit reasonable visitation rights to grandparents. Second, there are states with visitation rights limited to a few categories of persons. In those states, visitation rights occur only when one parent has died or when there is a divorce between the natural parents or a stepparent has adopted the child.

Finally, in more recent years some states have recognized a "psychological extended family of children," which allows not only grandparents but also others "to have a continued relationship with a child." There are also states that specifically recognize stepparents' rights to custodial care of a stepchild.[44]

Third parties may also incur support obligations for children otherwise abandoned. A few states have statutes imposing support obligations upon stepparents of minor children. No such statutes exist concerning grandparents or siblings, although states may be able to impose such obligations on third parties by enforcing the "poor laws" of several states.

Because the states vary so much in their requirements concerning the rights and obligations of grandparents, the Supreme Court has defined the meaning of the word "family" for the whole nation. On June 5, 2000, the Court struck down a Washington State law that granted visitation rights to grandparents and others over the objection of the parents of a child, if a judge ruled it would be in the child's best interests.

The Washington law permitted any person at any time to petition the courts to visit a child without the consent of the parents. Although all fifty states have grandparents' visitation laws, none were as expansive as Washington's. The principal issue in this case was the conflict between parent's rights and the rights of the state. The court came down six to three in favor of parent's rights and the rights of individuals to remain free from government interference. The facts of the case were that grandparents Jenifer and Gary Truxell wanted to continue to visit their son's two young daughters after their son committed suicide. However, the mother of the children wanted to limit the Truxells' visitation time. The Truxells then sued, which led to the court battle settled by the Supreme Court.[45]

Intergenerational families headed by grandparents, or surrogate parenting, is primarily a women's issue. Women, not men, are almost always caregivers for grandchildren abandoned by their parents. Such grandmothers are often vulnerable to losing their vested pension rights if they quit work too soon in order to take care of their grandchildren. Caregiving is seldom recognized in the media or in public policy debates because those who are most involved are socially invisible. A principal reason for this invisibility is the popular stereotype that children who failed to maintain their own families were poorly raised, so the grandparents are at fault, must have been poor parents, and are therefore obliged to raise their grandchildren. This "bad seed" theory prevents many grandparents from getting adquate financial and social support in their role as grandparents.

Grandparents have special health needs that parents, who are younger, do not usually encounter. There are many grandparents who neglect their own health, or at least downplay their own health problems, in order to focus on the children in their care. Much of this is due to the lack of health insurance coverage for poor Americans.

There are a disproportionate number of minority families, both black and Hispanic, represented among adults caring for children not their own. Therefore, the differences in culture, including family organization, of blacks and Hispanics should be given a good deal of consideration. It is noteworthy that in the Spanish-speaking community, relatives other than grandparents—such as aunts, uncles, and cousins—give abandoned children a home. There are also adults who raise the children of others not because they are the grandparents, but because the children, although not related, are known to them.

A good number of grandparents encounter social isolation and alienation because the PTA and other organizations of this kind have not become involved in the surrogate parent situation and have made no provisions to deal with this growing, but nevertheless unusual, trend.

When the Welfare Reform Act of 1996 was passed, little attention was given the impact of that new law on intergenerational households headed by grandparents. The act has had the effect of making grandparents de facto caregivers for children of teenage mothers.

It is evident at the beginning of the twenty-first century that the American family is more complex today than it has been in the past. There is now an "invisible" middle generation of parents who are unwilling or unable to take care of their children. These parents are generally viewed as "undeserving" because they are seen as irresponsible and immoral. Even if that is so, the children born to such parents cannot be included in the neglect public policy assigns to their mothers. This means that the increasing number of low-income families now suffering from this neglect should promptly be helped by financial and related services that will enable them to provide for their families.[46]

Because the American economy has done so well during the past several years, it is often overlooked that millions of Americans live in poverty. At the end of the twentieth century, an income of $16,000 for a family of four is the average poverty threshold. For a family of three consisting of one grandparent and two grandchildren, the poverty level begins as $12,641. It is among the poor that the surrogate parent situation is most acute, because the poor are most likely to abandon their children and leave them in the care of grandparents who are also poor.[47]

FOSTER GRANDPARENTS

Foster grandparents are an additional resource used to help children whose parents cannot or will not support them. There is a foster grandparent program in the United States that began in 1965. This program, then sponsored by the Office of Economic Opportunity, included eight hundred foster grandparents serving children to age five in the community or in institutions. In 1969 this program was transferred to the Administration on Aging and included children up to age seventeen. Then, in 1971, the foster grandparent program became the Community Action Network, and the age of children served was raised to twenty-one years. Since 1993 the program has been administered by the Corporation for National Service. Authorized by the Domestic Volunteer Service Act of 1973, the program allows income-eligible people aged sixty or older to provide person-to-person services in health, education, and welfare to children and adolescents with exceptional needs. Today there are more than twenty-five thousand foster grandparents serving ninety thousand children. Ninety percent of the foster grandparents are women and one-half are over seventy years old. The largest number of these volunteers serve in public and private schools and in day care centers, allowing children to receive individual adult attention that continues when teachers are absent or leave.[48] The foster grandparent program has had significant results in terms of mental health. The participation of foster grandparents has alleviated depression among the old, improved intellectual functioning among the young, and promoted social maturity among otherwise emotionally deprived children.

The success of the foster grandparent program has led to the establishment of other programs as well. In 1963 the Adopt-A-Grandparent program was established in Florida. This program involved weekly class visits by young children to nursing homes. Because of its success, the program was duplicated nationwide. In 1967 Serve and Enrich Retirement by Volunteer Experience (SERVE) was inaugurated. The elders who began this program worked with mentally challenged children. Later, this program grew into the Retired Senior Volunteer Program (RSVP), which became a national program under the Older American Retirement Act of 1965.

There are also programs run by students that provide services to the old. One of these is the National Student Volunteer Program. All these programs help to combat ageism, which may be defined as the unreasonable hatred and fear of the old. It resembles sexism and racism in that it is an emotional condition based on prejudice.

The Michigan Teaching-Learning Communities program seeks to combat ageism by bringing old and young together in the public schools. Another effort to associate the old with the young is Generations Together of the University of Pittsburgh, which was America's first university program devoted to intergenerational issues.[49] There are numerous other programs that have now diversified to include religion, community, government, and a number of clinical areas.

These programs have provided several benefits. First is the significantly better attitude of children toward the old. Such an improvement, in turn, leads to a more positive attitude of children toward their own aging. Another benefit has been the Generations United program, dedicated to developing cross-generational understanding and cooperation. This effort seeks to prevent the resentment some young people have because they must carry the financial and social burden for a growing number of the old in America. It is feared that those who have always lived in an age-segregated society and have had few contacts with the old will refuse to support them. The main purpose of Generations United is therefore to induce the old to share their experience with the young and for the young to seek out the old and learn from them.

SUMMARY

Longevity and fertility determine the status of grandparents. Currently one-third of children age ten and under have all their grandparents living. Therefore, families are now more vertical than in past centuries. Because many grandparents are now divorced and working, a new grandparent-grandchild relationship has evolved. Retirement is longer because life expectancy is greater. The National Survey of Families and Households found a greater emotional attachment between the grandparents and grandchildren of this generation than in any earlier generation. Grandparents have more money than in the past, and they spend an average of more than $500 a year on grandchildren.

A growing number of grandchildren live with their grandparents. This is a consequence of single motherhood, AIDS, divorce, and abandonment. There are ethnic differences in the proportion of children raised by grandparents. This leads some to explain this phenomenon with the "bad seed" theory. There are as many laws pertaining to grandparents' visitation and custodial rights as there are states.

In addition to the introduction of grandparents into the child-rearing situation, there are now also a number of foster grandparent programs in the United States.

3

Grandmothers

Grandmothers come in many shapes and sizes. They are first and foremost people with as many characteristics and needs as all of humanity. In addition to the common human needs, they crave the love of their family, their children and grandchildren. They are what they have always been. Perhaps they are a little more mellow, if they were kindly and mellow in their youth, or more easily hurt, if they were sensitive in their early years. They ache a bit—or a great deal—because of the aging process, bones that are brittle, limbs that are arthritic and don't work as well as they used to, intestines that don't have the same peristalsis and create abdominal pain, vision that is not quite as clear as they would like, and hearing that sometimes leaves them out of the more quiet conversations and may create some suspicion and annoyance toward the speaker. Grandmothers want inclusion, not exclusion. They want to be a part of the activities of their family, their grandchildren; they want to be needed. We will here describe the many different people that the label grandmother connotes. Viewed individually, grandmothers, like their male counterparts, are unique in looks, personalities, experiences, and behaviors. Here we will describe the expectations and characteristics the label "grandmother" encompasses. Our images of the gray-haired, over-indulgent woman with a child on her lap as she sits knitting in a rocking chair is a stereotype that has been perpetuated through the generations. The authentic examples of grandmothers that are documented throughout this chapter will dispel the age-old images of our female elders.

There is the grandmother then and now. The grandmother of yesteryear was of great help. In rural Europe and America, she would often care for the little ones while the parents worked diligently on the farm. She would care for their well-being, preparing their meals meticulously. She might rock them in the cradle when they were very young, go on walks with them, and tell them stories, perpetuating the family legacy through tales of ancestral greatness, their vicissitudes, and other interesting adventures and life events. She took great pride in the young generation and saw herself, her parents, and other ancestors in them. Since families generally lived in close proximity to one another, she had access to the grandchildren and was very much a part of their lives. There was little that escaped her. She had a "cure" for most childhood diseases, from alleviating the misery of coughs with the accompanying congestion to eradicating headaches and other ills. She would feed the youngsters Scotts Emulsion by the tablespoon to ensure their well-being and "make them grow big and strong." She would rub their chests with grease to ease their rasping breaths. She would place sliced raw potato on their aching heads to make their headaches disappear. In short, she enabled the children's parents to work without the encumbrances of having to worry about their offspring.

The grandmother of today is often too busy taking care of a very demanding job, where she might be occupied for the full day; returning home in the early evening to prepare dinner for herself and husband, do a bit of housework, and fall, exhausted, into bed.

Technology, too, has changed the function of grandmotherhood. Television, computer games, and a host of activities now occupy the lives of the majority of grandchildren. The crude stories that Grandma used to tell are replaced by sophisticated stories viewed on the television screen. Commercial baby foods in jars and cans have replaced the laborious cooking, chopping, and grinding that was once necessary to feed an infant. Ready-to-eat and fast foods have replaced the need for grandmother's help in meal preparation.

Urban grandmothers are no longer bound to the house and are seen driving cars, vans, and trucks and using public transportation to give them the freedom that was historically unavailable. If grandmothers are no longer among the working folk, they are frequently involved in volunteer activities, clubs of many varieties, senior citizen groups, and other pleasant outlets. They may be traveling to places near or far, or they may be golfing, playing tennis, or engaging in other sports.

The income levels of today's grandmothers have also changed from those of earlier times. Before Franklin Delano Roosevelt's time, Social Security payments were nonexistent. Most of the things grandmothers gave to their grandchildren were made at home: sweaters, blankets, dresses, trousers, and other pieces of clothing were created in their sewing rooms. Today, grandmother's may have more expendable income than that of their offspring. This gives Grandma the opportunity to do more for her grandchildren financially than her ancestors were able to do.

In summary, life has changed considerably for the generations in the last one hundred years.

The idealized grandmother of today is a benign, white-haired, kindly old woman who bakes cookies; hugs little children; holds them on her lap; kisses away their "boo-boos"; knits blankets, sweaters, and booties; and never speaks an unkind word. She is helpful to her offspring and baby-sits whenever she is needed. She is available at all times, but makes herself invisible when her presence is inconvenient. She dotes on her grandchildren, hangs unto their every utterance, and is certain that they will grow up to be Einstein—or at least a doctor. She attends all of their functions and beams with pride, regardless of the quality of their performance.

The working grandmother, too, enjoys the little ones. She sees her grandchildren when time permits; she is not as physically involved as the stay-at-home grandmother. She buys them the little extras that they might desire, attends their birthday parties and major celebrations, and is proud of their accomplishments, no matter how seemingly insignificant they appear. She may invite one or another to join her on a trip, and sends post cards to them when she travels to distant places. She may be a role model for an older grandchild—or a disappointment to an offspring who could use some inexpensive household help.

There is the grandmother who likes neither the title nor the role. She cannot face the aging process and may speak of her grandchildren as nieces and nephews. She may ignore the young ones altogether and "do her thing" without acknowledging the younger generation. The grandchildren barely know her, and their relationship with her is superficial at best. On the rare occasions she is seen with a grandchild, she may pretend that she is his mother.

Mabel never wanted to be a grandmother. To her the word in itself spelled "old age," and she wanted to remain young forever. In her mind, being a grandparent meant illness, gray hair, wrinkles, and death. By avoiding that status—even that title—she believed she would escape her age. Mabel is a seventy-five-year-old woman with artificial-looking bright red hair and heavy eye makeup. A very short skirt covers her very thin body. From behind, she is frequently mistaken for a teenager since she walks in very high heels with a brisk step, holding herself very erect. She and her late husband were the parents of two children and the grandparents of three. When she is asked about her family, she does not mention the grandchildren. On the rare occasions the teenagers visit her, she insists to folk who do not know her background that they are her nieces. In her mind, she has convinced herself that she is more desirable if she does not have the grandmother status; it makes her feel young. She declares that she can do all the things her "nieces" can do and that she has the same interests as the younger generation. She obviously does not view herself realistically and rejects her own being and that of others her age. In spite of her heavy makeup and unnaturally dyed hair, the image that she por-trays is that of a septuagenarian who is unable to accept herself.

Then there is the grandmother who, by accident of fate, lives far away from her grandchildren. She knows them mainly from pictures, telephone calls, and the rare times she can afford to visit them. She sends gifts when warranted and does what she can, given her circumstances. She would like to have them closer but is unable to alter the situation.

Dora is a pleasant, friendly, seventy-eight-year-old grandmother whose family lives out of town. Dora prides herself in living "her own life." She travels with a senior citizen group and makes a point to rarely discuss her grandchildren with the few male members of the organization. She enjoys flirting, and if there are fifty women and one male on an outing, Dora always "gets her man." She attributes this to the fact that she still has sex appeal, and believes that dwelling on her grandmother role would diminish her status as "girlfriend." With her female friends, she happily exhibits pic-tures of the grandchildren and speaks about their accomplishments. She is also known to send packages of toys and clothing whenever she has a few dollars to spare from her meager pension and Social Security income.

For one to be a grandmother, she needs to have grandchildren. Like their grandmothers, grandchildren are different because of their gender, their looks, their attitudes, their characteristics, their learning power, their expressions, and their ability to give and receive love and affection. Therefore, they react in their own unique ways to their grandmothers.

Just as children born to the same family have different personalities because of the factors mentioned above, grandmothers also are different and unique because of the combination of their genes, their birth order, and the reaction of their parents to their individuality. Added to this are the attitudes and reactions of the grandparents, who may feel closer to one child rather than another. Grandmothers may be able to identify more closely with a child who has similar tastes, looks, attitudes, or behaviors as a beloved relative—or the contrary may be the case if the child has Grandma's flaws, which may create some friction between them.

The Glatz family's five grandchildren (all from the same daughter) are Rebecca, age 17; Michele, 16; Albert, 14; Heddy, 10; and Robert 6. The grandparents dote on all five, especially since their sons have no offspring.

Rebecca is a very affectionate young person who has a very close relationship with her grandmother. As the first in the Glatz family constellation, she was adulated. There is much contact and caregiving between the two. She is an excellent student, just as Grandma was. She also exhibits the same interests in drama, books, and learning. She plays the violin, just as Grandma's beloved mother did. Rebecca frequently stays overnight with her "Nana," and thus has bonded with her in a special way.

Michele is a very interesting, giving child who is always ready to help—except when it comes to cleaning her room. She always offers to share food with her Nana, and is very unselfish. She struggles with schoolwork, which is very upsetting to her parents and creates quite a good deal of conflict in the home, especially with her father. He has very high expectations of the youngster, which she finds impossible to meet. This colors the behavior of her grandmother, who feels the need to advocate for and defend her granddaughter. The girl looks admiringly and enviously toward the achievements of her older sister. Michele's strength lies in having many friends who truly like her, but sometimes she overdoes the giving behavior in order to gain acceptance. She is resourceful and clever in many ways, and frequently goes out of her way to help her older sister. She, too, has a very special place in her grandmother's heart.

Albert is a very sensitive asthmatic, allergy-ridden adolescent. Although he is handsome, he is of short stature and is very self-conscious because of it. A bright student, he is admired by teachers and family. He enjoys baseball, basketball, and other sports, but is not particularly agile. Because of his severe, life-threatening allergies, he has always been very protected by his entire family. The food he eats has to be carefully screened for products that would send him to the hospital—or worse. He has had innumerable ambulance rides to the nearest health-care institution. Although his grandparents have taken him on a number of out-of-state trips, there are always precautions that must be taken. He was the first boy in his household, so he was adulated and received much attention. Both parents and grandparents were delighted when he made his appearance into the world.

Heddy is the blue-eyed, angelic eleven-year-old who, with a bat of her eyelashes, is able to win over anyone she chooses—including her Nana. She is a soft-spoken, compliant child, cuddly and lovable. For a number of years she was the youngest in the family and her father's favorite. She tries very hard to please and smilingly accepts any favors granted her. In spite of her gentle outer appearance, she sucked her thumb far beyond infancy, attesting to the fact that everything is not as calm within as it appears on the surface. Heddy weeps when she feels frustrated, which does not happen very often. This generally happens when she has forgotten to do her homework or has misplaced it. The tears mostly produce what she wants, especially around her grandmother. The child is easily satisfied and very well behaved most of the time.

Robert—or Bobby, as he is lovingly called—is the adorable live wire of the Glatz entourage. He was a very much wanted and planned child, born to his parents when they were already in middle age. They yearned for a second son and finally managed to produce him. He was instantly adulated and spoiled by one and all, including his siblings. His big sisters became little mothers to him, and his big brother was at last able to have a baby brother he could direct and dominate. Robert was the perfect final touch to the Glatz family. His chubby cheeks and winning smile reach his grandmother's heart. He is a strong-willed little boy who, when he does not get what he wants, will shriek and howl until he wins. He is aware that he is always forgiven very quickly for any outburst he might have, and he uses his power freely to attain his goals.

Clearly, grandchildren are very perceptive little creatures. At a very young age, they become aware that they can manipulate their grandmothers. This happens because they sense that Grandma wants to be loved and does not want to upset the little darlings, lest they not want to visit with her the next time. Unlike the parent on whom junior depends, Grandma is expendable. If she spoils the grandchildren and gives in to their will, they look forward to her company. Taking the children to interesting places and feeding them candy, cookies, pop, and other unacceptable nourishment will make Grandma popular. This, however, may create a dilemma in her relationship with the children's parents. If, upon a child's return home, he has a stomachache, refuses his dinner, or has a temper tantrum because he is no longer being spoiled, negative feelings toward the grandmother from her own children are not unusual. In addition, there is sometimes competition between the younger and the older generation for the love of the child. Parents need not fear, however: Under normal circumstances the young child always prefers his parents to anyone else in the family.

Grandmothers can be a real asset to frazzled parents, especially those with multiple children: They are able to take away some of the burden that constant interaction and demands place upon already overburdened parents. Grandmothers are an enhancement in the lives of grandchildren, adding a special dimension of unconditional love and caring that is invaluable for the emotional and psychological growth of the young beings.

Unfortunately, antagonism may arise between parents and grandparents, depriving the child of much that is wholesome for a healthy development. "Grandparents need to be aware that although they might want to play, the parents own the bat and ball and can go home anytime they want."[1] Grandmothers are sometimes used as scapegoats for problems between the parents or between the parents and their child. Some examples of these situations will illustrate this phenomenon.

Emily and her grandmother had an excellent relationship. She was the first grandchild and frequently stayed overnight at her grandparents' home. She often confided in her grandmother, who was always willing to listen. As a young teenager she had some disagreements with her father, Irving. One night she appeared at the grandparents' doorstep, weeping uncontrollably and showing welts where she had been hit by her dad after an argument. Not long afterward, her father arrived and ran up the stairs after the child. She was hiding in the bathroom. Her father pounded on the locked door so forcefully that the door nearly broke, and at the same time he threatened to hit his daughter again. Through the door the child begged for help in a sobbing voice. The grandmother asked her son-in-law to let things be and to think about the situation for a while, since she did not want her door broken. He promptly ran out of the house, returning later with the teenager's clothing, which he threw into the driveway. The following day Grandma convinced Emily to return to her own home with her clothing, which her grandparents had picked up and put into a bag. The clothing was dumped once again into the driveway by the irate father, who insisted that the grandparents keep the child. After a few days of respite, Emily allowed herself to be persuaded to return to her parents. The grandmother was the target of the buried anger of her son-in-law. Her part was merely to rescue a child who needed comforting at a difficult time in her life.

It sometimes occurs that in-laws have difficulties "replacing" their own parents. They are unwilling to address their parents-in-law as "Mom" or "Dad," feeling a disloyalty in doing so, and either address them by their first name, call them "Grandmother" or "Grandfather," or even call them nothing at all. This may even occur if they are antagonistic toward their own parents.

Leah, the daughter of a divorced couple, is unable to address the parents of her husband by name. She dislikes her own mother, whom she feels is a liar and an exploiter, left her maternal home as soon as she was able to do so, and has transferred her feelings of anger to her newly acquired family. She deeply resents her husband's involvement with and closeness to his parents and wishes he had been born an orphan. Although this young woman exhibits some superficial attention to "Grandma" and "Grandpa," her upbringing has left a mark on her personality. She overspends and suffers from panic attacks. She is a narcissitic personality who has difficulty relating intimately with children. Leah's characteristics, ways of thinking, and subsequent behaviors have their roots in infancy and childhood, as they do in all humans.

The age-old cliché "A look at your friends and I know who you are" may be more accurately translated: "A look at your parents and I know who you are." A similar statement in German is *Willst du um die Tochter bitten schau dir an der Mutter's Sitten*—"If you intend to ask for the daughter's hand in marriage, observe the manners of the mother."

Debby gave birth to a handsome little boy. She strongly dislikes her mother-in-law and used various excuses to keep her away from the child. She reached into the past in an attempt to convince her spouse that Grandma was unfit to participate in her grandson's life. Her reasoning appeared irrational from a normal point of view. She had marked differences with the older woman even prior to her marriage with Richard: She alleged that her engagement ring was "cheap" (in fact, she had it appraised) and insisted it was her fiancé's mother who "no doubt" had influenced his decision to purchase a "cheap" ring. Debby is very possessive of her husband and wants him totally to herself. Since he is a very busy professional man, he is unable to meet this need in his wife. That being the case, she now "possesses" her young son, not permitting him near his paternal grandmother and using him to fill the emptiness that exists within her psyche.

Leon and Ingrid lost their parents during the Holocaust and themselves hid in an attic in Holland during the Hitler era. They raised two successful sons under difficult circumstances; the oldest, Jacob, was born in Europe and came to America as a young child. When he grew up he became a physician and married an American girl, Jane, who disliked everything about her mother-in-law: the German accent, the fact that she loved her son so much, the way she walked, the way she combed her hair, the fact that she existed. The poor woman could do nothing that pleased Jane. Jacob and Jane's three young children were rarely in contact with their grandparents, since Jane did not want them influenced by "this foreigner." On the rare occasions the three youngsters were brought to their grandparents' home by Jacob, Grandma was overjoyed to see them. She showered them with affection, making special meals for them, giving them gifts, and spending time telling them stories and listening to their adventures.

Grandmother Ingrid was in great emotional pain over the rejection by her daughter-in-law, who denigrated her and took away the joy and pride of grandparenting. The grandchildren lost the intimate contact of knowing a loving grandmother who could have added so much wisdom and pleasure to their lives.

Jane is a rotund sixty-year-old grandmother of three, the offspring of Jane's two daughters. Jane looks like a storybook grandma, with her ready smile, graying hair, and oxford shoes, who wears her grandchildren's names on her sweatshirt. She also proudly displays their pictures for anyone who inquires. Although she professes love for her "adorable, gorgeous" progeny, she does not want to spend much time with them. She certainly does not want to take care of them or have them around her for long. She does not want to be disturbed or distracted from her daily routine by those "runny-nosed, snively children." She is willing to buy them sweets and toys and some gift items, but she cannot "bear" to be around them for an extended period of time. Susan, the younger of her two daughters, can accept this behavior on the part of her mother. She lives out of town, visits her parents infrequently. When she and her family visit, she has a friend supervise the children rather than having them stay at Grandma's. However the older daughter, who lives in town with her husband and one-year-old son, yearns for her mother's love and wants desperately to bring her son and her mother closer together—but to no avail. Grandma Jane rejects these attempts with vehemence.

Jane's reactions have their roots in her childhood. She was the product of an alcoholic, schizophrenic mother and a father who did not know his own dad and was raised by his single mother. Claudette, Jane's mother, was in and out of mental hospitals. When she was in the home she was verbally and physically abusive to her three children. She wanted absolutely nothing to do with her grandchildren and made this very clear to her children, Jane, Maurice, and Brenda. It was Claudette's inability to bond with her family, her self-involvement and rejection of her offspring, that formed Jane's feelings and behaviors. Fortunately for Jane, she was able to bond with her only brother, whom she could mother and "guide."

Ginny is the lovable Caucasian grandmother of Hyacinth, the nine-year-old child of an interracial union. Hyacinth's mother has never married and has to work to support herself and her child. The girl's father is an abusive man who has been in and out of prison most of his adult life. Ginny *feels very sorry for the little girl and took her into her home when she was an infant. Ginny identifies with Hyacinth, since she herself was raised by a brutal stepmother, her natural mother having died when Ginny was ten.*

In addition to Hyacinth, Ginny takes care of a bedridden husband and a grandson, Dayquan, whenever he needs care. Money is scarce in this household. The family lives on a small Social Security pension supplemented by welfare. Grandma Ginny is very resourceful. She is able to "stretch the dollar," and supplies Hyacinth with the little luxuries her mother cannot provide. Ginny visits garage sales in the neighborhood and frequently finds some real "treasures" for very little money. Hyacinth prefers being at her grandmother's meagerly furnished apartment than in her mother's house.

"Oma" is the name that Uschi called her grandmother. She was a kindly seventy-year-old who lived far away from her grandchildren. In spite of the great distance, Uschi bonded with her grandmother and had a close relationship with her. She would take the child to the farmer's market and buy overripe bananas, which they would share on the way home. Oma did not drive; she walked for miles to do her shopping and other trips that were necessary to sustain herself in her old age. On the three-mile walk home, time seemed to fly by as Oma told the fascinating stories of her own youth, together with the grisly fairy tales of the Brothers Grimm. Uschi held tightly to her grandmother's hand, all the while munching on a nearly brown banana, which tasted like ambrosia to the child. She was always disappointed when they reached home. Sometimes, when the weather was good, Oma would stop and buy Uschi an ice cream. This delicious treat was ladled into a boat-shaped waffle, which the youngster would lick ever so slowly, making the delectable flavor last so she could enjoy it longer. The times with Oma were some of the happiest times in Uschi's memory. Long after she reached adulthood, she would look back with yearning, wishing she could be back holding her Oma's hand, feeling protected and loved.

Jean was a very elegant lady; her grandchildren called her "classy." She and her husband, Duane, were a very close couple. They had "a life of their own." They took excellent care of one another and seemed to shut out the outside world. Although they did not interfere with their children or the raising of their two granddaughers, Jenny and Susie, they saw them occasionally. They did, however, endear themselves to the children. Once a year, they would take one of the teenagers on a trip. They were very careful to alternate between them, lest they be accused of favoritism. They made a special effort to include their guest on their agenda and would take the girls' interests very much into consideration. Jean would frequently tell her friends that away from their parents, their different personalities would emerge, and she found it delightful to "really get to know them." Through these intimate contacts, Jenny and Susie had the opportunity to learn a great deal about their roots, to view their grand-mother in a new light and to experience a warm and loving relationship between a couple. This was very important, because the parents of the girls did not get along with one another and were on the verge of a divorce. Jean and Duane were role models, a happy interlude in the girls' chaotic family life.

Hannah is the mother of four and grandmother of eight. Her history is one of poverty and deprivation. Her late husband was an alcoholic, and they parted when their children were very young. She raised them by her-self with the help of welfare payments and whatever she could get from the Salvation Army and various food banks. When her sons, Jadd and Jeff, became teenagers, she was no longer able to cope with their delin-quent behavior. Consequently, the court placed Jadd and Jeff into a very rigid, punitive children's institution. The daughters, too, had difficult teen years and felt deprived both materially and emotionally. Three of the four children had children of their own at a very young age. Five of the grand-children often visited Hannah in her senior citizens apartment complex. When they came to see her, they would create problems by pulling the fire alarm in the building, running around the halls in an uncontrolled way, making unnecessary telephone calls from Hannah's limited telephone, depleting her food supply very rapidly, torturing her parakeet, and stealing from her or begging for groceries or money. Hannah would give them what she could, but often resented their intrusion. At other times she would invite one or another of the youngsters into her apartment if she was lonely. She expected a great deal from her grandchildren. She wanted them to clean her rooms, wash her clothes, push her to the nearest store in her wheelchair, or do errands for her. The grandchildren had very mixed emotions about Hannah. Since they did not receive much affection from her, they generally visited her to exploit her in one fashion or another. In this way the relationship between this grandmother and her grandchildren became one of mutual exploitation.

Gertrude is the grandmother of three lively grandchildren. She enjoys seeing them and spending time with them. She takes them to playgrounds, the zoo, fast-food restaurants, and other enjoyable places. She is happy for them when they are having "good times." She is not as delighted, however, when they come to her house. Being an exceptionally tidy lady, she dislikes it when they play on her white bear rug, drop crumbs on her sparklingly clean kitchen floor, or touch the glass doors and windows with their not-so-clean hands. At times like these, she becomes very tense and anxious and is always relieved when the parents of the young cherubs come to take them home.

Gretel is a very wise grandmother. Although she does not baby-sit unless there is an emergency in her daughter's home, she does take the children into her house when the need arises. This gives her an opportunity to still take care of minor household chores, receive and make telephone calls, and play with the children as she is able. She does not have to wait for the parents of the little ones—who are invariably late in returning from their various sojourns. She is aware that she can't rely on the parents to pick up her grandchildren at a predetermined time. There have been occasions when the older woman has attempted to deposit the young ones at home, only to find that no one was there to receive them. With the years she has become wiser and now makes no plans for the times that she has the children under her care.

There is the grandmother who is unable to deny her offspring any request, the proverbial "girl who can't say no." She strongly dislikes the frequent babysitting chore, and although she loves the grandchildren she becomes angry at times. She feels that her children will not love her if she refuses to do their bidding; that the grandchildren will not know her well enough; that she should do what is asked of her; that refusal to comply with requests will place her in a bad, ungiving light; that if she refuses, future requests for favors from her children will be either refused or ignored, and so on.

Lilly had been invited to a dinner party when her son telephoned and asked her to babysit. She had so looked forward to an evening with friends, but after a few moments of hesitation and some pleadings from her son, she agreed to do his bidding, forgoing what she wanted to do. Her son had given her such a plausible argument—it was important to attend a work function with his spouse—that Grandma was afraid to refuse him. He said he could not get a sitter for his two overactive sons; that they would get hurt if he left them in the hands of a friend; that, after all, she is their grandmother and could do him that favor; and that the grandsons "adore" her. He implanted mountains of guilt in his mother's psyche.

That evening, as she grudgingly drove to her son's home, she thought of the wonderful dinner party she was missing—chatting with her friends, possibly meeting some new, interesting people. As the evening wore on and the grandsons became noisier, as tired children will, her feelings welled within her. Her patience wore thin, and the little ones could not understand how their beloved grandma could have changed so. The next day, she telephoned a childless friend and told her how fortunate she was not to have created grandchildren, who hold you back from a life of your own.

Being the person she is, Lilly will repeat the same act, even though it is against her better judgment and to her detriment. Her self-worth is lacking and she places her children's wishes before her own needs.

There is the grandparent, especially the grandmother, who frequently brags about the witticisms and accomplishments of her grandchildren. They range from "cute" little phrases to Einsteinian brilliance. For example: "Johnny said 'Mama' and he's only thirteen months old! Isn't he something?" "Melissa, at age two, combed her own hair! What an accomplished child, don't you think so?" "Little Doron got out of his crib by himself. He climbed over the rail with his little feet. I think he'll become a mountain climber someday and conquer Mount Everest." "Tommy threw the basebell directly into his dad's hand with such accuracy and precision. He will surely become the next Babe Ruth when he grows up—or maybe even a better pitcher or hitter at a younger age than the Babe." "Melissa will surely become an English teacher. She's only three and she says such big words, it's almost a miracle! I don't know where she picked up all that adult language at such a young age!" "Joey is so smart. He's nine years old and already he has straight A's in science, math, and English—and does he ever paint! Picasso couldn't do what this boy is doing, and at his tender age!"

Then there are the grandmothers who pull innumerable pictures of their little darlings out of their purse and expect the audience to *ooh* and *ahh* over each one. If that isn't enough, these listeners also get a history of the various traits of each grandchild and his genealogy. "This little girl's great-grandmother had blond hair and blue eyes just like Rosie. Her feet are small for her age, just like Aunt Bossie's. Her eyelashes are thick like her late Great-uncle John's. You can just tell that she's a Johnson, she looks so much like our part of the family." The speaker, often the grandma, enjoys attributing all the positive traits to her side of the family.

Grandmothers must not forget that other people have smart, talented, beautiful, and magnificent grandchildren also. It is all right to leave the pictures of those little cherubs in the purse or wallet—but if they must be exhibited, it should be done quietly, without the detailed history and background of each. Oh yes, we must not forget the recitation of all the diseases of each grandchild and its mother and that he would nearly have died if it had not been for Dr. Hotzenplotz who had the skills of a deity. Then there is the grandmother who injects herself into the miracle of this child's rescue by insisting that she was the first one to recognize that he had a disease called Krepansiere and she noticed it when the child turned its head a certain way when he was lying in the crib.

As we have shown, there are many kinds and varieties of grandmothers. There are those who love the little ones and will do everything in their power to please them and to have contact with them. Then there are those who do not want too much contact, and dread the term "grandmother" lest they be considered old and useless. There are those who want their freedom and feel they have met their responsibilities as soon as their children are grown and away from home. And there are those grandmothers who keep in touch, but only peripherally and from a distance—calling on occasion, writing letters, and sending packages for birthdays and other celebrations. Finally there are those who do not want the disorder and noise that children create, so they discourage visits to their homes.

Most grandmothers have special relationships with their progeny. They do not have the pressures that mothers have, taking care of the daily routines and requirements, nor do they have the responsibility of meeting their every need. They can be loving and generous and be in the good graces of the children. They do not have to discipline the children or to chauffeur them on a daily basis to all the places they want to travel. The same stresses that parents face, they do not.

Grandmothers are in a very enviable and favored position. They can be compared to the weekend father, the "Disneyworld Dad," who, because of divorce, takes his child out for good times and returns her to her mother for the rest of the week. In summary: Grandmothers are as different and unique as all of humanity. Their image has changed throughout the ages along with the enlightenment, discoveries, increasing longevity, and shifts in ways of thinking. Health and mobility have improved, and grandmothers are frequently still in the labor force, with their own careers and more education than has historically been the case. Because of this, many grandmothers are better able to contribute materially to the upbringing of their grandchildren. While some grandmothers have less personal contact with their grandchildren because they live great distances from their grandchildren, others have to act as substitute parents or daytime caregivers to their grandchildren.

Grandmothers cannot all be painted with the same proverbial brush. They are as different from each other as those younger than they—only they have had more time to develop. Grandmothers need latitude to express themselves in their own inimitable ways, to be respected and loved, and to be counted as integral parts of their families—a status they richly deserve.

4

Grandfathers

Grandfathers, like their female counterparts, come in many varieties. There are the young, the old, and the old-old. Each has a unique personality, a particular outlook on life, and an attitude toward grandparenthood and grandparenting. There are those who want to be actively involved with their progeny and those who want to be passive participants or observers. There are the storytellers, the fishermen, the baseball players, and any combination of these. Some take great pride in their grandchildren and others find them a bit burdensome. They are first and foremost people with likes and dislikes, like all folks. They want to be respected and honored; they want to count in their world. Grandfathers, like most men, take pride in their masculinity. For some males the label "grandfather" makes them feel they have lost their machismo, their virility. For others being a granddad is a badge of honor, a sign that they have sired offspring who in turn have created new life. They feel that they will live on in their grandchildren, especially if there is a boy among them. They love perpetuating their family name, their future. They may not take over the nurturing role of the ideal grandpa, yet they cherish the thought of being the head of a number of descendants that bear the same name. In sum, grandfatherhood is a blessing to many, but a denigration to some. Many young grandfathers are still very active people who hold either full- or part-time jobs and therefore are not as involved with the younger generation as they might otherwise be. The old grandpa has more time, giving him the opportunity to be more involved with the little ones. Most grandpas, like dads, prefer children when they are past the infancy stage.

They prefer the ambulatory ones who can enjoy walking, talking, and playing. As one grandpa aptly put it, "I like grandkids when they are fun."

There is the grandfather then and now. In 1900 Grandpa's life expectancy was around forty-seven; now it is seventy-three. Many people did not live to see their grandchildren. Those who did live worked very hard either on farms or in factories, depending on whether they lived in a rural or urban environment. Children and grandchildren were considered "woman's work." Diapering a child was unheard of for the male of that generation. Children in general were to be seen, not heard—and that, of course, included grandchildren. Grandchildren were considered useful for helping on the farm or with chores that had to be done in and out of the home. Grandfathers were there to pass on their skills and their religious beliefs, especially to their grandsons. In short, they were often considered role models for the younger generation.

The idealized grandfather of today is a kindly, benign gentleman who takes his grandchildren fishing and plays ball with them. If he is free of the physical disabilities of advanced old age, he buys them candy (if the parents don't object), gives them money to buy the small luxuries they enjoy, and spends time with them, telling them about their heritage. Grandpa will also, on occasion, give a money gift so that his grandchildren's future will be somewhat secure. He will never discipline or chastise them, but will guide them by example in the "right ways." He may tell them war stories in which he always appears as the hero who rescued his buddies single-handedly. He is masculine and gentle at the same time, and has all the attributes of the best qualities of both females and males—without losing his masculinity.

Grandfathers are often sole male role models for their grandchildren. This is largely due to the high divorce rate, large numbers of single mothers, and antagonism toward the birth father, and subsequently the absence of a father in the family. The grandfathers, therefore, play the role of surrogate dads. This has its positives for the children but also carries consequences. This robs grandfathers of being able to be traditional, doting grandpas and establishes a unique pattern that sometimes is not welcomed by the participants in their unexpected and unanticipated roles. This pattern will be discussed in greater detail in chapter 5.

Albert was a traditional grandfather. "Opa," as he was lovingly called by his grandchildren, was the father of three and grandfather of five. He was especially close to the three older grandchildren and spent a lot of time with them. On occasion, they were left with him for the day, as his daughter was employed and her childcare helper could not always be there. At those times he would allow the children a great deal of freedom to play as they desired. He would frequently play soldiers with them, using a broom for a rifle. He would march around as he had done in the German army in World War I. Although he spoke an accented English, the children seemed to understand him. They would giggle, imitate his goose step, and hang onto his shirttail. Even the little girl had a delightful time pretending to be a soldier. He would give them boxes of raisin nut chocolates that they would eat to their hearts' content. In the evening when their mother arrived to take them home, they were dirty and tired but happy. Grandpa, too, was tired but not unhappy to see them leave and be able to return to his routine. He always felt good to have been able to help his daughter in a time of need.

After his wife's death, Albert moved into the home of his daughter, who had moved to a distant city. He continued his previous role with the grandchildren; he also comforted them when they were unhappy. He would never oppose the limits that the parents had placed on the children, but he let them know by his actions that he was sympathetic and understood how they felt. They would come to him for hugs and reassurance. They felt good when they came home from school and found their beloved grandpa sitting in his favorite chair, reading his newspaper or smoking his cigar. He never failed to pay special attention to them as they walked into the room.

The grandchildren bonded to Opa Albert. They understood each other. They appreciated his quiet manner, his caring, his empathy when they were troubled, and his loving ways. When he died, his fifteen-year-old granddaughter composed his eulogy, which was engraved on his tombstone:

In the midst of laughter there is sorrow
In the midst of youth there is age
In the midst of life there is death
Oh dear God, why did you take him away from us?
Quiet he was, the calm center of a cyclone's wind
He lived peacefully and respected men of peace

He demanded nothing, he deserved everything.
Opa, as you are looking down on us
From skies above so blue
We hope that we our days spend right
And you'll bless all we do.

Joseph, grandfather of three and a widower since his own children were three and five years old, did not care to involve himself with the "little folk" at all. They "spelled noise and trouble," and he distanced himself as much as possible from them. After his young wife's death, he had placed his son and daughter in a children's institution so that he could continue to earn his meager living. He had struggled all his life and was short-tempered when he visited his youngsters and when, at ages six and eight, he finally took them home. He came from the "old school": he was of European ancestry and had the firm conviction that children should be seen, not heard. "Spare the rod and spoil the child" was his motto, and he practiced it often. When his children grew up and had children of their own, he paid little attention and had to be persuaded to attend their cel-ebrations. He looked at their births as "one more mouth to feed" and more commotion to tolerate. He became more and more withdrawn and rarely participated in celebrations. He did, however, have dinner with his family on occasion. The grandchildren knew him only as "Joe," and when he did come for a meal they paid very little attention to him. If they made some normal noise he would growl at them, and left immediately after he had eaten. When Joseph died at age ninety, there was little regret at his parting on his grandchildren's part. Out of respect for their parents they attended his funeral. The $10,000 he left each of the three young people was the only affirmation that Grandfather Joe had ever thought of or given any consideration to them.

George had divorced his wife when his children were very young. Because of the bitterness and fighting between them he did not see his children. He remarried after a number of years and became a stepfather to his new spouse's two daughters. When these two girls had children of their own, George became a very devoted grandfather to Robert and Molly. He spends inordinate amounts of time with them, playing games and building toys with them, and the three are very close. There is never any word spoken or thought expressed that these young folk are not his own grandchildren. George is very patient, watching cartoons with the children, drawing with them and building elaborate structures out of wood with and for them. Although he loves both of the children, eleven-year-old Bobby has a very special relationship with Grandpa George. He idealizes his grandfather, since George is a very large, macho man. When the children's parents moved out of town, Bobby grieved for his grandfather. He wanted to stay behind so that he could move into the home of the grandparents. Robert's father is a disciplinarian and travels a great deal, so the young boy used his grandfather as a role model. Because of this close tie with his grandchildren, George and Grandma visit as much as possible, even though they must travel three hundred miles to get there.

Grandpa Leonard was a fun-loving, playful fifty-nine-year-old man when he became a grandfather for the first time. He wasn't very much interested in infants, especially girls, since he was from "the old school." He felt that babies should be in the care of their mothers and, furthermore, that girls were not as valuable as boys. Thus he paid little attention to Delphine, the little one who seemed to scream more than he could tolerate. Two little boys were born in close succession. As the children grew older he began to show an interest in them. He played very active games with them and almost became one of the children in his ability to amuse himself and them. The boys enjoyed wrestling with him, and although they looked forward to visiting with him, there were times when he became overzealous and a little rough. He did not seem to realize that he was much stronger than his four- and seven-year-old grandsons. Several times he hurt the older grandson's arm rough-housing with him. Only when the child winced with pain and cried did Leonard realize what he had done. In his ardor to amuse the children and to "let them have fun," he forgot his strength. In spite of this, the boys looked forward to experiencing the entertainment that their very feisty grandfather provided for them. He was able to play on the floor with them, allowed them to climb all over him—and was able to relive his own childhood in the process.

Arthur, a very active fifty-four-year-old fireman, speaks animatedly about his two grandchildren: "From the time Louise conceived Samantha we recognized the blessing of being grandparents. It too was wonderful when the second one turned out to be a grandson, although I care about both of them the same. From the time they were babies I would diaper them, give them their baths, and when Kathy wasn't home I would give them their food. I didn't do all that for my own two daughters, but it's different when you have grandkids; I don't know why, but it just is. I attend all of the grandkids' baseball games, the boy's soccer games, and anything else they play in. I do things that my wife doesn't do. I pick them up from school and do whatever is needed. My wife was forty-three and I was forty-four when Samantha was born. The kids do have to mind me, and they do. They know I mean it when I tell them to stop or ask them to do something. I do get mad when parents don't control their kids, when the parents don't say anything when their kids fool with things that they have no business fiddling with, like turning on the VCR or the stereo, or pounding on the piano, or running around with muddy shoes all over the house. My grandkids don't do those things; they know better. My wife and myself, we don't interfere with our daughters even though we don't always agree with them . . . we don't do it."

Will is hardly a typical grandfather, although he has five grandchildren from three of his four children. He is a dapper-looking gentleman with a well-trimmed handlebar mustache and a modern haircut. He appears much younger than his fifty-eight years and at times is mistaken for his sister's son—and she is only two years his senior. He seldom talks about his children except when he is asked about them. His son Don has two sons and one daughter by his two ex-wives; son Dougherty has one son with his live-in girlfriend; daughter Dorothy has one boy with her boyfriend. Will freely states that he has no feelings regarding his grandchildren: "I don't care one way or another. You're proud like everybody else, I guess. I didn't have much family. My kids' past was bad. As impoverished Americans, they struggled and were often called names. They were raised in a poor neighborhood. They didn't have much chance for the good things that a lot of other kids have. I wasn't home much, since I worked very hard and had long hours. When I came home, I was tired and wanted to have my beer, eat my supper and go to sleep. As bad as my kids' past was they're functioning pretty well. I want my kids happy. I want to be happy and my grandkids should be happy. My oldest, Dorene, has no kids and isn't going to have children or to be anything. She smokes marijuana and even though she graduated from two years of college she stopped and is doing nothing. She has a one-legged boyfriend and a mother that too uses drugs. I don't feel about the grandchildren as much as I should. I don't go out of my way. When they were born I went to the Salvation Army and bought some stuff. I refinished it. I like doing stuff like that. I bought a buggy for the one and it looked good as new when I got done with it. I also buy other stuff for them once in a while. They invite me to the kids' birthday parties. Sometimes I go and sometimes not. You know my days are all turned around. I sleep days and am up at night. Nobody has birthday parties in the middle of the night. I don't go out of my way for the grandkids. I did what I could do, and the kids are on their own now. My kids bring the grandkids to me once in a while. I don't go to them. I like showing off the truck and showing off my fish to them. I'm happy being left alone most of the time. I love 'em, but I don't have the patience to deal with them most of the time. I haven't been able to get close to the grandkids with my oldest son's breakup of his marriage. Dorothy is not predictable; she brings her boy, Edward, to see me once in a while when she feels like it. She's good to Edward. I'd just as soon she wouldn't bring him when I'm sleeping. She's not married to her boyfriend, the father of the kid. It took me a while to grow up. I never cared if I had grandchildren or not. I just want them to be happy. My kids all grew up in poverty and they didn't really care if they had kids. They have to live their life, now I want to live mine."

Rudin speaks lovingly about grandchildren, mainly in the abstract. He was once married and divorced twenty years later. He had married a woman who had two young sons, adopted them, and raised them as his own. He also sired a daughter with his wife. He became the grandfather of four children, whom he rarely sees. He never sees the children from his younger son, since the antagonism as a result of the divorce is so intense that there is no contact between them. The other son allows him to see the grandchildren on very rare occasions, mainly to buy them gifts. He is not invited to their birthday parties since his ex-wife is present and does not want him there. Rudin feels extremely sad and rejected, but says he likes being a grandfather: "To see the beginning of life again is so wonderful; it's such a miracle. Stacy, my eighteen-month-old granddaughter, runs to me when I am allowed to see her. She runs into my arms. The things she does are so *wonderful. God's hand is there. It's a wonderful feeling. Someday I'll take the older one camping, take her out and enjoy her. With my other son's children I missed everything and they missed everything. I missed all the good things. They don't know me; I don't know them. My only daughter is moving; she's having a boy, I won't see them much. It's a shame. Birth is a continuation of life. You see the happiness on the parents' faces as they look at their little ones. Grandchildren are so full of life. They do things with such innocence. You must see them often, although their parents may not be forgiving. If you make a promise to them, you must fulfill this promise. You must not disappoint them. I know all about that kind of thing. I was in the orphanage after my mother died. My father left me there until I was seven. He almost never came to see me. I would stand by the windows every day to look for him. The other children had visitors; I didn't. I would wait and wait and no Dad. He would promise to come. When I did see him, which was very rarely, he would say that he forgot to come. It seemed as if he had forgotten me altogether. I don't do things like that to my grandchildren and I never will."*

Danfred, a sturdy-looking sixty-three-year-old man with a clean-shaven head, is the grandfather of three children ranging in age from four to eleven. Looking at him in his very casual outfits one would never guess that he is a highly educated individual. Although he still works in his profession, he spends a great deal of time with the three cherubs that are his daughter's offspring. He is also eagerly awaiting the marriage of his son so that a few more little ones might join the family. He professes that he thoroughly enjoys the children's company. This can be readily observed when one sees him in the company of young ones. He has been known to ignore adults completely when children are present. He can be deeply involved in reading, his favorite hobby, but when the grandchildren need his attention he abandons his books to be involved with them. When questioned about his feelings and his relationship with the young ones, he does not hesitate to express his stance: "I enjoy the grandchildren—their company. They're fun. I take the four-year-old boy, Dante, out at least once a week. We have power lunches together at McDonalds or other places. He looks forward to these and likes his special time. Eleven-year-old Lila likes going to the mall and my wife takes her. I like them all equally and have no favorites." He staunchly defends himself and his wife when asked if he has a favorite. "I go for walks with them, to the playground, to museums. I visit them at their house, take them home for supper. I give my daughter a break. It's important since she doesn't always feel too good. I have cookouts with the children. The only time they get on my nerves is when they're fighting with each other. My grandson Mitchell is a very deep thinker. He asked me about God the other day. Lila is charming, but Mitchell is the sweetest. Dante will go anywhere with me. They all adore their Papa—that's me. It's so much more fun to be with them than it was with my own two children. I don't have the pressure for their personality development. You can only get in their way and screw them up. With my kids I felt I had to show them the way. I was responsible for their development. It was circular reinforcement. If they did not turn out right I would be responsible. With grandchildren this is not so. With grandchildren, you are not responsible. There is no ownership. There is only a rental agreement; there is continuity. I expect nothing from my grandchildren. I love them and they seem to love me in return."

Gary is the grandfather of five children who range from first grade student to high school graduate. Gary looked forward with gusto to becoming a grandpa. He wanted as many as his three children would produce. To his dismay, his two sons were childless. The wife of his youngest son wanted none, and his older son is a bachelor. Gary enjoys seeing the little ones, and when the first, a girl, was born he was ecstatic, as he was with each of his own children. Although with his own youngsters he always wanted boys, with the grandchildren it did not matter to him. This is especially true because the young generation did not carry his last name. He enjoys it when he is asked difficult academic questions since he is an academician and his knowledge of literature, history, and other assorted studies is vast. He is the children's human encyclopedia. They need only telephone him and he has the answers at his proverbial fingertips. He enjoys his status with the young ones and likes teaching them whenever the occasion arises. He is patient with them and explains facts in a way that is understandable to them. He is not the type of person who takes children to the zoo or for leisurely walks, but he will take them to temple on a Saturday morning and proudly sits next to his oldest granddaughter, who shares many of his interests. He does not refuse the children when they need a ride and does not object to being a chauffeur for them when the need arises. He cannot accept that a married couple does not want children—unless, of course, they are unable to have them for physical reasons. He feels strongly that one of the most important aspects of marriage is to reproduce and thus to have a meaningful future. Gary is very busy with his own life and does not devote inordinate amounts of time to the little ones. When he does see them, at least once a week, generally for a family meal, he is satisfied and laughs heartily at their antics. At times, he even joins in with them and teaches them some nonsense syllables from his own childhood, which they frequently repeat to the dismay of their parents. He is concerned about their future and advises them whenever needed. Like all grandparents, Gary wants his children and grandchildren to have a satisfying and happy life.

Jim takes care of his four-year-old granddaughter, Annie. Her father works during the day and her mother abandoned her shortly after birth. Grandfather Jim has very little patience for the little girl. He is an invalid whose speech is somewhat garbled, and he does not hesitate to tell anyone who cares to hear it that he raised his own three children into adulthood and wishes he were done with it—often within the hearing of the child. He also teases her and enjoys this sport, even though it is painful for little Annie. Jim is very controlling and dictates what the youngster can and cannot do: "It gets on my nerves when she doesn't sit still and jumps around too much. She is evil and mean because she doesn't listen to me. She doesn't help her grandmother and me and sometimes even calls me names." It is impossible for the little girl to listen to him since he issues too many unrealistic orders. Annie has all of the attributes, habits, and behaviors of other children of her age, with an overlay of confusion and frustration at frequent intervals. Jim's expectations of her would be more appropriate for a much older child, one who has been raised with caring, reason, and love. He expects her to do the dishes, vacuum, make her bed, and organize her toys in neat rows before she is even finished playing with them. One day, Annie became so angry that she took a scissors and cut off her beautiful long hair. When he saw her unevenly cut hair he shamed her by telling her how ugly she looked, how no other child would want to play with her. He also threatened to hit her. Fortunately, she managed to escape the physical punishment since she was able to outrun him. The child has no recourse, since her own father will not hear of any wrong-

doing on the part of Jim. He has convinced himself that no one else would take care of his daughter, especially without remuneration.

At age seventy-five, Fred is a very vigorous man. He is the CEO of several businesses he and his wife own. He has many friends, plays bridge with skill, and works many hours each week. Although he claims to be "partially retired," this means he works only forty hours per week instead of his usual sixty. Although he is a wealthy man he is very humble: He lives in a small house, drives a small, inexpensive car, and patronizes a restaurant he says is " worth the money it charges." His tastes are very simple, and judging by his appearance and behavior one would guess he was a man of few means. Fred is the grandfather of two very handsome teenagers. He speaks of them with the utmost love and respect. His face lights up when he mentions their names. He only regrets that their parents, especially their mother, does not encourage their spending more time with him. "I never allowed myself to think that I would be fortunate enough to have grandchildren," he says. "It's a tremendous blessing. It's a great opportunity to do things for them. I can spoil them, since I don't have the day-to-day responsibility of caring for their total needs. Their parents give us one whole week a year to have the boys to ourselves. During that week we take them to a vacation resort, where they attend every cultural event they wish. Every evening there is a concert and during the day there is so much to do and to choose from that they are never bored. It is a joy for us to just have them around and to see them that time when they are with us. They are a gift to us. I often think about their future, the times they are living in, and the opportunities they will have. I so hope that they are well and capable of meeting the challenges of today and tomorrow. One of our grandsons asked why their dad is the only one of the four uncles that has offspring. The two boys feel deprived because they have no cousins. I explained that this is something I cannot change and each person has to decide for himself what he wants to do in that regard. My grandchildren know that I would do anything I could for them and they know that full well. Our grandchildren are a part of us. They are us. I see myself in them. Jean, my wife, looked at Andrew when he was born and saw her mother's smile in him. She felt her parent came back to life, and what a comforting feeling that was. When you have grandchildren you love them just the way they are. They are completely accepted no matter who they look like; how they smile; how short, tall, thin, or chubby they are. We as grandparents don't have to groom them. I loved my own children very much, but I was busy making a living, furthering our lives and our careers. With my grandchildren it's different, they are an extra bonus. It's even better!"

James is a very proud seventy-three-year-old African American. He is the grandfather of five and great-grandfather of one. During his working life, he was deputy warden of a large maximum-security prison. He graduated from high school but did not attend any institution of higher learning. His education came mainly through experience. He was a very ambitious man and achieved a great deal. He was the only child of a poor family. Because he was, for the most part, self-educated and attained a very high position in life through his own efforts, he expects that his progeny will do the same. His wife is a highly educated registered nurse. She has a doctorate and recently retired from a university. She is still very active in a number of organizations. She, too, pulled herself up by the proverbial bootstraps. The Romneys have two children, a son and a daughter. James is not terribly proud of his son's accomplishments. Through his son, Mirl, he became the grandfather of five, three girls and two boys. These grandchildren were the offspring of three different mothers, all girlfriends of Mirl. Because James had, for the most part, adopted a middle-class stand in these matters, he was not overjoyed at the birth of these youngsters, and he initially had minimal involvement with them. He believed in marriage, and it disturbed him to have grandchildren who were conceived out of wedlock.

His interest in grandparenting has gradually evolved. He goes along with his wife in dealing with them, but he does not initiate contact or involvement with them. He is closer to the girls than to the boys. He has a "thin armor." The girls, age twenty-three, twenty, and fifteen, insist on gaining his attention through teasing. They are manipulative and affectionate. James pretends not to like the affection but he really loves it. His grandsons reach him through tennis and chess. They have a competitive relationship, and both games lend themselves to this. Both grandsons have had educational problems, which creates animosity toward them on the part of grandfather, who finds it difficult to accept. He cannot help but recall that he did not have his grandsons' opportunities, that he was a self-made man and rose from corrections officer to deputy warden through competitive examinations, his love of books, learning, and hard work. He has no use for slovenliness, lack of ambition, and ignorance of the opportunities that are available. James feels that his son has wasted his life with side issues and hedonism. Instead of working and supporting the children he had created, he did whatever his impulses directed him to do. Mirl became a Muslim for a time and sired children before he was ready for the responsibilities of fatherhood. James was fifty years old when the first grandchild arrived, and he was in no way interested in playing the role of grandfather. His wife, on the other hand, kept a close relationship with the grandchildren and gave of herself to them. Through her relationship with them, James inadvertently became—reluctantly— somewhat involved. He always felt that his wife was overinvolved both with the grandchildren and their three mothers. He is unhappy that his eighteen-year-old grandson did not finish high school. He is, however, proud of his oldest granddaughter, who emulated his wife by becoming a registered nurse. James is now supportive of his spouse's advice regarding the grandchildrens' needs.

James sees his grandchildren approximately three times a month, mostly through the actions of his wife. He never takes the children anywhere on his own, only in the company of grandma, to whom the grandchildren mean a great deal. Through her he has formed a bond with the future generation.

Philip's father died when he was an infant, and he always longed to know his dad. He had a very difficult childhood, and as an adult he felt that he had no childhood at all. When he was four, he and his mother immigrated to the United States from Europe. The little family was very poor until his mother remarried. At that time he lived some of the time with his mother and some of the time with relatives. He had no acceptable male role model in his early life. When he eventually became a father and grandfather, he was uncertain of what was expected of him. His dilemma continued when he married a woman who was mentally ill, drank too much, and saw motherhood as an almost insurmountable task. When under the influence of alcohol, she was abusive to her three children and a burden to Philip.

Grandpa Philip has little time to spend with his grandchildren, six of whom live not too far from him. He is occupied with his failing furniture business and his emotionally ill spouse. He does pay some attention to the children of his middle child, a daughter who divorced her abusive, alco-holic husband when her two daughters were young. Since the little ones have no functioning dad, Philip takes over whenever he can and attempts to fill some of the void in their lives, even attending a father-daughter affair at his ten-year-old granddaughter's school. It was one of the rare times that he wore a tie and suit, a real sacrifice for him.

Heino is a rotund, gentle grandfather with a shock of salt-and-pepper hair. Although he is retired from his job as systems engineer, he is still active with his personal computer and now with his grandchildren. His son died in November, and he and his wife have had their two grandchil-dren, Timmy and Dana, in their home since then. He does not know how long they will be able to stay, since he does not have legal custody of the children. Before November, he was not overinvolved with Timmy and Dana. He saw them in the company of their parents three or four times a month, usually sharing meals together as a family. He went fishing with his son and grandson. He was never a "game player." Now he is fully involved with the children, taking them to doctor's and dental appoint-ments, chauffeuring them to school, helping them with their homework, and tending to their needs. Heino readily admits that he and his wife have had to make an adjustment. Their life has changed; the routines that they used to have are gone: "We're not accustomed to this lifestyle. It's hard. We've had our routine and nothing has disturbed it. Sometimes it's a real burden. We're doing more adjusting to it than the children are. [Our daughter-in-law,] Blanche won't give them up legally because of the Social Security and the veteran's payments she's getting. We don't want to alienate the mother. She is financially incompetent. Before my son died they filed for bankruptcy, since she didn't know how to handle money. She wasted it all. My wife is now managing her accounts for her. Blanche can't do much of anything. She has never even loved the children or anyone. She used to beat the children, but they still seem to have real feeling for her. Blanche doesn't visit them now, even though they live only a few streets away from her. She calls them on the phone once in a great while. I am very careful about punishing the kids, knowing what they went through, especially the boy. I seldom discipline them. If I have to, it's through restrictions and distractions. The boy is out of control sometimes. He's what they call ADHD. He jumps around like a wild man. His med-

ications haven't been adjusted in over a year. The hardest thing about all this is doing the right thing for my grandchildren."

Grant is the grandfather of five children, three boys and two girls. Although he now lives in Florida, he keeps in touch with them on a regular basis. He visits his family in New York State at least twice a year and telephones them at least on a monthly basis. At seventy-five, he is still a robust, active man, practicing his trade of carpentry on a part-time basis. Although he is now married to a very compatible woman, he has had a difficult life fraught with hard work and unexpected illness. He was married for many years to his first wife and got along well with her. They were happy together until she became disabled with multiple sclerosis. Although at the beginning of her illness she was still capable of walking and taking care of her responsibilities, this ended when she gave birth to twins. When her children were very young she could no longer fulfill the mother role. She was unable to walk, her speech was garbled at times, and ultimately she had to be fed. Since Grant had to work to make a living for his young family—there were four children—he could not be at home to help. On his meager carpenter's wages, he did not have the means to employ a caretaker for his very ill, incapacitated wife. She ultimately became wheelchair bound, and the children were often left to their own devices. As much as he loved them, he could not change the situation. He would frequently come home at midday to feed his wife and children, rushing back to work as soon as he could.

Grant became a grandfather after his wife's death. This was a different experience for him. He did not participate in his grandchildren's care, but he was pleased at their births and happy to assume his new status. Since he remarried he has not been "superinvolved" with the little ones. He does see them at his children's homes on occasion and is always interested in their welfare. He remembers their birthdays and Christmas with little gifts, and is proud of their accomplishments. He is pleased to know that his growing grandsons are also interested in and skilled at carpentry and attempt to emulate him in a number of ways. It is a joy for him to hear that they are healthy and doing well. Grant has a good relationship with his family. His grandchildren are his affirmation that his life has been worthwhile and that he has accomplished something in this world.

Dusty is the devoted, young-looking grandfather of a six-year-old boy. He is a most unusual man, a distinguished college professor who, as a single parent, raised his only child, a daughter. His marriage was dissolved when his child was young and he was happy to have her and to take care of her. He was very proud of her as she grew into womanhood and attended college away from home. Dusty was dismayed to learn that his unmarried daughter was pregnant. When he returned from an overseas sabbatical leave, he saw his four-month-old grandson for the first time. He felt no immediate bonding with him and no visceral genetic response. It was just another infant, a baby that interrupted his daughter's education and her opportunity to be self-supporting.

In retrospect, he feels that this now very much wanted child gave his daughter a meaning, an anchor, and a purpose in life. He remembers the birth of his daughter, Lesandra, and recalls that the first time he saw her he felt a tremendous sense of attachment to her. "I did not feel this immediately with Tipper until he was almost a year old," he says. "I cannot distinguish within myself the difference between my father or grandfather role. Tipper has called me 'Daddy' for a long time, but recently he fluctuates between that title and 'Grandpa.' It seems that Tipper leads a double existence between his image of father and grandfather all within the same person. The child was born not knowing his dad. My daughter eventually married the man who impregnated her, but divorced him not long afterward. This man, Gard, is not meaningful in the boy's life. He has seen him only once within the last four years. Gard's life is not sufficiently cohesive and purposeful to be a good father. He is not a reliable and steady figure in the child's life and would only make him unhappy. It is no doubt very good that there is no contact between these two individuals, Gard and Tipper. Lesandra is thirty-five years old. She sets the guidelines between certain types of behavior. Although she did live for a brief period of time on her own, it did not last for long. She has purchased a million toys for the young one; she is no doubt compensating for a deficiency that she experiences in their lives. I do not interfere in my daughter's fashion of upbringing of her progeny, although I do not always agree with her. I am more conservative than my daughter. My daughter takes the child to places like Chucky Cheese, etc., but I would never do this. I would make him more introspective. I only listen to classical music; she likes popular music. Tipper is almost constantly in motion except when he is watching video games or television. I do not like to let him ruin his young brain with television. I take him out very often. We take excursions to farms, country fairs, adventures to expand his mind and his life. I'll take him far and wide to let him experience some historical event. I would rather travel three hours with him than to let him engage in television viewing. He is spoiled and often says, 'We never do anything.' He is accustomed to leading an active life. He's just like my daughter was and asks, 'What are we doing today?' I can never satisfy his desire to be on the move and to be amused constantly.

I very much like doing things with Tipper. On the other hand, my freedom is limited as the result of these commitments. My daughter lives with me for economic reasons. Unless you have a supportive parent or grandparent, you cannot go back to school. My daughter was not eligible for welfare. As a result of helping to raise my grandchild I have no assets. In spite of the negatives there are gains. Yesterday Tipper said to me, 'Grandpa, you know more than anybody else.' I've always liked children, but this one is special to me. I don't know how much of this is genetic and how much is history. Temperamentally, I always responded to the disadvantaged, the underlings, the children. I worked as a camp counselor, also with handicapped children. I believe I could love any child that was put at my feet. I love writing, I love travel, and I love children. I visited fifteen or twenty countries. Had it not been for the baby I would never have come back from Hong Kong, a place which I really enjoyed. It is such a cosmopolitan place; both English and Chinese are the major languages. It is a mecca of the world. I taught at the University of Hong Kong. I returned from there when Tipper was four months old. The prospect of travel makes my life interesting. My academic life has enabled me to do this, to feel fresh and renewed. My daughter is thinking of moving to Florida with Tipper; it's a terrible wrench. When my grandson with his mother moved to Chicago for a year, I visited them every two months. I guess I can do this again, especially since my eighty-six-year-old mother lives in Florida also. If their life can be put on a stable economic basis as a result of their moving, it will be a relief to me. I know I'll become the backdrop in my grandson's life because his peers will become very important. I adore him and love him dearly and he is very important to me. I have spent more time with Tipper than any grandparent that I know. I like to play and this helps. Being an academic has given me a great deal of flexible time to do this. We created the extended family through necessity and it has worked for us."

Ralph is the father of three adult children. Ralph and his wife, Irma, have struggled with their marriage for years. Ralph is a retired college professor who enjoys the company of women. His wife, a highly educated woman who worked hard as a teacher, is very unhappy in her marriage and has separated from her husband a number of times. These separations took place when she learned of his frequent but brief affairs. During those times she felt useless and self-recriminatory. She would always keep her children with her while her spouse moved. The three children knew of their father's escapades and did not appreciate the quarrels that resulted from his absences. His daughter would often weep with frustration, and his sons became alienated. In addition to this unacceptable behavior, he was also very strict and expected great things from his "boys." Julie, while in her early teen years, made an aborted suicide attempt. She felt that she was never understood by her father, and that in any event he disliked her and did not attempt any sort of meaningful relationship with her. She could not wait to leave home, where she felt helpless to be of assistance to her mother and felt alienated from her father. At age twenty-two, she moved far away from her parents. Having had a poor role model at home, she was unable to relate to men. She turned to women for solace and lives with her lesbian mate six hundred miles from her parents' home. The oldest son had a great deal of difficulty in his youth. He was involved in the drug culture, worked in a factory for a living, and "did his thing"— to the dismay of his very educated parents. He did eventually complete his schooling and followed in his father's footsteps, becoming a college professor at age forty. The middle child, a son, would occasionally visit his parents without his wife and children. The only one who had any attachment to Ralph was grandson Eugene, the only child of Ralph's oldest son. Grandpa adulated him. He took him places when he was a teen, sent him gifts when he was attending an out-of-state university, and paid some of his college expenses. Their relationship seemed based to a large extent on financial advantages for Eugene. Ralph and his wife grieved the loss of a close relationship with their children and grandchildren. In his old age, Ralph made a number of attempts to be a part of his two other grandchildren's lives, but nothing seemed to be effective. His son's wife refused to participate in any visits with her in-laws and convinced her husband that Ralph was not a man that she wanted in her children's lives.

When Gregory became a grandfather, he was very unhappy. He refused to talk with his daughter, Heather, and asked her to leave and to take the "little bastard" with her. Johnny was a beautiful little brown-skinned infant. He was conceived from an out-of-wedlock situation involving a Caucasian mom and an African American dad. Heather was the daughter of a middle-class Protestant family whose "morals" did not include illegitimate children, especially not if they were from a mixed racial background. When Heather was fourteen years old, her parents divorced. Heather was very unhappy. She had not had the best relationship with her father, yet she was bonded to him and always wanted to be accepted by him. She is a beautiful young woman, but her poor self image declined further as a result of her parents' separation and subsequent remarriage. Because of this need for acceptance she chose to move in with her father. She wanted desperately to be loved but she did not feel much affection in her father's home. Her stepmother was not pleased to have Heather in Gregory's house, especially since she always seemed to be underfoot. She found fault with everything the girl did, and made sure that her husband knew her feelings. Heather was devastated by the rejection. At age seventeen she met a twenty-two-year-old African American man in a bar. They were attracted to one another, and nine months later Heather gave birth to Johnny. After being evicted from her father's home, she lived with the child's father for a time. The situation became unbearable for her since the couple had very little income and their relationship left a great deal to be desired. When Johnny's father, James, got a well-paying job in Atlanta, Heather agreed to let her son go with him. It was a very painful time for her, but she felt that the child needed his father more than he did her. Johnny's paternal grandparents were also in Atlanta. Grandfather Rufus, a retired railroad man, was delighted to see young Johnny. He and his wife took great interest in the boy and would take him fishing, on pleasant country rides, and would frequently watch the youngster while James was working. Johnny and Rufus became very attached to one another. If Grandpa was doing something that he believed would be enjoyable for the little boy, he would take him along. Johnny was his only grandson and the two became almost inseparable. Observing these two

*people together, it could easily be concluded that the grandfather gained
as much from his relationship with the boy as the grandson did.*

*Theodore, or Teddy as his friends called him, was the doting grandfather
of three children, two grandsons and one granddaughter. To this man
children were a very precious "commodity," especially since he lost his
only son in Israel during one of the country's many skirmishes. Teddy
himself was a survivor of the Hitler era, a man who had escaped to Israel
at the beginning of the Holocaust. When his daughter, now his only child,
presented him with children he was overjoyed. When they were very small
he would visit them frequently and would imagine what great accomplishments they would have and how proud he would be of them. He
would often call one or the other of the boys by his late son's name, which
sometimes annoyed the designated grandson. He was especially pleased
because Fred, the younger of the two boys, looked very similar to his late
son. Teddy spent hours telling the children about his life experiences, his
boyhood adventures, his religious education, the school he attended, and
the teacher that educated him. He would speak of the Holocaust, his
escape to Israel, and the hard life he had there. He spoke of the chickens
he raised when he made an attempt at chicken farming in Israel. He spoke
of his failures and successes and always impressed upon them that they
must be ready for anything, because "life is unpredictable and you never
know what will happen." The grandchildren were enraptured listening to
their granddad and never seemed to get enough of the story of their roots.
Ted was always ready to share his wife's delicious pastries which all three
children ate with gusto whenever they visited him. He would give them a
few dollars for their "piggy banks" and would always accompany these
monetary gifts with the caution that they should save as much as they
could for "rainy days." Theodore was a very interesting and unique
person and to his three grandchildren he was absolutely "the greatest!"*

In conclusion, we have seen grandfathers and their infinite variety.
Having had many years to live and to gather experiences, they are who
they were—only more so. In their later years, they now have the opportunity to see a third generation and to be a part of their lives. They have
a chance at a second fatherhood, one that is more relaxed; one that is of
help to their grandchildren. They are as unique as all other people. They

are often of great help to the young ones and their parents. Where there is an absent father, they often take his place, giving the boys an opportunity to emulate them and giving the girls the presence of a male in their young lives. Grandfathers are an integral and important part of every family and, together with grandmothers, help children to realize their roots.

5

In Loco Parentis

Raising Grandchildren

Raising children is a difficult task best reserved for the young. Raising grandchildren is an even more difficult task. It is a labor of love. Parents are rewarded by seeing their progeny grow up and become self-sufficient adults; grandparents, because of their advanced age, are often deprived of that pleasure. They sacrifice their own needs and desires to give a home to the young ones who would otherwise have no permanence or security in their formative years.

The emotional hazards of substitute parenthood are many. For the most part, children will always love their parents best; they yearn for the absentee parent most of their waking hours. They sometimes project their disappointment onto grandparents who are trying hard to make them happy. Grandparents have the impossible task of explaining to the grieving child why a drug-addicted mom never comes to see him; why an alcoholic dad has abandoned him; why a single mom disappeared; why dad died; why mom committed suicide and will never return, and so on. Grandparents have to answer all of these queries without hurting the child, and yet not lie to him. In addition, Grandma may be poor and/or alone, and may have great difficulty stretching her Social Security pension to feed and provide for the young one. She may be frail and have a number of age-related physical problems; she may have to cope with many losses at the same time she is attempting to comfort her grandchild. She may be criticized by outsiders for raising her own children "the wrong way," thus attributing the problems of the problematic parent to her. She may find socializing very difficult because her friends are finally free to enjoy the company of other adults and do not appreciate having a child "tag along." They long for adult conversation rather than the constant prattle of young children. Grandma or Grandpa may not be in a financial position to employ a baby-sitter when they do want to enjoy outside activities, or they may feel that they must not leave the child with strangers since the child has already lost his parents.

Grandma may feel exhausted from a day's work and yet force herself to attend a parent-teacher conference that she has been asked to attend. She may feel very much out of place among all the young and enthusiastic parents, and as a result she may feel ostracized and snubbed.

Those grandparents who were enjoying a leisurely retirement may have to return to a job, often of a menial nature, in order to have enough income to support a child or two. This creates a great hardship for these elderly people, who are trying hard not to let the grandchild feel their resentment. There are also those grandparents who give up a satisfying job in order to remain at home with a grandchild.

Some grandparent "moms" experience hostility and jealousy from their adult children, who may feel that the live-in grandchild is monopolizing all of their parent's time and energy. They may feel shortchanged since the grandmother must give much more to this "new" permanent addition than she does to the other children and grandchildren in the family. They project their anger toward their absentee sibling onto the grandmother. Often the caregiver grandma faces the collective hostility of the child's natural parent, her own son or daughter; her husband, who feels ignored; and possibly also the grandchild she is raising.

There are also often problems with the absent parent who comes in and out of the surrogate parents' house, perhaps in an inebriated condition. He or she may make all sorts of promises that are never kept and creates unhappiness for the child, who doesn't understand what is happening and why. The child is frequently unhappy for long periods of time after the parent has left. There is also the parent who takes the child with her temporarily, perhaps introduces him to current or previous lovers, and disappears again, dropping off the young one at the grandparents' home or just leaving him without supervision. This causes a great deal of confusion and turmoil in the child, often with subsequent unacceptable behavior toward his upbringers. Regression to an earlier stage of life is not an unusual symptom that the grandparents have to deal with. This sometimes is exhibited through uncontrollable crying, incontinence of bowel and or bladder, smearing or retention of feces, and so on.

The grandparent has the duty to raise a well-behaved, healthy, well-adjusted child, but at the same time she worries about disciplining the young one, since she wants the child to be happy and to love her. The caregiver grandparent has a Herculean task before her and is forever hoping that she will have the stamina to live long enough to complete her job. This is particularly the case with the elderly grandparent, whose concerns are not unfounded.

There are also those grandparents who thoroughly enjoy the excitement and adventure of once again having a child in their household, a human being they can mold and love and hopefully bestow with a happy and satisfying life. It is a time when they can feel young, worthwhile, and fulfilled again.

SOME CASE HISTORIES

No one becomes a grandparent of his own volition. Grandparents attain that status because of decisions made by their children, and have no control over the timing of their becoming grandparents. Likewise, grandparents cannot control their children's divorces, or the use of drugs or alcohol and other family threatening lifestyles. Sociologists have used the term *countertransition* to indicate the involuntary changes in lifestyles to which grandparents are subject.

In part, these changes in lifestyles are the outcome of demographic conditions. As life expectancy increases, multigenerational families involving four or more generations are more common than ever before. This means that a grandparent may have a father or a mother, or both, living, and that constant alterations to these statuses are produced by the departure of the adult children and the birth of children in the next generation. Therefore, the greater the number of generations living at one time, the greater the number of roles held by each family member. This situation leads to a variety of interpretations of the grandparent role, derived from the differences in the ages of grandparents and great-grandparents and the differences in the occupational and health condition of each grandparent. There are grandparents who work full-time. There are grandparents who are in excellent health, have a youthful and active appearance, and keep busy in their work and their outside interests. There are, in many families, other grandparents who are quite old, ill, poor, and incapable of working or participating in social affairs, who give children a totally different impression concerning the status and role of grandparents than some of their other grandparents exhibit.[1]

Even under normal circumstances, grandparents are faced with a number of role conflicts. One of these pertains to those grandparents who are working and to whom the grandparenting role is of minor importance because it conflicts with their self-definition.

Grandparents also face a conflict inherent in diverse expectations placed on them by their children and children-in-law. Grandparents are expected to be supportive but noninterfering. That distinction is hard to discern and may also be seen from the viewpoint of the grandparents, who find the natural birth parents to be interfering in their efforts to support grandchildren abandoned by their mother and father. Particularly among divorced parents, it is common to expect grandparents to provide support and maintain family stability and a sense of history, but not be involved—since such involvement is viewed as "interference." This dilemma has no resolution but continues for years. In cases of divorce, in which the mother almost invariably is granted custody of her children, the relationship between paternal grandparents and their grandchildren often deteriorates as paternal grandparents are denied visitation with their grandchildren.[2]

Because divorce, desertion, drug use, and illegitimacy are so common in the United States at the beginning of the twenty-first century, an ever-increasing number of American children live with their grandparents. In 1998 the census found that 6 percent, or 3.9 million American children, were living with grandparents. In 2001 4 million children in this country lived with their grandparents. This represents a 2 percent increase over three years. In some of these households, the parent is present. This is particularly true in the case of unmarried mothers, who have given birth to approximately one-third of all American children born each year since 1997.[3]

This important development has received some attention in the media and in the academic literature over the past ten years. Information concerning grandparents raising grandchildren can be found in the media. In addition, politicians and family sociologists are speaking about this trend with ever-greater frequency.

Current trends concerning grandparents who care for grandchildren are more visible than ever before because the Welfare Reform Act of 1996 requires teenage single mothers to live with their parents and attend school if they seek government money for their support. This provision increases the burden of child care for grandparents almost ipso facto, because 4 million children under the age of eighteen are living in the homes of their grandparents. These range in age from those just born to those seventeen years old, among whom there are additional pregnancies and births. Additional provisions of the law restrict cash benefits to a limited number of years and require cash assistance beneficiaries to work, meaning those with children must find day care—often provided by the grandparents. Because many unwed parents are drug users, the limits recently placed on treatment for drug use by Medicaid have had the unanticipated consequence of ensuring that more and more children of such drug users become the responsibility of their grandparents.[4]

It has been estimated that in one-third of the homes in which grandchildren live with grandparents, neither parent is present, so the grandparents are the sole primary caregiver for their grandchildren. Drug use is not the only reason for the abandonment of children by mothers and fathers in favor of grandparents. AIDS and parental death are other reasons, as are emotional problems, teenage pregnancy, and incarceration.[5]

Arnetta, a forty-seven-year-old African American woman, was suddenly confronted by the death of her oldest daughter and the necessity of caring for her motherless granddaughter, Eloine, who was three years old at the time. Arnetta had raised seven children on a meager practical nurse's salary. When she discovered her daughter on the floor of her apartment, the victim an apparent cardiac arrest, she attempted desperately to revive her, to no avail. Her little granddaughter was crying unconsolably, calling "Mommy" to the still figure of her mother. It was a very long day for Arnetta. Not only did she have to cope with the death of her beloved daughter but there was the child who had to be consoled and cared for. With very little hesitation, Arnetta decided to give little Eloine a home. In the beginning she did not know how she was going to keep her hospital job and take care of the child at the same time. She switched to the night shift, enabling her to be with her granddaughter during the day. After much searching, she found a neighbor who was willing to watch over

Eloine at night. Her life became a hectic one. She had to abandon her hope for a more restful and leisurely life with nothing but her job to think about. She had recently begun to work three twelve-hour shifts, thus freeing her to pursue her own interests and socialize with friends the other four days. This was not to be. She now had to come home directly after her shift in order to feed, dress, and meet the needs of the sad little girl, who was mourning the untimely death of her young mother. Eloine regressed in her behavior. She frequently wet her bed at night and often cried without apparent cause. The grandmother tried hard to cheer the child up, but because she was grieving herself she had a very difficult time making the little one happy. Sometimes Arnetta would sit in her rocking chair after a night's work and weep quietly while holding Eloine on her lap. Eloine became the shadow of her grandmother, following Arnetta wherever she went. She clung to her with the fear of death and abandonment. At age five, Eloine began attending the neighborhood school. She could not understand why people spoke about mothers when she had none. She asked Arnetta many questions about death and why her mother died. It was very difficult for the grandmother to deal with all of the questions for which the little girl sought answers.

It took many years for Grandma and grandchild to adjust to their situation, but adjust they did. The two became very much attached to each other. Arnetta included Eloine in almost all of her activities. She attended school functions with her and brought the little girl along when she visited friends. When Eloine was a sophomore in high school, Arnetta got the teenager a job as a nurses' aide in the hospital where she herself was employed. This position cemented their relationship, ultimately leading the child into the field of nursing. In spite of the emotional pain that both Arnetta and Eloine suffered because of the death of the child's mother, the grandmother had rescued the child from estrangement, abandonment, and neglect.

It has been estimated that nationwide approximately seventy-five thousand grandmothers must care for their grandchildren because the children's mothers are in prison. One such example is Jessielean Smith, the Milwaukee grandmother whose daughter was imprisoned for stealing $11,000. This forced Smith to take on the responsibility of two toddlers, aged two and three, left behind by their incarcerated mother. According to reporter Jason DeParle, "The children have clogged her toilet, colored her walls, and reduced the wood paneling in her dresser drawers to a pile of splinters." Smith's story, which appeared in the *New York Times*, recites a litany of unending deprivation and difficulty even the strongest and youngest among us could hardly bear.[6]

The hardships depicted in the *New York Times* story are mainly the product of the reduction in welfare payments, which are now down 43 percent nationally. In Wisconsin the welfare rolls have been slashed 91 percent. Consequently, the fate of children of imprisoned mothers has become even more uncertain than it was under the old welfare system. This has led to the organization of Aid to Children of Imprisoned Mothers, Inc., (AIM) a resource available to address the needs of grandmothers who are faced with new and increased burdens resulting from their daughters' imprisonment.[7] Originally, AIM was organized to help imprisoned mothers, but quickly it became evident that help was needed by entire families. These concerns relate to the worry by the imprisoned mothers concerning their children, the clarification of their legal status, hope for the eventual reunification of mothers and their children, and the family need for economic support and self-sufficiency.

Tahisha is the sixty-year-old caregiver/grandmother of her two grandsons, ages five and eight. Her son, the father of these children, is in prison for drug trafficking, molestation of a young girl, and burglary. He is serving a long prison term and will likely remain in jail until his sons are adults. His wife left long ago and had not been heard from in more than a year, when she sent a postcard from another state with greetings for Jake and Jimmy, her two little boys. Tahisha continues her work as a cleaning woman, a job she has held for a number of years. She cleans offices at night, and during the day when the children are not in school, she supervises them. At night, her sister "looks in on them" while they are asleep. Between her meager earnings and what she receives from Social Security for the young ones, she is able to keep the children fed and dressed. She walks the boys to the bus stop every day and sometimes is so tired she can barely stay awake. One weekend a month she travels many miles on a bus to the prison where her son is incarcerated, so her two grandsons can visit their father. She believes it will keep her spirits up and will give him something to look forward to, while at the same time, her grandchildren will get to know their father and hopefully will bond to him in a positive way.

Tahisha saves all month so that she has enough money to take this journey regularly. At the prison, the boys meet other young visitors and do not find anything unusual about their father's or their own circumstances. On occasion they mention their mother's name, but most of the time it does not enter into their conversation. At school they seem to blend in with the other children. Tahisha does worry that the two boys will follow in their father's footsteps, and hopes that they will get an "honest job." She is also concerned that their mother will appear one day and disrupt all of their lives—only to leave again. She is very much concerned that she herself may not be alive long enough to lead Jake and Jimmy into adulthood. She worries about the many young men in her area of the city who have been shot, and others who have been sent to detention centers and other institutions for children and adolescents. Tahisha takes the boys to church consistently and believes that her faith will prevent some of the prevalent problems, and that the children will be influenced by the teachings of the church and the example that she herself sets.

There are those who hold that the number of African Americans incarcerated in American prisons is the product of racism alone, and that the rich get richer while the poor get prison. While this point of view may be debatable, it is certain that a high proportion of imprisoned African Americans leads to unmet needs of children thus abandoned by their fathers and mothers. Such imprisonment affects about seventy-two thousand women at any one time. One-half of these women are of African descent, while the other half are almost entirely of European descent. Because blacks constitute only 12 percent of all Americans, the effects of the more than fourfold disproportion in presence of black mothers in prisons is often cumulative in that many of the grandmothers who now care for the children of their imprisoned daughters were in prison themselves when they were young.[8]

The pressures and responsibilities that descend upon grandparents when their grandchildren come to live with them illustrate how many of these disadvantages are passed on from generation to generation, not only because of the high incarceration rate, but also because poverty, disease, illegitimacy, and divorce are also disproportionate in the black community. Because of this, AIM works mostly with African Americans.

The phenomenon of grandparents raising grandchildren indicates that there is indeed a considerable bond between the generations in the United

States and a great deal of solidarity within families despite the rise in divorce, desertion, and abandonment of children.

Rhoda is the sixty-two-year-old grandmother of four-and-a-half-year-old Haley. The child is the product of Irving, Rhoda's drug-addicted son, and Diane, an irresponsible, alcoholic, promiscuous young woman who found it impossible to raise her infant daughter. Diane met Irving in the drug rehabilitation center that both were attending at the time. When Diane became pregnant, the couple decided to marry. The child was born in California, far from the couple's home state of New Jersey. Rhoda remained in close communication with the young couple. She sensed from their conversations that neither her twenty-eight-year-old son nor his twenty-one-year-old wife were doing much for their little girl. When Haley was four months old, Rhoda sent a plane ticket for the mother and child to come home. Her son remained in the rehabilitation center and eventually graduated to a halfway house. The couple ended up on welfare because they had no means of support in their condition. Diane decided to move in with another man and left Haley with Rhoda. Grandma was very happy to have the little girl because she feared for the child's welfare. Rhoda bought everything the child needed, furnished an entire room for her, and planned for her care and education. "I did not want my little grandchild to be raised by that tramp," she says, speaking of her daughter-in-law. "She sleeps with many men. She has been in many relationships and never stays very long with one man. I have joint primary physical custody of the child, together with the mother. I don't want the child to be exposed to all these so-called fathers, men who come in and out of Diane's apartment and usually sleep with her. I've fixed it so the child is not allowed to stay with her overnight. I have control. I feel totally divorced from that woman, although I have to deal with her for the sake of little Haley. Diane comes to see the child in erratic ways; three hours, maybe, once in a while. She throws the child into strange family situations. She and my son never filed papers for divorce, although they are never together. Diane is really not involved in a good or regular way with the child.

"Haley is very much attached to me. I am her full-time caregiver. I gave up my job as administrative nurse to take care of our little girl. My now-husband never had children. He simply adores Haley. We take her to the ocean, for vacation, and everywhere. Wherever my husband and I go, *so does Haley. I have a forty-five-year-old lady friend who is a widow and who also has a child Haley's age. We have a great deal in common and we relate to each other. The two little girls go to nursery school and play together. We have so much fun, Haley and I. She's my life now. John, my husband, is so different from my son. My son is not dependable; John is. Whatever my son did he messed up.*

"I know what it's like to be an orphan. My mother died when I was four years old. My dad remarried when I was eight. I was raised by a paternal aunt and uncle. I have no regrets about having given up my job and my lifestyle. I know how important it is for a child to have a good family life. Haley calls me 'Mommy' most of the time. When she's happy, I'm happy!"

Evidently, grandparent caregiving is not rare. Today, such caregiving cuts across class, race, and gender lines. Three-quarters of custodial grandparents took in their grandchildren when the children were younger than five years old. More than half of such grandparents provide care for at least three years, and for many such obligations last much longer. Furthermore, many such grandparents are responsible for their own children and multiple grandchildren at the same time.

African American grandparents become full-time caregivers at twice the rate of those in other ethnic groups. This is in part the product of a long tradition in black families of intergenerational caregiving, which has its roots in West African culture. Principally, however, grandmothers in the black community assume the role of caregivers because of their daughters' drug addiction, incarceration, AIDS infection, and early pregnancy.[9]

It is no surprise that a significantly larger number of caregivers for grandchildren are female rather than male. Nevertheless, one quarter of the caregiving grandparents in this country are grandfathers, a fact that has been ignored by the media and academic researchers alike. This is because grandfathers are generally secondary caregivers, either because men are employed more often than women and are therefore less likely to be home or because American culture demands a caregiving role from women, not from men. In fact, suspicion of homosexuality often rests on men who pursue caregiving careers.[10]

There are also a good number of grandparent caregivers who are unmarried, either because they are widowed or divorced or because they themselves were unmarried mothers whose daughter(s) have repeated this pattern.

As the number of grandparent caregivers has increased, support groups for such grandparents have proliferated across America. These groups are necessary because so many grandparents willingly accept the responsibilities their own children have left behind. In fact, many grandparents intervene and volunteer to take in grandchildren who have become the victims of parental neglect or abuse. The acceptance of these roles has led to a number of problems among grandparents who play the surrogate role. Illness is the leading problem for such grandparents and great-grandparents, including depression, insomnia, hypertension, back and stomach difficulties, and other conditions caused by the new emotional, physical, and financial demands made upon them by their surrogate parent status.[11]

Grandparents raising grandchildren also face economic difficulties, particularly since more than half of such grandparents are already living on a low income. The overrepresentation of the poor among such grandparents is evidently associated with the reasons for the abandonment of the grandchildren in the first place. As we have already discussed, these reasons frequently involve the use of drugs and alcohol but also include unemployment, desertion, divorce, and incarceration. For grandparents, these newly acquired demands can mean quitting their jobs, reducing the number of hours spent working, and making other changes that place their economic security in jeopardy. This is particularly true of the many grandmothers who are suddenly confronted with the need to spend their time with their grandchildren at the expense of their economic future. Frequently such grandparents have to sacrifice the savings they have accumulated to protect themselves from poverty in their old age.

Retired grandparents can also suffer economic hardship from being called upon to raise grandchildren. Many Americans have inadequate pensions and are living on Social Security checks, which will not cover the added costs of supporting grandchildren. "Such grandparents sometimes report spending their life savings, selling the car, giving up such 'luxuries' as shopping for a new pair of shoes," and making other sacrifices.[12]

One of the most astounding distinctions made by the federal government concerning surrogate grandparents is the support given to foster care parents, which is not available to blood-related grandparents. Such grandparents qualify only for low and stigmatized welfare payments, while foster parents receive psychological counseling, a clothing allowance, and substantially higher government financial compensation.

This means that, in effect, blood-related grandparents are penalized for helping their grandchildren. This penalty exceeds the financial burden placed on grandparents in that it also includes social isolation. Because the care of children takes up so much time, many grandparents must restrict their social lives as they have less time to spend on family and friends, who are generally unwilling to give surrogate grandparents any support. In fact, many friends and relatives avoid surrogate grandparents because their own days of changing diapers and dealing with small children are behind them. Furthermore, a good number of grandparents are embarrassed to discuss the fact that their own children have abandoned the grandchildren. Many younger grandmothers who are forced to quit their jobs feel dreadfully isolated when they are suddenly limited to the exclusive companionship of small children. Like so many working people, these grandmothers enjoyed the social ties that are part of the work situation. These ties cannot be maintained once the former worker becomes the full-time caregiver for a child. Because drug use by parents is often the reason for the assumption of these responsibilities by grandparents, there are a good number of abandoned children who are the victims of prenatal drug and alcohol excesses by their mothers, which can cause further cognitive and emotional problems.[13]

Custodial grandparenting can be a stressful role. Nevertheless, there are also a good number of emotional rewards that come with raising one's grandchildren. Surely, not all custodial grandparents experience difficulties. In addition, even those who encounter some difficulties gain a good deal of satisfaction from their grandchildren's accomplishments and from the presence of the grandchildren in their lives.[14]

THE AMERICAN ASSOCIATION OF RETIRED PERSONS

In 1993 the American Association of Retired Persons (AARP) instituted the Grandparent Information Center.[15] This center provides grandparent caregivers with information, resources, and services related to grandparents rearing grandchildren, as well as referrals to grandparent support groups. In 1997 the center obtained a Ford Foundation grant permitting the development of a minority grandparent component. Additionally, the

AARP Grandparent Information Center received a grant from the Freddie Mac Foundation, allowing the center to develop a book of quotations from grandchildren reared by grandparents.

Because the center receives thousands of letters and calls each year from grandparents and others, a contact form has been developed that is used by many of those who contact the center. This has led to the establishment of a database of demographic information concerning surrogate grandparents. There are, of course, numerous grandparents who do not supply any information about themselves. Nevertheless, a sufficient number of grandparents have done so, enabling the AARP to develop a picture of grandparent-headed families.

Even in grandparent-headed households in which the mother is present, the children are usually raised by the grandparents and not the single parent. The parent or parents are often transient visitors in the grandparents' home, caring only intermittently for the child. A good number of these young parents are addicted to drugs. They occasionally visit their child or children in the home of the grandparents, causing disruption and excitement and threatening to take the child away.

By conducting numerous interviews with custodial and surrogate grandparents, the staff of the Grandparent Information Center has gained further insight into the phenomenon of surrogate parenting. In recent years the number of grandparents willing to publicly speak of their responsibility to raise grandchildren has increased dramatically, as public acceptance of this situation has become more widespread and as almost everyone has met a family whose children are being raised by grandparents. The AARP Grandparent Information Center receives communications from every part of the country and from rural as well as urban areas.[16]

The AARP survey found that custodial grandparents range in age from the thirties to the seventies. Nearly 75 percent of custodial grandparents are fifty to seventy years old. Sixty-six percent are less than sixty years old and have not yet reached the traditional retirement age of sixty-five. Many of the older grandparents are also great-grandparents raising great-grandchildren. This indicates that in many such families there is not one lost generation, but two.

The AARP study found that half of the custodial grandparents are living on a fixed income while the other half are working. More succinctly, 12 percent of these grandparents are on a fixed income and are working because they need the extra money to augment their small pensions, 46 percent are living on a fixed income only, and 42 percent are working. Four out of ten such grandparents have incomes of less than $20,000 per year. Only 20 percent of custodial grandparents report annual incomes of more than $40,000.

Two-thirds of the grandparents in the AARP study are married. The remaining third, who are single, are almost all grandmothers (96 percent). Furthermore, two-thirds of the grandmothers raising grandchildren are maternal grandmothers, illustrating once more that child rearing is viewed as a female responsibility in this country.

The average household in which grandchildren are raised by grandparents has three persons, and the average number of children raised therein is 1.59. In some cases, grandparents raise two or more siblings to insure that the family remains intact. This may also mean that grandparents raise two or more cousins when more than one of their children are not available to parent their own children. Several studies have shown that African American grandparents are twice as likely as European American grandparents to be caregivers to their grandchildren.[17]

Forty-four percent of custodial grandparents reported in the AARP study that they are raising their grandchildren because their children are on drugs, including alcohol. Crack cocaine, however, is the principal drug of choice for such parents. Grandparents often use the phrase "the living dead" when speaking of their addicted children. Other than drugs, these reasons for raising grandchildren were reported to the AARP investigators: child abuse, neglect, or abandonment, 28 percent; teenage pregnancy and inability of the mother to handle her children, 11 percent; death of the parent, 5 percent; parental unemployment, 4 percent; divorce, 4 percent; and other reasons, 4 percent.

New York City's Orphan Project has estimated that in 2000, at least one hundred thousand children in that city became orphans because their parents died of AIDS. The deaths of the parents, as well as other reasons, leads three-fourths of grandparents to conclude that their role as primary caregiver is permanent. Between 1993 and 1994 alone there was a 27 percent increase in the number of children raised by grandparents. Nearly one-half of all grandparents rear a child who is attending elementary school. Eleven percent in the AARP study are raising a child under the age of two, and 18 percent reported caring for a preschooler aged three or four. Twenty-two percent are raising adolescents or young adults twelve years or older. Grandparents in the AARP study who need financial assistance constitute 36 percent and use such federal programs as Aid to Families with Dependent Children or Medicaid.[18]

The most frequent request from custodial grandparents who contact the AARP's Grandparent Information Center concerns referrals to a grandparent support group. The reason for this lies in the principal difference between normal grandparents, the contemporaries of custodial grandparents who do not have the responsibility of rearing grandchildren, and custodial grandparents. These "normal" contemporaries of grandparents raising second families do not want to hear about diapers, pediatricians, school problems, and that great host of other frustrations that are the lot of every parent everywhere. Yet those parents who are young and are raising their own families do not care to associate with grandparents raising grandchildren. Our ageist society precludes such contacts. Hence, grandparents raising grandchildren often feel utterly alone in that role and need to be given an opportunity to meet others with the same problems.

There are now more than five hundred such support groups in this country. Most of these were founded by custodial grandparents themselves. They began informally as grandparents with second families met each other. Today, many of these groups have been sponsored by social service agencies; others, by employers. These support groups are now forming state, regional, and national organizations to lobby for their interests in state legislatures and the federal government.

Many grandparents are involved in conflicts with their own children concerning custody or guardianship of the grandchildren. These conflicts are the primary reason for grandparents seeking court intervention. When the parent or parents of a child go to court to demand that their child be returned to them, the grandparents are forced to pay huge legal fees to fight their battle. States differ in their laws concerning guardianship, visitation rights, and custody (see appendix). Furthermore, many judges make decisions in these cases that may fit their private prejudices but which can destroy a good relationship between grandparent and grandchild.

Finally, like many parents, grandparents find it extremely difficult to find child care so they can be relieved of the pressure some of the time.

SOME LEGAL ISSUES

There are several legal and financial issues that relate to the assumption of parental responsibilities on the part of grandparents. These legal issues arise from the several ways in which these responsibilities may be met. One of these is the informal arrangement resulting from the abandonment of a child by her parents in favor of the grandparents. Such an abandonment permits the parents to resume their legal right to the guardianship of the child at any time. This means that the grandparents who are taking care of the child have no legal standing to do so and are therefore not eligible to receive medical care for their grandchild unless they pay for such care themselves. In some states the specific consent of parents must be obtained before the public health law will allow doctors to perform any procedure on a child.[19]

In an emergency, some hospitals will provide treatment to a child without the consent of parents, although hospitals largely require payment in advance of treatment, either in the form of cash or using an insurance card. Grandparents who cannot make informal arrangements for medical treatment must obtain legal guardianship or custody to safeguard the child.

School enrollment presents grandparents with another legal problem. Like many states, New York permits anyone who is the "custodian" of a child to enroll the child in school. "Custodian" includes persons other than the parents who are caring for a child whose parents are dead, ill, or incarcerated, or whose whereabouts are unknown.[20]

In some states parents may delegate some of their responsibilities, such as medical care or school enrollment, to someone else by signing a consent form detailing the responsibilities so delegated. In California a parent may authorize a grandparent or other caregiver to enroll a child in school and authorize school-related medical care.[21] In Washington, D.C., a parent or legal guardian may authorize another person to consent to medical, surgical, dental, developmental screening, and/or mental health examinations or treatments.[22]

In states such as New York, which do not authorize the practice by statutes, a written statement from a parent giving a third person the power to take certain actions on behalf of the child is often effective. Even in the absence of a written statement, a nonparent caregiver is often able to obtain needed medical care or enroll the child in school by explaining the situation and documenting her relationship to the child.

In every state an order of custody gives a person the legal right to the physical possession of a child, although parents have a presumptive right to custody. That means that a parent does not need an order of custody to be in control of his or her own children. This issue, adjudicated in 1972 in *Stanley* v. *Illinois*, was reinforced in 2000 in *Troxel* v. *Granville*, in which the U.S. Supreme Court affirmed the right of a parent to be free of the interference of the state.[23]

Whenever a nonparent files for custody of a child and one of the child's parents objects, the nonparent must prove that both parents are unfit to be in control of the child. It is not sufficient to argue that it is in the best interests of the child to be supervised by a nonparent. A nonparent who obtains custody can make day-to-day decisions about the care of the child, although a nonparent does not control the child's property nor does he assume financial responsibility for the child. One example of this arrangement is the code of Ohio, but other states have similar laws.[24]

Children who are abused or neglected by their parents may be placed under the guardianship and custody of the state official charged with the protection of children. Children who have been removed from their homes are usually placed with relatives or in foster homes. In most states relatives may become foster parents; and in New York a child must be placed with a relative before he is placed with strangers. Such relatives must be informed about the "kinship foster care system" and be given the opportunity to apply to become a kinship foster care parent. Those accepted into the system are paid by the state for their services. Because many grandparents know nothing about these benefits, many grandparents raise their grandchildren without the financial support the "kinship foster care system" could give them.[25]

If a relative is approved as a kinship foster parent, the child is eligible for kinship foster care payments and Medicaid. Kinship foster care payments include payments to meet the food, clothing, shelter, daily supervision, school supplies, personal, and special needs of a child. Since foster care payments are much higher than public assistance benefit levels, kinship foster care appears much more attractive to low-income grandparents than public assistance can ever be. Legally, children in foster care are in the custody of the bureaucrats who are charged in each state with the protection of children. Since these bureaucrats seldom know anything about the children in their charge, it is not unreasonable to say that their "custody" is only academic, perfunctory, and uncaring. Unfortunately, the grandparents of children in the "custody" of government agencies have no authority to consent to medical treatment or make any other decisions the guardian or custodian is normally entitled to make. Payments are not available to all grandparents, only to those whose grandchildren were subject to abuse or neglect and who were placed with the grandparents by an agency authorized by the parent or guardian. Most states view foster care as a temporary measure allowing plans to be made to either reunite the child with his parents or promote the child's adoption.

Adoption severs all rights and responsibilities of the biological parents, and the adoptive parents become the child's legal parents. This means that the adoptive parents make all decisions concerning education, medical care, and support for the child. In most states the adopted child inherits from the adoptive parents but not the biological parent.[26]

If the biological parents do not consent to the adoption, their rights can be terminated in a legal proceeding by proving neglect, abandonment, or mental illness. The definition of "mental illness" is, of course, arbitrary, as Thomas Szasz has shown. The diagnosis of "mental illness" is made by psychiatrists. Szasz explains in his influential book *The Myth of Mental Illness* that psychiatry is not a branch of medicine, calling psychiatry and mental illness a "double impersonation." It is, therefore, entirely possible for a parent to lose her rights to her children through the pretenses of psychiatry.[27]

Adoptive parents become financially responsible for their adopted child and possess all parental rights and responsibilities. This also applies to grandparents who have adopted a grandchild, so these grandparents must meet all the financial needs of the grandchild.

In those cases in which the grandparents have accepted responsibility for more than one grandchild, the burden may become overwhelming. Some grandparents who are already retired must go back to work to meet the financial needs of their grandchildren. Other grandparents use public assistance and other sources of income to make the support of their grandchildren possible. To help in these situations, former president Bill Clinton signed the Personal Responsibility and Work Opportunity Reconciliation Act of 1996. That law eliminated the Aid to Dependent Children Program and instead created the Temporary Assistance to Needy Families (TANF) program. This program provides block grants for states to use to provide cash benefits to poor families with children. Under TANF, states have far more discretion to decide how to distribute benefits than was the case under the old Aid to Dependent Children law. Therefore, benefits vary from state to state and even within one state. TANF is not an entitlement, so not all needy children will be helped, particularly since there is a five-year limit per adult-headed household on the receipt of these benefits. Therefore, grandparents raising grandchildren may find themselves without federal money after five years. This does not mean that a state cannot provide assistance beyond five years, and some states have decided to assist indigent adults and children by giving them vouchers instead of cash.

The Personal Responsibility and Work Opportunity Reconciliation Act requires that any adult seeking to qualify for assistance must engage in work or job training no later than twenty-four months after first receiving assistance. The act requires that states must impose sanctions on recipients who refuse to go to work. States can also require that recipients engage in community service after receiving assistance for two months. If all these requirements are applied to grandparents seeking assistance in raising grandchildren, then a large number of grandparents cannot receive any assistance because they are too old to get or hold a job.[28]

Grandparents can also apply for food stamps for themselves and their grandchildren. Food stamps are distributed to households rather than individuals. This means that a child who may be eligible for food stamps might not receive this aid because the resources of the grandparents are considered in determining the food stamps allocated to that household. Therefore, many grandchildren receive no food stamps or very few.

Supplemental Security Income (SSI) is a program designed to help those who are disabled and have an income below the poverty threshold. In some states, such as New York, grandparents who receive SSI benefits are penalized for having grandchildren in their house, as the presence of grandchildren results in fewer benefits allocated to the grandparent than if he lived alone.[29]

Medicaid is a government program that provides comprehensive health-care coverage for low-income people. Many grandparents and grandchildren who have a low income and few resources may qualify for Medicare. If children alone are applying, their grandparents' income need not be considered, nor do grandparents have to have custody or guardianship in order to apply for Medicaid for the grandchild.[30]

Housing is another problem that confronts many grandparents who assume care of grandchildren. Many poor grandparents have only small apartments, not large enough to accommodate a grandchild. It is often difficult for such grandparents to find affordable larger homes. Some grandparents live in housing built exclusively for seniors with the understanding that children are not allowed to live there. Furthermore, a child living in a senior housing development would be deprived of the company of other children and would feel totally out of place in such a situation. There are also landlords who can restrict the number of occupants of a rented accommodation, although discrimination against families with children is prohibited by federal law. Those grandparents who live in public housing must notify the management when an additional person has moved into their apartment.

These difficulties are added to the legal issues that the acceptance of a grandchild creates for grandparents. In sum, then, grandparents who include abandoned grandchildren in their households need a great deal of help in doing so unless they have the money and the resources to deal with all these issues alone. The fact is, however, that those who are most often faced with the challenges of surrogate parenting are the poor, who can least afford these burdens.

LIVING WITH GRANDPARENTS

We have seen that about 4 million American children are now living with their grandparents. This number is slightly higher than the number of children born in the United States each year. Because the parents of the grandchildren now living with grandparents abandoned their responsibilities, these grandparents must deal with the issue of blame for their adult children's behavior. Although trapped in a situation they did not cause, these grandparents are often blamed by relatives and outsiders for the behavior of their children. In addition, they generally blame themselves, wondering what they have done or should have done with their own children so as to prevent the difficulties their own children are experiencing, which led to the abandonment of their grandchildren. If their children are in prison, on drugs, or are alcoholic or otherwise impaired, parents may well blame themselves. There are also those grandparents who place the full blame for their circumstances on their children. In both cases grandparents and grandchildren must talk to each other about the parents, who are truly responsible for their children but have abandoned them.

Psychotherapists have developed a technique called contextual family therapy (CFT), designed to help grandparents raising grandchildren in crisis. This technique allows grandparents to describe and discuss the impact that parenting grandchildren has had on them and on the children involved. Children who rely on grandparents generally undergo "intense emotional and behavioral adjustments."[31] In plain terms, this means that many of these children will test the limits of authority and/or push grandparents away because they feel that others have abandoned them and that this may happen again. Children who have been abandoned feel grief, guilt, anger, fear, anxiety, and embarrassment, even as they hope for their parents' return. Many suffer from excessive eating or sleeping disorders; others engage in "clinging" or in regressive behavior. Some of these children have been sexually abused, been exposed to pornography, or observed a parent with various partners, leading to sexual "acting out" on their part. Many abandoned children often want to contact their parents, although this is almost always a useless effort.

Grandparents are generally unable to understand the irresponsibility of their own children, who have left the little ones in their care. Many of the parents of these children are not only unwilling to assume their responsibilities toward their own children, they are also unwilling to acknowledge the help given them by their own parents. Many grandparents find, then, that their own children are using them to shirk their responsibilities even as their grandchildren blame them for the misconduct of their parents. It is the purpose of contextual family therapy to deal with all these issues involving three generations whose lives are inextricably tied together.[32]

SUMMARY

Grandparents frequently sacrifice their own needs to accommodate the needs of their abandoned grandchildren. They face additional burdens, both material and emotional. These include giving up good jobs and having to explain their children's absence to their grandchildren. Nevertheless, there are those grandparents who are happy to help their grandchildren in crisis.

Demographic changes and the drug-abuse epidemic have increased the number of surrogate parents in recent years. Because the majority of these grandparents are poor, the Welfare Reform Law of 1996 affects them considerably. Many receive no financial help from the new Personal Responsibility and Work Opportunity Act, but must rely on private support groups, such as those offered by the American Association of Retired Persons.

A disproportionate number of those grandparents who must raise their grandchildren are of African ethnicity. There are, of course, millions of other grandparents whose ethnicity is derived from other cultures. We shall concern ourselves with those grandparents in the next chapter.

6

Grandparents in Various Cultures

ETHNIC FAMILIES

Any study of ethnic families in America reveals at once that there are clear differences between the majority of Americans and various subcultures with regard to the relationship of grandparents to their children and their children's children. There are additional differences between ethnic groups concerning the status of grandparents. These differences depend on both the culture of the nation of origin and the economic and social condition of a subculture. There are, however, also a number of distinct similarities in the status of grandparents from various otherwise disparate groups. One of these similarities is the high status that age generally confers on all who come from predominantly rural, agricultural societies, and the decline in that status in urban, industrialized America. It is, of course, a gross exaggeration to claim, as some do, that Americans are utterly uninterested in their "old folks" and abandon them ipso facto.

As we examine various ethnic and other groups and the roles family members play in these groups, we find that the structure of families in various cultures is determined by the distribution of responsibility and authority among family members.

In the traditional German family, the father was undoubtedly "king" and the grandfather was a man of authority. Women, in that scheme, had little authority and were relegated to the kitchen and child rearing. Yet Scandinavian women, who lived so close to Germany, had much greater freedom than German women, participating in the labor force when German women could not, because Germans viewed it as a disgrace if a wife worked outside the home. Slavic, Italian, and Mexican families likewise supported the division of labor that favored male employment in factories and farms and female domestic work.

Families such as these are generally organized vertically. This means that a man guides the younger generation even as he submits his own conduct for review by his old father, no matter what his age. This certainly differs from the present middle-class American family organization, which views fathers as "buddies" of sons and gives grandfathers only minimal attention.

For older adults, families are the most important source of support. Yet these family relationships take place within the boundaries of cultural expectations. This support varies among different ethnic groups. In Italian and Hispanic families intergenerational interaction is frequent. In the 1970s, for example, the sociologist Andrew Greely found that 79 percent of Italian Americans visited their parents and/or grandparents once a week.[1] Then, as now, Italians tended to live close to other family members and to stay in the same neighborhoods longer than people of other backgrounds. Polish families likewise live in close proximity to each other, and according to Greely, 65 percent visit their parents and/or grandparents each week.[2] In fact, younger members of the Polish community do heavy cleaning or shopping or bake Polish treats for grandparents even as the grandparents watch the children. Unlike Italian and Hispanic grandparents, Polish grandparents do not believe that support from their children is to be expected as a matter of course, but as a matter of contribution by them. Germans, on the other hand, have a tradition that differs from that of Italians. German families are more independent than Italian families, and it is not therefore surprising that they are less likely to live in the same neighborhood as their parents. Likewise, Jewish parents receive more visitors than Scandinavians, who have the lowest rate of visitation from their grandchildren.

There is also a great deal of variation in retirement lifestyle. Retired Italians show a great deal of involvement in the roles of parents and grandparents, with little involvement in activities outside the family.

Maria, a grandmother of three, exemplifies the importance of kin in one

Italian American family. Maria and Giuseppe had a host of close friends in the city in which they had spent most of their professional lives. They were very popular among their peers and were known by most of the people in their professions. They had established an excellent reputation among all who came in contact with them. They never lacked invitations and had a very active social life. Their children were raised and went to school there, and the family appeared to be happy in their surroundings and with what they had accomplished. After their children grew up and moved away, Giuseppe and Maria returned to the small American town where their siblings, nieces, and nephews lived, a place that was close to their children and grandchildren. They felt strongly about the importance of family, who to them ranked much higher than the close friendships they had enjoyed.

Gina was the beautiful daughter of an Italian American family. She was a very talented young woman who played the piano flawlessly, had an operatic voice, and was the pride of her mother and father. At eighteen she became pregnant by a casual boyfriend, and when she refused to marry him she was sent away to an institution for unwed mothers. Although she was pressured by her parents and the institution to place her unborn child for adoption, she adamantly refused. Pleading by her mother and threats by her father were futile. When she saw her little girl for the first time, she was ecstatic, and insisted on taking her home. Her family refused to have anything to do with baby Mia, and were determined to have their way. They felt it was an embarrassment to have their child bring shame upon their household. They strongly believed they would be ostracized by their family and friends.

Gina eventually applied for welfare benefits and moved with her little one into a small efficiency apartment in a poor area of town. It was extremely difficult for this young woman to care for her child and go about her life. After many arguments about the situation, her mother finally visited her daughter and saw her grandchild for the first time. One look at little Mia and she fell in love. She picked her up and wept tears of pity and joy. Before long, Mia became an important and integral part of the family. Gina found a job, and her mother took over care of the baby. Mia was very happy with Papa and Grammy, as she called her two grandparents. She was the apple of their eye, and they were overjoyed at her development; they were filled with pride when she spoke her first word, took her first steps, and smiled in her winning way.

When Mia was six years old, her mother married. Gina wanted to take her daughter into her new home, but her husband was very critical of the little girl and saw her as interfering in the new marriage. After much pain on all sides, it was decided that the little girl would remain with her grandparents. Gina reluctantly agreed to accept the situation, and visited her daughter regularly. Although she loved her parents, her feelings toward them were never the same. She knew the child was happy, which resulted in rivalry between her and her mother. Mia's grandparents were excellent and loving caregivers for their little grandchild, yet they never fully forgave Gina for the heartache she had caused.

Poles are more likely to engage in hobbies and crafts and to work past normal retirement age than those of other ethnicities. Jews and Japanese seek support in the community itself. These two groups seek out age peers who share the same culture, language, and heritage.[3]

THE ETHNICITY OF AMERICAN GRANDPARENTS

An ethnic group is a collection of people who are distinguished by others and by themselves on the basis of culture and nationality. American ethnic groups share several characteristics: They exhibit unique cultural traits such as language, clothing, holidays, foods, and religious practices. Ethnic groups also recognize a sense of community and a feeling of *ethnocentrism*, which refers to the belief that one's own culture and way of life are superior to that of anyone else. Membership in an ethnic group is ascribed from birth. In American cities there are a number of areas that are distinctly marked as the territory of one or another ethnic group. Such territories may be called "Little Italy," "Little Havana," or "The Gilded Ghetto."

There are, of course, many Americans who do not participate in any ethnic functions and do not view themselves as "ethnics." These are mainly the descendants of western Europeans.

There are, however, others who actively seek ethnic relationships and identify with an ethnic group. These are Americans who choose to perpetuate the culture of their grandparents or great-grandparents. They feel a common identity with others who have similar characteristics such as language, religion, and politics. Ethnic groups are influenced not only by their own history and culture, but also by the ethnic domination or subordination they may experience in this country.[4]

The manner in which we conduct our human relations is also influenced by ethnicity. Therefore, the status and role of grandparent is, in part, a reflection of the ethnic group in which the grandparent lives. Family lifestyle is decidedly influenced by ethnicity, which in turn relies on the ability of the family to socialize its members into the ethnic culture. Such socialization insures that at least one more generation will continue the distinctive lifestyle of that ethnic group. Normally, the past of an ethnic group is of major importance, as is understanding the personality of a group, called the *group ethos.*

The conditions that led a group to come to North America and the situation in which its members lived here are important factors in creating a group history and a group mentality. Family activities are the best way in which members of an ethnic group can express the heritage, values, and beliefs of any group. Some family values and attitudes continue from generation to generation because experiences within the family are intense and emotional.

Included in the attitudes of families toward one another are the distribution of authority, status, and responsibility and the network of kin relationships. For example, there are socioreligious ethnic minorities in this country such as the Jews, the Mormons, and the Old Order Amish, whose cultural traditions have allowed them to maintain a separate identity over many years. Furthermore, their traditions have given each of these groups a chance to survive in its unique fashion. This includes the Jewish concern with education and literacy, a concern that has helped that group immensely in achieving a high socioeconomic status in this country. The belief that education and literacy are of the greatest importance, brought here by the Jewish immigrants of the late nineteenth century, transformed that group from an underclass of beggars and pushcart merchants into an affluent, educated, and professional group that has made major contributions to American culture.[5]

This illustrates how the culture of grandparents and great-grandparents lives on in generations of people born in this country and not at all acquainted with the places from whence their ancestors came.

Included in the cultural heritage of the American Jews, who stemmed almost entirely from Yiddish-speaking eastern European immigrants, was the belief that one must take care of the old. "Particularly strong was the obligation to take care of elderly parents although there is a great reluctance on the part of the elderly parent especially the father to accept aid."[6]

Grandparents in the Yiddish-speaking culture had great prestige and were treated with utmost honor and respect, as were parents, particularly fathers. We will see that the same attitude prevails in many other cultures as well.

The modern-day American Jewish family is, of course, one century removed from its principal immigrant contributors. The great-grandparents of modern Jewish Americans were largely integrated into their families and have been described as choosing family solidarity and cohesiveness as their most important value. This was undoubtedly also true of the Eastern European Jewish grandparents of American Jews. However, almost all of the generation of the grandparents of modern American Jews were murdered by their European neighbors between 1939 and 1945. Few escaped that slaughter, so the culture of American Jews today derives from those European Jews who came here before the Holocaust.

Today, there are still some Jewish grandparents who speak Yiddish and who recall the horrors of World War II as a personal experience. Largely, however, American Jewish grandparents are native-born professionals and businesspeople. The Yiddish culture is now mainly a memory in the Jewish community, including family myths and legends often centered upon the grandparents' stories of religious persecutions in Europe and anti-Semitism in America. In the Jewish community anti-Semitism is regarded as a constant in the Western world and among the 187 million Arabs of the Middle East. Jews generally believe that as long as Christianity survives, anti-Semitism will exist as well, although few Jews are Semites, or speak a Semitic tongue. Jews are, of course, necessary in Christian mythology as the "outgroup" whose history illustrates the superiority of the Christian story, which cannot well be sustained in a world in which Jews live in security and prosperity and have even established themselves in Jerusalem, contrary to Christian teachings. This is all part of the legacy of the grandparents' generation, now included in the modern-day Jewish American psyche. It is this anxiety that is responsible for the defection of some Jewish voters from their usual Democratic affiliation in 2000, after the Democratic candidate for New York's seat in the U.S. Senate, Hillary Clinton, was accused of having made an anti-Jewish remark in 1974.[7]

Mormons, also called the Church of Jesus Christ of Latter-day Saints, are, like Jews, a socioreligious ethnic community in the United States. Unlike Jewish Americans, Mormons are not the children or grandchildren of immigrants but rather the descendants of born Americans who fled religious persecution in this country. Organized in Fayette, New York, in 1830, the Mormon faith is based on the "visions" of the prophet Joseph Smith. The faith attracted a number of followers, but soon ran into opposition from the nineteenth-century individualists who dominated American life. Mormons sought to establish a theocracy and "dominated the economic and political aspects of life around them,"[8] so they ran into constant hostility from non-Mormons in New York, Ohio, Missouri, and Illinois. Added to this collective lifestyle, which annoyed most Americans, was the institution of plural marriage as practiced by Mormon church leaders and others. With the murder of Joseph Smith in 1844, the Latter-day Saints had a martyr, leading to the trek to Utah under the leadership of Brigham Young.

All of this is part of Mormon history and myth and is the foundation of the Mormon worldview. That *Weltanschauung* includes the view that the family is eternal, as illustrated in the favorite Mormon hymn: "In the heavens are parents single? No, the thought makes reason stare." The tremendous emphasis on ancestry therefore elevates grandparents to a height not known in any other Christian denomination.[9]

One of the principal aspects of Mormon theology concerns the extended family. This belief involves the "work for the dead," which is based on the belief that only baptism in the Church of Jesus Christ of Latter-day Saints permits anyone to have access to God's presence in the next world. Since millions throughout history did not have the opportunity to know about the teachings of the Mormon Church, it is now the obligation of Mormons to seek out the names of their dead ancestors and to act as proxies for them, experiencing baptism in the names of deceased relatives. One of the consequences of this belief is the building of the most extensive genealogical library in the world. The other consequence is the promotion of fathers and grandfathers to an exceptionally high status, based on religious principles, and subjecting women to be ruled by men.

The top echelons of the Mormon Church are all men. The leaders keep their positions until they die. The president of the Quorum of Twelve

Apostles assumes his position as president of the church on the death of the previous president. The old members of the church participate in sacred dramas and rituals and play proxy for the dead. Such work, however, is reserved only for the "worthy" and cannot be undertaken by those whose lives do not warrant temple work.

The sum of this system of beliefs is the fairly strong position of grandparents in the religious sphere among Mormons, although the secular life of Mormon grandparents does not differ from that of other Americans living in nuclear families.

The Old Order Amish are another socioreligious community still living in America. As it does with Jews and Mormons, history separates the Amish from the majority community in the United States. Followers of Jacob Amman, these seventeenth-century "dissenters" are socially self-sufficient. Old age is not well defined among the Amish, as there is no retirement age. Instead, retirement is gradual and related to health and family needs. Grandparents who wish to retire move to a "grandfather house" adjacent to the main farmhouse. The grandparents, therefore, remain physically and emotionally close to the family. Whenever one of the adult children lives in a separate household, the grandparents travel from household to household for monthly visits. The middle-aged Amish farmer discusses farm problems and other issues with his father. Mothers ask advice concerning children from their mothers. Grandparents have an increasing obligation to visit the sick and to keep in touch with all relatives in an extended family. Grandparents among the Amish, and among all peoples, have the function of holding the family together. History and genealogical relationships are an important function of grandparents' responsibilities. Amish grandparents who become ill are cared for at home, and grandparents die at home. Because the Amish are generally related to almost everyone in their community, funerals usually involve a large crowd, sometimes more than five hundred people.

Home care is not seen as a burden among the Amish. Instead supporting the old is regarded as a natural obligation receiving no particular attention. Furthermore, Amish families are usually so large that the support of the old can be spread among a number of family members without much cost.[10]

The Amish support an "unwavering feeling of familism" that permeates their generational relationships. Older Amish know that their families will support them whenever needed. The definition of "family" includes primary and secondary kin as well as other members of the Amish church. In short, church members are family and are treated as such.

When an old Amish enters a hospital, she has a large number of visitors from among her family and her other brethren. The extent of such a family is immense. The sociologist William Kephart reports that one Amish widow died at age eighty-nine with 350 descendants and that an Amish man who died at age ninety-five was survived by 410 descendants.[11]

The Amish provide support for their old people because they will not accept Social Security payments or welfare. This is the consequence of their wish to separate themselves from the world, so outside support from government or anyone else is strictly forbidden among them.

Most of all, young Amish are willing and indeed eager to provide for their grandparents and others who need help.[12]

OUR ORIENTAL HERITAGE

In addition to our socioreligious ethnic minorities, we also have several early ethnic minorities that have been able to maintain their unique culture in this country. Among these are the Chinese, who first came to San Francisco in the 1850s. The Chinese are probably the best example of the meaning of the phrase "marginal men," since no group of European immigrants to America was as foreign and distant from American civilization as the Chinese.

The 1990 U.S. Census revealed that other than Hispanics, Chinese Americans are the fastest growing ethnic minority in America. Although Chinese have come to the United States since 1850, one-half of those now in this country are foreign born.[13]

Cleo was the adopted Chinese child of Angela and Catherine, a young lesbian couple. Angela's parents idolized the little one. They could not have loved her more if she had been their biological grandchild. Every weekend they looked forward to visits from Cleo and were disappointed when she did not come. They had always been very accepting people and had adopted their own children as infants from a social service agency. Cleo was, to them, as much theirs as their own children had always been.

As is true of any group, Chinese grandparents provide support for their families even as they need support for the conditions facing all who experience old age. The contributions of the old to the welfare of younger family members has only a short history, because prior generations of the old were too feeble and too poor to give much to their children or grandchildren. It is only in the last fifty years that this has changed; there are now innumerable grandparents who are in good health and who have money past retirement age.

Filipino families have very similar attitudes and behaviors toward their family as Chinese ethnics.

Amelda and Miguel Ramos moved into a three-bedroom Manhattan apartment with their adult children and grandchildren. Both their daughter and son-in-law worked full-time, and they did not want "outsiders" to raise their children. They wanted their son and daughter to retain their Filipino identity, to understand their language, to be comfortable with their culture and themselves. Amelda did the cooking, baking, and cleaning, as well as taking good physical care of the children. Both she and Miguel spent time on a daily basis telling the young ones about their ancestors, about the Philippines, and about their heritage. They also stressed the importance of a good education and how many possibilities and opportunities life in America would hold for them. Hard work was an example the grandparents furnished by pointing out how much better off the children's parents were because of it. In return for the grandparents' loyalty and helpfulnes, their daughter and son-in-law were ready to assist them if they became ill or incapacitated. Grandma and Grandpa also reaped the reward of the love of their grandchildren, which means so very much to them.

Grandparents can, of course, contribute financially to their grandchildren's upbringing. They can also act as advisers because of their wisdom and experience. That advice may well be in the tradition of the "old country" among those who came as immigrants. Nevertheless, there are innumerable similarities between European and American values, so the views of an immigrant grandparent may not substantially differ from the views normally expected in America. Not so for the Chinese and other Asian immigrants. Asian Americans are indeed marginal people who live in two cultures at once and whose traditions sometimes differ sharply from those of the majority.

If we look at grandparents as a family resource instead of a burden, it will become evident that grandparents represent an opportunity to deal with problems, with important family decisions, and with the implementation of such decisions.

Marianne, a widow of British descent, is the grandmother of five children. She is a nurse and a very health-conscious woman who tries to see to it that her grandchildren are well nourished and have a "correct" outlook on life. She is the mother of two adult sons and the grandmother of two boys and three girls. She is particularly concerned about the two daughters of her divorced son. She is very angry with her former daughter-in-law and is convinced that she is using the children as pawns to try to get "as much money as possible" from her son.

Marianne gets the girls on and off the bus five days a week, or whenever she is not occupied with her many other responsibilities; celebrates their birthdays and other occasions with them; and attempts to correct their "faulty" upbringing. She worries about the girls' punitive, anorexic mother, who does not feed them nutritious foods, punishes them harshly, and sets a poor example for them. The mother is involved with an older man who frequently sleeps in her house while the children witness the "goings on."

Marianne is very protective of her two granddaughters and has been known to buy them clothes that are not supplied by their parents. She feels that her former daughter-in-law is not meeting the children's needs, spending the support money sent by her son on herself and on frivolous items. Interestingly enough, she does not hold her son, the children's father, responsible for the problems inherent in this situation. This is not atypical of parents, who look only at the shortcomings of the in-laws or former in-laws.

Although the girls love Marianne, they cling to their mother and do not see her as an antagonist. Marianne is a wise woman and does not berate the children's mother in their presence. She comforts them, tries to diminish the pain they feel from the divorce, dries their tears, and intervenes whenever possible. She is definitely a grandmother who fills the gap when no one else has time to be with them, a caring person who adds to their well-being and enhances their lives.

We have already seen that the United States permits grandparents to choose from a variety of roles, which is not true of Chinese, Filipino, and other Asian groups. Because individualism and independence are so highly prized in this country, a great number of American grandparents are not very involved with their grandchildren. This is also the outcome of the nuclear family arrangement so common in this country. Such an arrangement generally excludes grandparents from the residence of their children and grandchildren. Intergenerational obligations are not prescribed in this country; instead, they are recreated by each family member throughout his life.[14]

In some families, grandparents provide a great deal of emotional support and assist with day-to-day needs as well. Mothers who are attending school or are employed outside the home are most likely to enlist their own mothers for childcare. Grandparents are also role models and provide historical continuity to the family.[15]

In other American families, grandparents play a marginal role. In some situations grandfathers and grandmothers seldom see their grandchildren, particularly if the grandparents live at some distance from their children and grandchildren, a situation very common in the American professional class.

Seventy-seven-year-old Ernst, grandfather of four, rarely saw his grandchildren. He exhibited little interest in them and knew nothing of their personalities, since he saw them less than once a year, and then only for the last five years of his life. A professor of human services, Ernst was very much self-involved. He had written a book and had taught in universities in this country and overseas on visiting professorships. He was a man who traveled extensively, had divorced two women, and had married three times. All were highly educated professional women. His first wife gave birth to a daughter; his second, to two more. Ernst abandoned them all, leaving the little girls with their mothers. He insisted that he was forced to leave his young children because he needed to further his career. When Ernst's second ex-wife died, suddenly leaving two little girls, he did not take them but readily turned them over to the care of their maternal grandparents. Ernst rationalized his actions regarding his divorces, stating that his first two wives had a different "worldview" from his own. Regarding his children, he was convinced that he was justified in his desertion of them since he needed to take care of himself first and foremost. He moved from one prestigious university to another until he finally retired at the age seventy-three. His third wife, a practicing physician twenty years his junior, had established a lucrative practice, so he remained in the community in which he had held his last position. In spite of his age-related physical problems, he continued to travel extensively with and without his spouse. Rarely did he give much thought to his grandchildren, who lived in distant cities. He felt justified in his actions since he had not had the best of childhoods. Ernst never equated his loneliness in his retirement years to his own actions, but forever held his deceased parents responsible for his unhappiness and his fate.

The role of grandparents in the lives of grandchildren is also largely determined by the attitude of the parents of children toward their own parents. Parents can easily prevent the involvement of grandparents in the lives of their children—or they can encourage such involvement.[16]

In contrast, families in the traditional culture of China were patriarchal and patrilocal. Multiple generations lived in one household, permitting children to see their grandparents at any time. Because of the Chinese emphasis on the male line of the family, paternal grandparents were part of the extended family more than maternal grandparents; in fact, maternal grandparents were generally remote from the children of their daughters.

Because the Chinese family relied on the teachings of Confucius (Kung-fu-tzu 551–479 B.C.E.), heavy emphasis was placed on the hierarchical order of Chinese society. Here, the grandparents were given great authority and power because they were viewed as the top of the pyramid in the Chinese family organization. Although mothers were mainly responsible for child rearing, the opinion of grandparents was always solicited. This arrangement also meant that there was a great deal of reciprocal aid available to all members of the Chinese family.[17]

During the second half of the twentieth century, the traditional Chinese family changed a good deal in the United States. Industrialization and urbanization led to an increase in the number of nuclear families and a corresponding decline in the prestige of the old in Chinese families. In the United States, the loosening of intergenerational bonds within Chinese families has become pronounced. Assimilating mainstream American values, both Chinese seniors and their adult children agree that it is not desirable for the old to move in with the young.[18]

Over the past thirty years, natives of China who have been admitted to the United States have been mainly students. These students became professionals in this country and then sent for their Chinese families. Because of this "chain" immigration arrangement, the typical Chinese American family is nuclear. In fact, the sociologist M. G. Wong found that in the United States, nuclear families represent 87 percent of all Chinese American households. A nuclear family consists of a married couple and their children. Since most Chinese immigrants come alone or with only their spouses and children, the children seldom have grandparents or other relatives in this country. This development is due to the great physical distances both between the United States and China and within the United States. Many grandparents of Chinese American children live a great distance away from their families. This has come about because so many Chinese immigrants are professionals who have had to relocate for economic reasons.[19]

Unlike the traditional Chinese family, Americans of Chinese origin include the paternal grandparents of both sexes in their extended families. Gone is the authoritarian, patriarchal, and patrilocal dominance so common in traditional Chinese families.

Nevertheless, many Chinese families have brought their maternal grandmother to the United States, where she is engaged in child care while both parents work. Some Chinese immigrant parents even allow their children to stay in China with their grandparents while they work here. These arrangements are made because many Chinese want their children to be enculturated in Chinese folkways and mores. Because many of the Chinese immigrant grandparents do not speak English, grandchildren under their grandparents' care learn Chinese at home. They are also useful in teaching their grandchildren Chinese cultural practices. In sum, grandparents are useful to parents in providing child care and socialization in Chinese culture.

Not all Chinese immigrants seek the help of grandparents. Some respect their parents' freedom and do not want to create a cultural "prison" for their parents. Others do not believe their parents are of help, viewing them as an obstacle to freedom and autonomy, which reflects the adoption of American values by many Chinese immigrants.[20]

HISPANIC AND AFRICAN AMERICAN GRANDPARENTS

Mexican Americans have lived in this country since its inception and are as much part of the American experience as the English. Hence, the traditional Mexican American family has always been a feature of American life. Familism, male dominance, and the subordination of the young to the old are the major features of Mexican family life in this country.

Familism refers to the great importance of the family to all its members. Among Mexican Americans, the needs of the family supersede the needs of the individual so that "mutual financial assistance, exchange of work and other skills and advice and support in solving personal problems are ideally available in the extended kin group."[21]

This view of the Mexican American family has been challenged by D. Gallego, who studied Mexican American grandparents living in Utah. He wrote that "Mexican-American family solidarity and reciprocity and friendship support systems are a myth and this need for human interpersonal relationships is absent in the Mexican-American elderly population."[22] It is, of course, certain that there is more than one Mexican American subculture in the United States, depending not only on the length of time a family has been in the country but also on the area in which the family lives. Those who have moved a good deal farther away from Mexico, in this case those living in Utah, have evidently accepted lifestyles that do not substantially differ from the family support network of Anglo-Americans.[23]

Much has been made of the Mexican concept of *machismo*, which implies manliness and includes all those qualities of male conduct elevated in the Latin culture. This includes sexual prowess, but is not limited to virility. Machismo includes the authority of the male over his family, which is delegated through male members of the family, while women and children carry out orders. Included in the concept of machismo is the view that a Mexican man provides fully for his family, despite the permission machismo gives a man to engage in occasional extramarital sexual encounters. Machismo consequently includes the notion of female submissiveness. Child rearing and homemaking are the only occupations in which the traditional Mexican American culture allows women to work. Nevertheless, increasing urbanization and greater length of time in the United States have produced more egalitarian Mexican American families, as is also true of so many other ethnics. As this egalitarian leveling becomes more widespread, it also affects the historical respect and honor that have heretofore been accorded parents, and particularly grandparents, in the Mexican American community.[24]

The subordination of younger to older family members in the traditional Mexican American family is reported to be a good deal greater than it is in Anglo homes. Respect for grandparents is reflected in speech patterns, manners, and behavior. The belief that the old must be respected even includes the relationship between older siblings and their younger brothers and sisters.

Yet those Mexican Americans who are raised primarily in an Anglo environment do not normally continue these behaviors. Mexican Americans who have lived here a long time or who were born here tend to devalue old age, as is common in American culture. Nevertheless, grandparents in the "barrio" areas of large American cities still play an important role in child rearing and an influential role in family decision making. No doubt, the authority of grandparents has declined in the Mexican American family because assimilation reduces foreign characteristics from any culture to a level less prominent than when they first encountered American values. Of course, traditions do not disappear in one or even ten generations. On the contrary, we can expect that Mexican and other ethnic features of American life will always be with us.

The African American family includes a history of slavery not known to any other ethnic group in America, despite the Jewish experiences in Europe. The 35 million Americans of African descent comprise 13 percent of the U.S. population. There is, of course, no such thing as one African American culture. African Americans are of diverse origin, having come from several cultures in Africa, the Caribbean, and South America.

The proportion of African Americans who live in extended families is a good deal greater than among European Americans. This means that the extended family among African Americans often provides individual family members with emotional and financial support not otherwise available. In emergencies, three or more generations may work together to care for one another. This contributes to the well-being of children, but also of the old, who benefit from relationships with their children, grandchildren, nieces, nephews, and more distant relatives.

Nine-year-old Daquina lives with her mother and grandmother; the youngster's father left soon after she was born. He moved to a distant state and has shown very little interest in his daughter. The grandmother is with the child all day while her mother works. The grandmother takes great pride in seeing that her little granddaughter is well cared for. She meticulously braids the child's hair, sees to it that she wears clean clothes to school every day, prepares her meals, and even looks at her homework before she retires for the night. Grandma herself had seven children, of whom six survived. One boy was killed in an auto accident while another ended in prison. Another son recently became very ill and is currently living with his mother during his recovery. Whenever one of her "kin" needs her help, the grandmother is ready. In addition to Grandma, Daquina's great-aunt lives upstairs and is always willing to be of assistance to the child should the grandmother need to be on an errand.

Jasmine, a ten-year-old African American child, has been taken care of by her Caucasian grandmother since she was an infant. The child is the product of a Caucasian mother and a black father. Her father, Daquin, has spent most of his adult life in prison. When he was free he met Jasmine's mother, Rowena, and the two lived together for a time. This union did not last very long. Daquin was a drug dealer who "earned" a living by selling narcotics wherever he could find a buyer. When Rowena strenuously objected to his occupation, he became physically abusive toward her and the child. Following a number of injuries as a result of Daquin's outbursts, Rowena became frightened and reported him to the police. It did not take long before Rowena found another male, and from this union another little girl, who is being raised by Rowena, was born. The grandmother keeps Jasmine and tends to her needs. Grandma also has a very ill husband who needs her attention. Jasmine is "the light of her eye," as the grandmother often declares. The two walk to the store together and feed the baby rabbit that the child keeps as a pet. They seem to have a special understanding between them. The grandmother, being very poor, cannot afford everything that the more affluent schoolchildren have, but Jasmine does not seem to notice or feel deprived. The child is only too happy to be apart from her mother, the mother's boyfriend, and her half sister. Jasmine has found her haven with her grandmother, and the grandmother has found happiness raising this child, who was so much in need of her affection and caring.

Conandra, a mother of nine, was delighted when her youngest child turned eighteen and went on her own. She had raised seven sons and two daughters virtually by herself. Her husband was an alcoholic who came and went as he wished. He was often gone for months without Conandra knowing his whereabouts. After many years she permanently separated from him, went to school on a government grant, and became a practical nurse. She was able to earn a living without having to depend on the welfare system or on her undependable, alcoholic husband. When she was fifty, the unthinkable happened in the life of this very capable, kind woman: her favorite daughter died, leaving behind Jekina, a six-year-old child. Although Conandra was devastated with a loss that seemed insurmountable, she immediately took in her orphaned granddaughter. It was not an easy task for her since she had, after so many years, put her child-rearing days past her. She rearranged her work schedule to accommodate little Jekina: She had been working the night shift, where she earned more money, but she quickly changed to accommodate the little girl's school schedule. Conandra struggled this way for a number of years until Jekina was fifteen years old and could be trusted alone overnight. At that time, Conandra resumed a night job in the hospital in order to better meet the financial needs of her granddaughter and herself. Conandra taught Jekina many things. She taught her how to sew her own clothes, how to make the most of the money that is available in a household, the importance of saving even small amounts, the necessity of an education and the need to study diligently, and so on. Conandra raised Jekina into adulthood, and was able to see her enter college and earn a degree, and to have a more satisfying life than she herself had experienced. Through her granddaughter, she felt that her life had been fulfilled.

It should be noted that among that small group of African Americans who have attained upper-middle-class and upper-class status, the nuclear family dominates—with the same consequences for the old as we have already noted among the Chinese and others.[25]

Traditionally, grandparents in the black community have been viewed as the central stabilizing figures in the extended black family. This role is rooted in the age-graded system of West African culture. In America, the role of the grandparent also became a survival mechanism under the adversity of slavery and beyond. We have already seen many cases in which black grandparents have raised their grandchildren. Black grand-parents have been the transmitters of family history and folklore, served as family advisers, and mediated disputes between family members. These tasks are also undertaken by grandparents in other ethnic groups in America.[26]

Some African Americans have adopted the traditional lifestyle of the white upper-middle class and therefore live in nuclear families to the exclusion of the old. Urbanization, the entrance of the white individual-istic value system into the black community, and high rates of black male unemployment have altered the traditional black family together with the role of the grandparent in that family. Most important is that demographic changes in intergenerational family structure have had a great impact on the familial role of grandparents in the black community.

The first of these demographic changes is that today blacks live longer than was ever the case heretofore. Aged grandparents may well now be part of a four- and even five-generation extended family. Fur-thermore, black grandparents—and many white grandparents as well—are now presiding over families that include a number of single mothers and fathers.[27]

The decline in mortality that has led to the increase in the number of older Americans has been pronounced for whites and for blacks, although not to the same extent. A black American male born in 1950 was expected to live fifty-nine years. A black female born that year could expect to live sixty-three years. In 1996 this expectancy had risen to sixty-six and sev-enty-four years, respectively. White males born in that year could expect to live seventy-four years, while white females had a life expectancy of eighty years. This decline in mortality was also accompanied by a decline in black fertility since 1940, from about 4.4 children per woman to around 2.2 chil-dren now. The third factor affecting the intergenerational black family has been a dramatic increase in single-parent, female-headed households.[28]

The interaction of these factors has had a considerable effect on inter-generational family relationships and roles, because these factors deter-mine the content of family life. Family roles are a function of family structures; as structures change, roles change. One kind of family that has emerged from these demographic changes is the verticalized intergenera-tional family. This kind of family is the product of a decline in mortality and fertility. This means that the living members of a family increase as the old live longer, even though fewer babies are born and as there are fewer family members in each generation.[29]

For this reason older blacks must assume several roles at once. There are aged parents, grandparents, and great-grandparents—but with fewer children, grandchildren, and great-grandchildren than in earlier generations. Therefore, these old people are able to spend more time with their progeny, although the smaller number of descendants reduces the number of those who can deliver care to the old when needed.[30]

Because at least two-thirds of black children in America are born to single mothers, the age difference between generations is only twelve to seventeen years. In most American families, the age difference is twenty to twenty-six years, and among professionals who delay marriage and child bearing the difference is thirty to forty years. The youthfulness of black mothers, therefore, affects the lives of older blacks. First, this practice led to more levels of grandparenthood than is known in any other American ethnic group, because there are so many great-grandmothers. In a study of forty-one black females, Linda M. Burton, professor of human development at Pennsylvania State University, found mothers aged eleven to eighteen, grandmothers aged twenty-eight to thirty-eight, and great-grandmothers aged forty-six to fifty-seven. Burton interviewed a ninety-one-year-old woman who was a great-great-great-great-grandmother.

Teenage pregnancy also increases the workload of grandmothers in the family, workloads that are not welcomed by the young grandmothers who have to bear them. Because young grandmothers do not want to care for unwanted grandchildren, the care of such children is often pushed up a generation in black families so that great-grandmothers become the frequent caregivers of children who would otherwise be abandoned. Of course, many of these grandmothers are themselves single parents who are often still raising their own children.[31]

Some studies have revealed that older blacks are more supportive of their adult children, both financially and with advice, than are whites. Young blacks are also more supportive of their grandparents and great-grandparents than are whites. A study by the gerontologists Charles Mindel, Roosevelt Wright, and Ruth Starrett found that the family supports grandparents in a variety of ways, transportation being the most frequent. Checking services, homemaking services, and administrative or legal services, in that order, are also high on the frequency list of help offered grand-parents. The majority of older blacks also report that their children help them when they are sick, in financial crises, and in emergencies, and also advise them on numerous matters of importance in their lives.[32]

We have discussed the surrogate parenting role of black and other grandparents. Yet another role played by black grandparents has been given the label "kinkeeper," a role that almost always accrues to women. The majority of older black women have outlived their husbands and have become the most respected and dominant figures in the family. The kinkeeper attempts to perpetuate and maintain the family network by passing on the history of the family, living by a family theme or ethos, promoting family unity, and helping with family responsibilities. This, once more, includes the need to deal with children abandoned by their parents. Usually grandparents take care of these children at great expense to themselves.

THE "HIGH-MOBILITY" GRANDPARENTS

During the last twenty years of the twentieth century, a new subculture developed in the United States, which sociologists call the postmodern subculture. Those who participate in this lifestyle are best identified by their use of computers and the Internet. Located almost entirely in the upper-middle class of business and professional people, this postmodern culture is marked by the permeable family. That family is unstable and, unlike the modern nuclear family, assumes no permanence. Sexual rela-tions in the postmodern group are based on current needs without neces-sarily leading to marriage; even marriage is frequently seen as temporary. The autonomy of each family member is valued a great deal more than the family unit in the postmodern subculture.[33]

Applied to the role of grandparents, the postmodern attitude differs from that of traditional grandparents, who are concerned with future generations. This traditional attitude has heretofore been almost universal among grand-parents. Postmodern grandparents, however, view their families in the light of a new "social contract" that is narcissistic rather than altruistic, as was for-merly almost always the case. In the age of the computer, cyberspace, and high incomes, these grandparents live according to a materialistic, acquisitive philosophy that emphasizes consumerism and personal pleasure.

In this world children are vulnerable to the materialistic attitudes of their parents who were, of course, raised by their grandparents. Such grandparents are no longer willing to support their children and grandchildren either financially or, more important, emotionally. When adversity strikes postmodern families, they often turn to strangers or official agencies rather than their parents and grandparents, who do not care to be involved. Many of those who live the postmodern life are divorced and remarried; their new spouse is not truly the grandparent of their grandchildren. And divorce includes the grandparents and their children: In cases in which adult children have divorced and remarried, it is likely that the second spouse has her own children, so the grandparents now also become "step-grandparents." Such step-grandparents are seldom well accepted by their step-families. Despite every effort to cover up the differences between natural grandchildren and step-grandchildren, these differences remain and are highly influential in the relationship grandparents have to their biological and step-grandchildren.[34]

In short, a great deal of discretion is given grandparents concerning their relationship to their grandchildren, particularly the children of divorce. Unlike the traditional biological grandparent, the "after-divorce" grandparent and his step-grandchildren make decisions as to the extent of their relationship, if any. The relationship is not involuntary, but calculated. It is, of course, true that blood relations do not guarantee a family. However, it is a common experience that grandparents and grandchildren, by choice or otherwise, have no guarantee that their union will succeed.

Not all divorces have the same consequences. Researchers have found that if a daughter divorces, the children tend to continue to see the grandparents regularly. When a son's marriage breaks up, however, it is unlikely that the ex-wife will allow the paternal grandparents any further visitation rights.[35]

It is reasonable to predict that if the new "social contract" continues, as can be assumed, then the consequences of this kind of grandparenting will be the erosion of the quantity and quality of grandparent-grandchildren relationships. This is already visible in the numerous situations resulting from the high mobility of those now included in the business and professional upper-middle class of Americans. Because so many college-educated, upper-middle-class people move from their hometowns in order to seek financial and professional advantages, grandparents in that subculture see their grandchildren only on occasions such as holidays, vacations, and major life events. This means that a truly strong emotional tie between grandparents and grandchildren cannot develop.

This feature of the postmodern subculture is visible in these statistics: Between 1983 and 1990, the Northeast lost 108,000 residents and the Midwest lost 196,000 residents, mostly those with a college education. The South gained 133,000 residents and the West, 171,000 residents. Of these, 304,000 were migrants. This trend has, of course, continued since 1990, and it demonstrates how the grandparent-grandchild relationship, at least among the upper-middle class, has been sacrificed for economic advantage.[36]

Added to the removal of grandparents from the everyday experience of grandchildren is the influence of the media, which teach stereotypes to their viewers. Included in these stereotypes regarding older people are depictions of grandparents as people to be scorned. Fear of old age is also taught by the media.

Examples of stereotyping the old in the media include children's literature, which portrays the old as unimportant, unexciting, dull, inarticulate, unimaginative, and boring. Other portrayals of old people in children's literature show them to be disabled, ill, and ready to die. In some of these books, the old are constantly knitting, cooking, or fishing, but are never shown as creative people.[37]

Television also portrays the old in a negative light. This comes about because the number of the old shown on television is very small. Studies have shown that only 8 percent of television characters are old. Of these, the bulk are shown as professionals, mostly doctors and lawyers, while more than 25 percent are shown as belonging to the upper class. Such a portrayal of older Americans does not correspond to reality at all. Commercials seldom show the old. Studies indicate that only 2 percent of commercials on television show the elderly at all.[38]

The parents of grandchildren are also affected by the great physical and social distance that the postmodern subculture imposes on them. Many feel very lonely because their parents are not available to them, either because they live far away or because the grandparents do not care to be involved. Many divorced couples believe that their marriages could have survived if they had had the support of their parents.

Many grandparents who work all the time and spend most of their time with their peers do not foresee the isolation and alienation the post-modern attitude produces. Fearing that interest in family members is controlling or "meddling," those devoted only to their economic concerns soon find that they have neither a common history nor a common future with their children and grandchildren. As an increasing number of mothers leave their young in the care of others, emotional connectedness is unknown to many children.

Business and social institutions are now taking the place of grandparents and even mothers. This can be best observed by the boom in psychotherapy, largely resulting from the social and emotional distance that has overtaken college-educated American family members. This means that people seek in group therapy or in bars what the natural family freely offers and what grandparents have given to so many generations over so many years: love, understanding, and unconditional acceptance.

Finally, the removal of grandparents and others from the intimacy of the family has led to the substitution of human contacts with technological devices such as television and the Internet. There are large numbers of Americans in the postmodern subculture who have the money to buy these devices—and who spend an inordinate amount of time dealing with strangers they meet in chatrooms on the Internet, while rejecting the companionship of their families. Included in this dehumanization are additional electronic devices such as personal radios and video games. At least one society lost its judgment based on an inhumane ideology, ending in the mass murder of 11 million innocent people. Is it possible that our gradual divorce from each other, both horizontally and vertically, will lead some to argue that euthanasia is the best policy in dealing with grandparents?

A number of programs have developed that seek to counter the trends postmodernism has imposed on the 25 percent of Americans who live in that world. Included are the Retired Senior Volunteer Program, Senior Companions, and the Foster Grandparent Program.[39] These programs seek to promote interaction between the generations and give both grandparents and grandchildren a continued opportunity to benefit from the most satisfying relationship life has to offer.

SUMMARY

The status and role of grandparents depends largely on the subculture in which they live. Traditionally, a vertical arrangement existed among the generations. This was true among various ethnic groups who came here over the years, including the Jews, the Old Order Amish, and the Mormons. All three are religiocultural groups holding grandparents in high esteem. In fact, the Mormons elevated grandparents greatly because of their intense interest in their ancestors. Likewise, Jews and Old Order Amish followed biblical injunctions concerning the honor owed the old. All of these groups are engaged in familism.

The Chinese, a distinct marginal group, and other Asian Americans shared the notion of elevating grandparents to a high social standing with other, non-Asian groups in America. However, the latest arrivals from China, almost all professionals, have loosened the ties they once had to their grandparents in favor of independence.

Black families in America, more than any others, protect and support grandparents with their limited resources. Various demographic changes have recently contributed to the strain felt by black grandparents, who have traditionally been the foundation of the black family in America.

The postmodern subculture has negated almost all the traditional roles played by American grandparents. Instead, high mobility, a search for the "good life," the use of electronic devices, and the atomization of the family have contributed greatly to the dehumanization of the grandparent role at the beginning of a new century.

7

Grandparents in the Media and in Literature

GRANDPARENTS IN FILMS

Any review of American movies released for the past eighty years depicts an attitude toward the status "grandparents" that exhibits the ageism so common in the American psyche.

The word "ageism" was coined by Robert Butler, M.D., in 1968 and published in his 1975 book *Why Survive? Being Old in America*. Butler used this definition: "Ageism can be seen as the process of systematic stereotyping of and discrimination against people because they are old."[1]

The movie industry lives by the use of stereotypes. This is done with reference to almost any group or situation seen in films, whether in theaters or on television. This is due in part to the nature of the medium itself. Once something has been photographed, it can hardly be changed. Furthermore, movie producers know that they must appeal to a large audience consisting almost entirely of people who already "know" that the old are feeble, confused, poor, and mildly retarded. The audience "knows" that Grandpa plays with small children because he is in his "second childhood" himself, that Grandma is either a helpless old woman who interferes in the lives of younger people or an active "old lady" who cooks incessantly, bakes endless pies and cookies, says soothing things, and smiles all the time.

Expectations make reality, so many grandparents act out the bigotry directed against them. It is, therefore, not uncommon to meet grandparents who act out the roles the media assign them.

We looked at films released during the greater part of the twentieth century and found that the status of grandparent is never associated with a working, decision-making, dominant person.

Two Bits is a movie released in 1996 concerned with life during the depression of the 1930s. It deals with the experience of a twelve-year-old boy and his grandpa, who has promised to leave him a quarter when he dies. The grandpa has terminal heart disease. True to stereotype, the old man is depicted as sick and debilitated.

The child is obsessed with the wish to see a movie for which the admission fee is twenty-five cents. The tension that arises in that boy's situation rests in the fact that he can only gain the needed money at the expense of his grandfather's life. Despite a number of contrived obstacles that must be overcome, the boy finally does attend the movie after his grandfather dies and, as promised, leaves him "two bits." The old give way to the young, as usual, even if the price of a life is a mere twenty-five cents. The message is clear: Better an old man die than that a twelve-year-old should be deprived of a show.[2]

Perhaps one of the most boring, lame-brained movies ever made is *Father of the Bride, Part II*. A 1996 sequel to the 1991 remake of the 1950 production by the same name, this version of *Father of the Bride* includes the reaction of the principal male protagonist in this story, the father of the bride who is terrified at becoming a grandfather. Played by Steve Martin, the father is so upset by the unwanted grandfather status that he gets a so-called youthful makeover.

Again, the message is clear: It is horrifying to be reminded of old age by involuntarily becoming the patriarch of the family. Old age must be hidden. Cosmetics will hide our age and make us acceptable. Of course, if cosmetics really work, then they serve the purpose of lying about our age. That is fine, according to the "makeover" point of view, because age is a sin not to be revealed if at all possible. This movie plays directly into the hands of every ageist in America.[3]

Another example of an ageist film is the 1997 picture *The Evening Star,* which was reviewed as being "geared toward morons of any stripe."[4]

This story deals in the main with Aurora, a grandmother who drives her three adult grandchildren crazy with her meddling ways. She criticizes her granddaughter's boyfriend, has the "gall" to visit her grandson in jail and bring him brownies, which he cannot tolerate. Her other grandson's girlfriend is also the target of the grandmother's ire.

When her maid arranges for her to see a therapist, Aurora falls for the younger, male therapist.

This idiocy ends when all Aurora's grandchildren have resolved their problems. Since she has no more meddling to do—and no other purpose than to interfere in the lives of younger people—she dies.

The message is that old women, old grandmothers, have no life or interests of their own. They have no function or purpose other than to get on the nerves of other people.[5]

Yet another example of utterly stereotyped, wooden characters are the grandfather and the grandmother in the 1997 movie *The Education of Little Tree*, based on the novel by Forrest Carter. This movie not only caters to the usual negative view of grandparents and old people, it also reflects common beliefs about Native Americans which have as much credence as the most racist imagery will allow.

Little Tree is an eight-year-old boy who comes to live with his grandparents. The grandfather is white, but is married to a Cherokee woman. He tells his grandson that his long association has taught him the "evils of civilization." This stupidity appears in almost all movies involving so-called Indians, despite the evidence gathered by years of anthropological research that primitive life is unsanitary, difficult in every possible way, and therefore short. Instead of going to school, Little Tree learns reading by having Grandma recite a dictionary to him, and Grandpa teaches him all about nature.

Along come some cruel state welfare agents who force Little Tree to attend a school where he is treated like a criminal. The boy tells his troubles to the Dog Star, which leads to Grandpa coming to the school and helping Little Tree escape. Having successfully evaded the evil welfare agents, both grandparents die—leaving the child in the hands of some stranger.

The message is that grandparents who live in nature are superior to civilized people, that schools are intolerable prisons, and that real people and particularly grandparents are primitive "know-nothings."[6]

Wide Awake was released in 1998. This deals with a little boy's effort to find a reason for his grandfather's death. The entire movie is so overladen with religious symbolism, angels, and other supernatural personages and events that it has little to do with real grandfathers and a lot to do with infusing the viewer with the Roman Catholic view concerning the old, death, and the so-called spiritual life.[7]

Another boring effort is *I Love You, I Love You Not*. This 1997 stupidity focuses on the relationship between an adolescent girl and her grandmother. The grandmother in this story is a Jewish Holocaust survivor who discusses her experiences in the Nazi death camps with her granddaughter. That is truly unbelievable. Real Holocaust survivors very seldom discuss their horrible experiences with anyone, least of all grandchildren. Even more unbelievable is the fraudulent "suicide" attempt by the granddaughter who is saved in the last minute by her grandmother. Of course, the granddaughter is snubbed by other high school students, who cannot tolerate a girl who reads too much.

The grandmother in this confused presentation is never demanding, always attentive and supporting. In short, she is not human. Once more, the lesson is that grandmothers are victims, but never contributors or successful people in their own right.[8]

Movies made earlier in the twentieth century fare no better at viewing grandparents as real people than the later films already discussed, as in *A Walk in the Spring Rain*, with Ingrid Bergman and Anthony Quinn. The thrust of the movie is a story of geriatric love. Both protagonists are married to other people. Unreasonable demands are made on these two grandparents by a selfish daughter who wants them to baby-sit. The "lovers" really get nowhere—because they cannot deal with real adultery. Overall, the message is that old grandparents can still fall in love, even if it is temporary; but neither of these grandparents is in any fashion productive or capable of carrying out any project of substance.[9]

A "cantankerous old coot" is the principal protagonist of the 1968 movie *The One and Only, Original Family Rand*. The family's grandfather argues politics during the Cleveland/Harrison campaigns of 1892 and believes in freedom of speech "as long as it is Democrat." Once more we are treated to a grandfather who is all mouth and no substance.[10]

Likewise, the grandmothers in *Open the Door and See All the People* are hard to tolerate. Twin sisters, one of these grandmothers is a superstitious, domineering hypochondriac; the other, a happy-go-lucky fool who works as a cashier in a supermarket. Neither grandmother has much of a contribution to make to this world; neither has an education. They are not capable of assuming any kind of leadership in anything. They are both "superfluous people."[11]

In *Misty*, released in 1959, we once more find a grandfather who associates with little children and horses because he has no real adult status. He has returned to his "second childhood," in accord with every movie stereotype ever invented. Grandfathers love animals and grandchildren. They all deserve each other since none of them can think much.[12]

More stereotypes of grandmothers can be found in the 1940 production of *Granny Get Your Gun*, in which a domineering old woman teaches the police and the district attorney a thing or two about detective work. This is an utterly improbable story that does not fail to illustrate that grandmothers are hard to tolerate—even if this particular grandmother exonerates the innocent and finds the real murderer.[13]

If we now review some of the earliest efforts to portray grandparents on the silver screen, we find the monotonous repetition of the usual stereotypes. There are the domineering grandmothers, ruthless old women, grandmothers interfering in the lives of young lovers, idiotic grandmothers who are eternally swindled out of their life's savings, and "scheming" socialite grandmothers who will do anything to break up the romances of numerous granddaughters. Anyone wanting to see these devilish grandmothers may find them in *Let Us Be Gay*, *The Truth about Wives*, *Satan and the Woman*, or *On Your Toes*, all movies from the late twenties and the thirties.[14]

GRANDPARENTS ON TELEVISION

The representation of grandparents on television is no more positive than that in the movies. George Gerbner, the "father" of cultivation theory, argued in 1993 that "mass media are the most ubiquitous wholesalers of social roles in industrial societies" and "the world of aging (and nearly everything else) is constructed to the specifications of marketing strategies."[15]

Even when grandparents are depicted in a favorable light on the television screen, the images of grandmothers are unrealistic. Grandmothers are often shown as having young faces with gray hair. They are pictured as if they could be the sister of their own son or daughter, instead of a grandmother. Grandpa is portrayed as the image of the proverbial "whiskey advertisement" male with silver hair, big muscles, and a strong, masculine figure.

Grandparents are utilized in advertisements to enhance sales in a manner that reinforces the stereotypes that already exist in our culture. A number of examples are readily available: There is Ensure, where the daughter is shown in a role reversal: She becomes the mother figure to her own parents. She tells her parents that she is now taking good care of them by providing this food supplement in order to keep them in good health. Other examples include the adult diaper advertisement in which a well-known movie actress lauds this product for incontinent old folks; the Celebrex medication for arthritis, which shows a grandparent walking along the beach with her grandchild, allegedly free from arthritis as a result of using this drug; or the grandfather who is now capable of taking his grandson fishing and performing other playful tasks with grandchildren now that he is medicated. He is also now capable of assisting his adult son in the garage since his hands and fingers are now pain-free. The use of denture adhesives picture grandparents capable of sharing apples with young ones without the slippage of their artificial teeth, and so on.

Meredith Tupper claims that "in American culture, increasing age seems to portend decreasing value as a human being," and quotes gerontologists Butler, Lewis, and Sunderland, who suggest that there are six major causes of the disrespect and contempt aimed at the old in the United States.[16] These are: a history of mass immigration, mostly consisting of the young and leaving the old behind in Europe and Asia; a nation founded on the principles of individualism, independence, and autonomy; the development of technologies that demand rapid change and specialized skills; a general devaluation of traditions; increased mobility of the population with a large continental space; and medical advances that have relegated most deaths to later life, producing a tendency to associate death with old age.[17]

According to Tupper, the old are either ignored or given a negative evaluation in television programming and advertising. This is probably an expensive mistake for American marketers whose prejudices against the old are so strong that they are evidently willing to lose a great deal of money in order to foster their disdain and contempt for the old among us. Americans over fifty now represent 25 percent of the population, have a combined annual income of over $800 billion, and control 70 percent of the total net worth of U.S. households—about $7 trillion.[18]

This potentially large source of income for producers has been neglected because many businesspeople continue to cling to the belief that the old are poor. Furthermore, the old are believed to be so fanatical about their consumption habits that they will buy the same brand over and over and cannot be persuaded by advertisements to do anything else.

New research has discovered that older people are more likely to read newspapers and magazines than watch television, and that advertising to them is therefore better accomplished by the written word than the electronic message. In addition, old people, mostly retired, watch television much more during the day time than do working younger people. The old are also heavy listeners of AM radio. Furthermore, the old tend to make their buying decisions by asking friends and relatives about products rather than consulting advertisers. Therefore, the belief that the old are less amenable to persuasion by commercial interests than are younger people does indeed confirm some of the inclinations of advertisers concerning the old consumer. From this we may abstract that ageism is not the only cause of the failure of advertisers to deal with the old population.[19]

Nevertheless, aversion to the old in the media is ubiquitous. This is visible first of all by the discrepancy between the number of older people in the American population and the number of the old, mostly grandparents, depicted on television. Today, 12.6 percent of the American population is sixty-five years old or older. Swayne and Greco examined the portrayals of grandparents in television commercials and found them to be both misrepresented and underrepresented, with a significant underrepresentation of old women as compared to old men. The sexism is evident. Grandfathers are not only more likely to appear in television shows and commercials than grandmothers, but grandfathers are also projected as more active, more powerful, and more productive than grandmothers. According to television, grandmothers are invariably passive and nothing more than "useful accoutrements" to males. In addition, grandmothers and grandfathers "tend to be shown as more comical, stubborn, eccentric, and foolish than other characters. They are more likely to be treated with disrespect."[20]

Today, the picture of grandparents on television is somewhat better than it was ten years ago. This more positive attitude is reflected, in part, in such TV entertainment as *Murder, She Wrote*, *The Golden Girls*, *Crazy*

Like a Fox, and *Mr. Belvedere*. There is, then, a slightly more positive portrayal of the old on television, although underrepresentation persists.

Perhaps the most powerful grandmother shown on television was the character Jessica Fletcher, who was the principal focus on *Murder, She Wrote*. Cancelled and then reinstated, and visible in reruns, this "detective" is depicted as more intelligent, more versatile, and more insightful than many younger persons in each episode. This is not true of *The Golden Girls*, who are befuddled, not very competent, and humorous because of their incompetence. Some grandparent characters on TV are healthy, strong, and physically active. This is particularly true of *Matlock*, an ever-winning lawyer with white hair and a furrowed face.

There are those, on the other hand, who are seen as frail and vulnerable, in need of adult diapers, as recently portrayed by actress June Allyson. There are the grandparents who need guidance and direction from their children and/or grandchildren, as shown in advertisements for "caring, compassionate nursing homes," or Ensure, a product to keep the old folks healthy. Then there are the denture advertisements where Grandma and Grandpa are able to eat apples along with their grandchildren without having their artificial teeth move or fall out. Sexuality, is of course, utterly absent among all of these old TV characters—because everybody "knows" that the old have no sexual interests.[21]

Television also agitates against the old in this country by pretending that health-care costs for the old are so immense that they are used up on futile efforts to deal with the old, who are dying anyway. Grandparents are labeled "greedy geezers," a term that turned up sixty-eight times in just over two years in national news databases as the media recycled this pejorative with reference to health-care costs.[22]

GRANDPARENTS IN THE NEWS

The treatment of grandparents in print journalism does not differ much from the images drawn on television. Grandfathers and grandmothers in newspapers are invariably depicted as idle, disabled, and poor. There are also "age pages" in some newspapers that seek to address the concerns of senior citizens. These "age pages" contain material deemed "cute," but which is, to be honest, condescending. Unexamined stereotypes are used to illustrate so-called human interest stories that deal with interpersonal relationships, health, and exercise. These "age pages" have much in common with "women's" or "colored" pages, which define the media's judgment concerning the interests of women and/or minorities—based almost entirely on canned stereotypes recycled again and again. Such specialized pages also contain the achievements of grandparents or women or blacks, achievements not mentioned in the other pages on the assumption that the general reader would have no interest in the achievements of such people. Women and African Americans have recently succeeded in eliminating these stereotypes by labeling such reporting as racist and sexist—a success not yet attained by the old.

New magazines use similar methods to indict the old. "Rusty"— meaning corrupted, eroded, deteriorated, rotten, and stale—is a common term used by newsmagazines when describing grandparents. These newsmagazines also reduce discussions of grandparents to the level of bodily discomforts and body functions. In the world depicted in these media, grandparents never do anything worthwhile but sit all day and complain.[23]

The only exception to the constant negative stereotyping of grandparents in America was the coverage afforded America's most famous grandfather, John Glenn. When he returned to space in 1998, after first achieving fame in 1962 for being the first American to orbit Earth, he was seventy-seven years old. Articles about John Glenn appeared in *U.S. News & World Report*, *Time*, and *Newsweek*. None were demeaning, although there was a good deal of comment as to the "deterioration" of all body parts in the old. This is a physical stereotype so commonly accepted that it is rarely challenged. The reason Glenn was given a rather objective coverage not focusing only on his age was that he did something courageous and made a contribution not normally associated with old age.[24]

GRANDPARENTS IN POPULAR MUSIC

Grandparents have been a topic in popular music for years and have been characterized, in country songs in particular, with reference to the reputed mental deterioration of grandparents. Here are the lyrics to "Granny's Off Her Rocker":

Granny's off her rocker and the family is upset.
She took her life's savings and bought a red Corvette.
There's talk of putting her away; her new lifestyle is a shocker.
Since she met this man they're saying Granny's off her rocker.

The message of these lyrics is clear. An old grandmother has no right to drive a sportscar and even less right to have a boyfriend. Both the car and the boyfriend imply that Granny may be spending her money on herself and not leaving it all to a greedy family. Furthermore, Granny may even be involved in sex, an unthinkable offense for grandparents.

Then there is the song "Grandpa," recorded by the Judds. Here are the lyrics:

Grandpa take me back to yesterday, when the line between right and
    wrong didn't seem so hazy;
a time when lovers fell in love to stay;
people kept promises, families prayed together, and Daddy stayed
    home.
Grandpa let me fill your whiskey glass;
then paint me a picture of long ago.

Those who believe that the "good old days" were really good are evidently ignorant of the history of social conditions. The belief that in earlier years all men were pure and simple is as simplistic as it is wrong. There are even those who claim that Thomas Jefferson and others of our Founding Fathers were great Christians, when exactly the opposite is the case. Perhaps there is no more common stereotype than the belief that the past was glorious and that things are just terrible now.

Here are the lyrics to "Grandma Harp," a song that rests on a similar basis:

Just think about the times that she lived through
and think about the changing world she saw.
Somehow she raised a decent family out of poverty;
and for seventy years she stayed married to the same old Grandpa.

Such lyrics omit telling the listener that Grandma had no choice but to stay with Grandpa, because women could rarely get a divorce even if victimized by abusive husbands. Furthermore, divorce was a "scandal" in any family before 1960, an era that was far from idyllic—as is our own.

Neglect of Grandma and withdrawal are also frequent themes of country music. "Rocking Alone in an Old Rocking Chair" includes these lyrics:

Sitting alone in an old rocking chair
I saw an old mother with silvery hair.
She seemed so neglected by those who should care.
Rockin' alone in an old rockin' chair.

Other songs deal with grandparents who no longer see their grandchildren because their children have no time to visit them. Here is Harry Chapin's "Cat's in the Cradle":

I've long since retired, my son's moved away;
I called him up just the other day.
I said: "I'd like to see you if you don't mind."
He said: "I'd love to Dad, if I could find the time.
You see my new job's a hassle and the kids have the flu;
but it's sure nice talking to you."

This song accurately reflects the fate of many grandparents whose children have moved away so that they seldom see them or their grandchildren. In the upper-middle class this is so common that grandparents who have two adult children and five grandchildren "in town" are endlessly envied by the many whose children left them long ago. It also reflects the reciprocity (or lack thereof) between parents and children and grandparents. Grandparents cannot expect to be treated with deference and love if they did not have time for their children and grandchildren.

Another portrayal of grandparents is that of death and the longing for the departed grandmother or grandfather, as illustrated by the Collin Raye song, "Love, Me," quoted below:

I read a note my Grandma wrote back in 1923.
Grandpa kept it in his coat and he showed it once to me.
He said, "Boy, you might not understand but a long long time ago
Grandma's daddy didn't like me none but I loved your grandma so.
We had this crazy plan to meet and run away together;

Get married in the first town we came to and live forever.
But nailed to the tree where we were supposed to meet
Instead I found this letter and this is what it said:
If you get there before I do don't give up on me.
I'll meet you when my chores are through; I don't know how long I'll be.
But I'm not gonna let you down, Darling wait and see.
And between now and then till I see you again, I'll be loving you.
    Love, Me."
I read those words just hours before my Grandma passed away.
In the doorway of a church where me and Grandpa stopped to pray.
I know I'd never seen him cry in all my fifteen years
But as he said these words to her his eyes filled up with tears:
"If you get there before I do, don't give up on me
I'll meet you when my chores are through;
I don't know how long I'll be.
But I'm not gonna let you down, Darling wait and see.
and between now and then till I see you again, I'll be loving you.
    Love, Me."*

A general review of the role of grandparents in country music con-
cludes that grandparents fare somewhat better than "the old" in these
depictions of the last part of life. This means that grandparents can relate
to children and grandchildren, and therefore seem to have at least some
purpose in their old age, a status the lyrics will not allow "the old" in general. Nevertheless, the overall message of country music lyrics concerning the old, including grandparents, is negative.

GRANDPARENTS IN LITERATURE

There are so many novels, dramas, and short stories that include grandparents that it is impossible to discuss even a fraction of that vast literature. Therefore, we will confine ourselves to a few examples of writings
involving grandparents, beginning with the nineteenth century and
ending in the 1990s.

---

*Written by Skip Ewing and Max T. Barnes. Published by Acuff-Rose Music, Inc., and Write On
Music. Reprinted with permission.

No doubt *Martin Chuzzlewit* by Charles Dickens (1812–1870) is the most prominent of nineteenth-century novels dealing with grandparents.[25] Dickens tells the story of grandfather, Martin Chuzzlewit, who believes that everyone he knows has designs on his money. His grandson, also called Martin, resembles him physically as well as in character. He, too, believes that money is everything. Old Martin has a ward and companion, an orphan named Mary Graham. The old man hopes that she and his grandson will fall in love.

When this finally happens, Old Martin allows his suspicions to rule him, and in his fear that the young couple are seeking his fortune, he turns his grandson out of his house. The grandson then becomes an apprentice to an architect, and the events that follow all end in the redemption of the old grandfather, who finally acknowledges his family and their right to live "happily ever after."

There can be no doubt that Dickens was one of the foremost English novelists of the nineteenth-century. His novels, therefore, had a great deal of influence on the views of English-speaking people everywhere. Dickens's *Martin Chizzlewit* adds to the stereotype of the old and greedy "geezers" who are so "tight," they still "have every nickel they ever made." This novel has also been dramatized by Thomas Higgie and Thomas Hailes.

Remembrance of Things Past was written by the important French novelist Marcel Proust (1871–1923).[26] This novel seeks to portray the wasted life of a wealthy yet empty-headed aristocracy who spend their lives on intrigues and jealousies. The only unselfish and decent person in this vast novel is the grandmother of Marcel, the protagonist of this story. The principal purpose of this truly Freudian novel is to illustrate to the reader the purpose of life and the need to do more than indulge in selfish pursuits. In this novel, only the grandmother has any admirable characteristics, so we here have a book that enhances the esteem of the earlier generation.

The drama *The Intruder,* by Maurice Maeterlinck (1862–1949), features a blind grandfather who, despite his disability, has better "vision" than those who can see.[27] The grandfather "hears" the intruder—death—arrive and enter the house where the family is gathered because of the illness of a mother who has just given birth. The grandfather is viewed as irrational by his children because he claims to know things he cannot possibly see. Yet, in the end, the grandfather is proved right—the sick woman dies, just as the blind grandfather foresaw.

This play promotes the idea that life and death are the same, that they cannot be controlled by reason, but that the intuition of a blind old man is superior to the arguments of those who are younger. The grandfather is the only rational person in the drama because he understands all this.

Grandfather Stories, by Samuel Hopkins Adams (1871–1958), deals with events occurring along the Erie Canal between 1820 and 1888.[28] The protagonist in the story is a young boy who has two living grandfathers, which was most unusual in the nineteenth century. The novel contrasts a stuffy doctor of divinity, Grandfather Hopkins, with Grandfather Adams, who turns out to be a horse thief. The stories in the book are autobiographical. They reflect life in nineteenth-century America as lived by a generation that had witnessed the Civil War but had not yet seen the outcome of industrialization. Both grandfathers are seen in a positive light because both are contributing members of their boring society.

Glenway Westcott (1901–1987) published *The Grandmothers* in 1927.[29] This novel deals with a grandfather, Henry Tower, a Civil War veteran. Seeking his fortune in the West, Grandfather Tower moves from New York to Wisconsin, only to fail at farming. He suffers the death of his wife, a loss from which he never recovers, although he marries a second time and has a number of children. The entire novel seeks to exult the past and its advantages. The family portrayed in the novel includes grandmothers who were nineteenth-century pioneers and endured drunken husbands, abject poverty, and finally prosperity. The purpose of the novel is to feature American pioneers, both female and male. Thus, the grandparents are real heroes for all they endured so that subsequent generations could succeed.

In *The Grandfathers*, Conrad Richter (1890–1968) also portrays nineteenth-century American life before the automobile and the supermarket.[30] Like Adams, Richter contrasts two grandfathers and their families: one is a "squire," the other a "squatter." One family is all order and respectability, and the other embraces disorder and violence. The story also deals with the effort of a woman to discover who her father and her grandfather are. The grandparents portrayed are real people. One grandfather is in jail for theft, but he is, nevertheless, a functioning person and not a stereotypical "old geezer." The grandfather who is not in jail is a real upper-crust, "old money" gentleman, honored and respected. He makes his living as a justice of the peace, and is therefore feared by some. Richter gives grandparents a good name and lets his readers know that grandparents are important people.

The play *The Dining Room*, by Albert R. Gurney (1930–), seeks to show that the white Anglo-Saxon dominance of American culture has come to an end and that the younger generation views any pretense of superiority on the part of grandparents concerning their membership in that social class ridiculous and irrelevant.[31] The play illustrates a permanent generational contrast. The dining room table represents the era of grandparents who sat around that table with their families while servants served large dinners that led to hours of discussion around the table.

These novels and plays are only a small sample of the numerous works that include grandparents as either principal characters or participants in the action. Overall, these fictional grandparents are treated far better than grandparents in movies, on television, or in advertisements. Evidently, novelists and playwrights have more time and more skill than those in the other media, who endlessly portray grandparents as ignorant old fools who play with dogs and grandchildren.

Likewise, grandparents appearing in short stories are treated far better than in the film media. Furthermore, grandparents appear frequently in short stories, but less so in novels and seldom in films. For example, between 1994 and 1998, a period of five years, 65 short stories appeared dealing at least in part with grandfathers. Grandmothers fared even better, as 117 stories including grandmothers were published during those five years. There were also 16 short stories published during those years that discussed grandparents, and another ten dealing with grandchildren.[32]

GRANDPARENTS IN CHILDREN'S STORIES

Grandparents are included in children's literature to a considerable extent. Nevertheless, the picture of grandparents presented to the young readers of such literature is not very encouraging. Grandparents in children's books engage in little, if any, social activity or interaction; they are endlessly employed in dull activities requiring no mental or physical ability; and they are almost always portrayed as very old, quite sick, and not at all self-reliant. In children's stories grandmothers are always in the kitchen preparing food. Grandfathers are endlessly interested in fishing, animals, and telling stories about the "good old days." Grandparents, who are always gray-haired individuals sitting in rocking chairs, are passive and always pleasant. This depiction totally overlooks the fact that there are many Americans who have become grandparents in their forties.

In these children's stories, grandparents may be kind and friendly, but old people who are not portrayed as grandparents are generally disagreeable, if not downright mean. A good part of children's literature involving grandparents reflects "culture lag." This means that the picture of grandparents drawn in current children's books reflects life in earlier centuries, even though the world has changed a great deal. The old—that is, grandparents—are not generally sick or poor. On the contrary, older Americans are normally healthy and even wealthy. Few live in rural settings, many are fully employed, and a large number are college-educated professionals. Grandmothers, too, are generally working women who do not spend the day in the kitchen. Furthermore, both grandmothers and grandfathers are a good deal younger than portrayed in most children's literature, some of which is more than a century old.

One example of such a story is *Heidi,* which was written by the Swiss author Johanna Spyri (1827–1901) in 1880.[33] This story has been in print in English for more than a century and is still popular among American children. The story deals with the adventures of a little Swiss girl who lives with her grandfather and grandmother because her parents are dead. Her life centers around her grandfather, who spends all his time with goats and other animals in the Swiss mountains. When the grandfather takes Heidi to visit a goatherd's grandmother, it turns out that the grandmother is blind. Of course, in these children's tales old people are always disabled in one form or another.

This nineteenth-century novel contrasts life in the big city, Frankfurt, with the idyllic life in the mountains and other rural areas. The rural life is, of course, painted as far superior. The grandfather, who lives in the mountains, is not well educated, but in children's stories, uneducated grandfathers who live with goats are far superior to "city slickers" who live in corrupt surroundings, far from the truly healthy life "up on the farm" in the Swiss Alps.

The Patchwork Quilt by Valerie Flournoy was written in a similar vein.[34] It portrays a grandmother, otherwise utterly incompetent, who is endlessly working on a quilt using rags from the family's old clothes. As usual in such stories, Grandma becomes ill, and the little girl continues to work on the quilt because it is so important to the family.

True to the children's book formula, *Grandaddy's Place* by Helen V. Griffith takes place in the country.[35] The grandfather is, of course, involved with animals, and tells stories that make his once-frightened granddaughter feel much better. The grandfather is a near idiot who can hardly be distinguished from the animals he keeps—although the author does not attach such a label to him. Nevertheless, here, as elsewhere, Granddaddy is certainly not a professional man or a success in Modern American terms.

There is also *Oma and Bobo* by Amy Schwartz.[36] *Oma* is a German term meaning "grandmother." In this book, the grandmother is involved in training a dog, which will not obey anyone other than Oma. She speaks in German to the dog, which wins a blue ribbon when Oma shouts German commands. Other than training a dog, Oma has little to contribute and locks herself in her room when the dog causes a problem. As always, the grandmother is concerned with little children and animals and has no adult role.

It may be that *What's Under My Bed?* at least has the function of relieving children of their common fears.[37] The author, James Stevenson, ridicules common children's fears by having Grandpa remember how he, too, was afraid of all kinds of things when he was a boy and was comforted by his grandparents. The highlight of this book is the experience of sharing some ice cream with Grandpa, who has no interests other than telling stories to his grandchildren.

In *The Wednesday Surprise* by Eve Bunting, an illiterate grandmother is taught to read by her granddaughter.[38] That is the nature of the "surprise," which occurs at the birthday party of a child's father, who is a truck driver. The number and proportion of illiterate adults in the United States may be around 2 percent these days. Of course, it makes for a great story to teach an old lady how to read. The impression a child reader will get from this book is that grandmothers and other old people are stupid and illiterate.

On the converse side, it illustrates that children can teach their grandparents. This has been observed as Grandma and Grandpa have learned from their grandchildren how to use a computer. While on vacation at her grandfather's home, fifteen-year-old Heather taught him how to use e-mail to stay in touch with her and other family members. Johnny, a fifth grader, taught both of his grandparents to operate the computer. These experiences helped cement already excellent grandparent-grandchild relationships.

An African American family is portrayed in *Grandpa's Face* by Eloise Greenfield.[39] Here, the grandfather is interested in acting in theater productions. Little Tamika is frightened because Grandpa distorts his face as he practices his role in an upcoming play. Of course, Grandpa explains all about acting as he and little Tamika go for a walk together. Here, at least, Grandpa has an interest in acting and is not only spending all his time with animals. Nevertheless, his companion is a little girl, not an adult, and his conversation is at a child's level as well.

In *The Best Present*, we find that the grandmother is in the hospital.[40] The author, Holly Keller, tells the story of an eight-year-old girl who is not admitted to the hospital room where her grandmother is staying. She sends flowers to grandmother by way of an adult who is permitted to visit the upper floors of the hospital, and Grandma gets "the best present," as the child learns after Grandma's return from the hospital. Again, true to script, Grandma is sick.

Then there is Mrs. Medley, a grandmother who is utterly confused and returns home four times on her way to the beach with her grandson. In *Not the Piano, Mrs. Medley!* Evan Levine portrays the grandmother as disorganized and incapable of planning ahead.[41] It takes a little boy to straighten Grandma out and teach her that there is no need to drag all kinds of things to the beach just to spend an afternoon there. This story also teaches that the old are ipso facto confused.

Some American history can be learned from *Three Names* by Patricia MacLachlan.[42] In a typical "boy and his dog" story, the great-grandfather describes life on the American prairie in the early twentieth century. The great-grandfather is the storyteller who remembers attending a one-room schoolhouse in his youth, always accompanied by his dog, Three Names. The book describes the change in the seasons, which impinged a great deal more on the early pioneers than they do on those living in cities now. It is a wonderful history lesson that the child enjoys and feels connected with as it is related by his beloved great-grandfather.

MacLachlan is also the author of *Journey*, which deals with two children who live with their grandparents on the family farm because their mother has abandoned them.[43] Their grandfather takes photographs of the animals as well as of the family, as he and Grandma reminisce about their youth by looking through old photographs. In fact, Grandpa even goes so far as to develop negatives of old pictures that reconstruct the children's earlier years. Once more, grandparents are full of devotion, affection, and rural love—but have no other characteristics. At least in this book, the grandparents are not sick.

Grandmothers are not always portrayed as sick. In *Thunder Cake*, Patricia Polacco depicts a grandmother who helps a little girl overcome her fear of thunderstorms.[44] Grandmother bakes a cake during a thunderstorm and uses the occasion to teach the child that fear of thunder is unnecessary. Grandma is engaged in baking, once more a stereotypical occupation for old people.

The exception to the rule that grandparents are simpletons is illustrated in *Gentlehands,* a story by M. E. Kerr.[45] Here, the grandfather is in fact a cultivated and cultured man. He loves opera and has a "style and wisdom" seldom found. The dramatic aspect of this novel for junior high school students is the revelation that the grandfather was a brutal concentration camp guard during World War II, and that adulthood may come with the painful lesson that people may not be as kind and pleasant as they seem on the surface. The principal lesson here is that some values are more important than attachments to people, including an abominable yet pleasant grandfather.

Likewise, *Homecoming* by Cynthia Voigt is the story of four abandoned children who find a home with a grandmother who is, at least at first, an obnoxious and rejecting old woman.[46] It is then revealed that she is a widow who became the village oddity when she lost her only son in Vietnam and felt that she had nothing more to live for. However, her grandchildren, who arrive looking for a home, change all that. Her grandchildren give her something to live for and make her a different person. She gives the grandchildren a real home, thereby saving herself and them. The book discusses the problems of homelessness and the value of family life.

The 1990 novel *Everywhere*, by Bruce Brooks, deals with a grandfather who is the victim of a heart attack.[47] The book portrays a grandpa at death's door who is saved and restored to health by the use of magic and the "power of love." No doubt this kind of story has some appeal to ten-year-olds even as it perpetuates the usual stereotypes about the old.

Dennis Hasley is the author of *Shadows*, which deals with a grandfather who teaches his grandson how to make shadow pictures with his hands. The grandson saves Grandpa's life, reaching him just as he is overcome by smoke from a fire in his cabin in the woods. The grandfather also suffers from the memory of his dead son, the boy's father, who died in an industrial accident. Once more we have a grandfather who lives in the woods, is a tragic figure, lives in the shadows of his imagination and memory, and needs a lot of help to stay alive.[48]

The books we have mentioned are a representative sample of the thousands of children's books published each year. They depict grandparents invariably as rural simpletons who are not only sick all the time but who also spend a large amount of time with every kind of animal. Compared to middle-aged adults, grandparents are shown as incompetent, but invariably interested in animals and little children.

GRANDPARENTS IN JOKES AND HUMOR

Jokes reflect the culture in which they are told. It is for that reason that we often find no humor in jokes from another culture and/or a setting not known to us. The jokes of outsiders seem dull and not humorous, although our own jokes provoke boisterous laughter.

There are a number of jokes illustrating the status and role of grandparents. Almost all of these jokes convey a negative message. Psychiatrist Joseph Richman has studied jokes concerning grandparents and found that 66 percent were derogatory, while only one-fourth of jokes about children were negative.

Below are three of Richman's jokes.[49] Both reflect the popular view that the sexual interests of grandparents are not to be taken seriously. The truth is that sex plays a role in nursing homes and never ceases to interest us at any age. However, puritan assumptions prohibit the old from being sexual unless in a jocular context.

> An eighty-year-old grandmother complained that she had a lot of trouble during the night that prevented her from sleeping. The trouble

was that a man kept banging on her door. When asked why she didn't open the door, Grandma replied, "What? And let him out?"

Grandma is held up by a robber. The robber frisks her for her money but, after some search all over her body, he gives up. "Heaven, young man," shouts Grandma, "don't stop now! I'll write you a check!"

A ninety-year-old man married an eighteen-year-old girl and promptly dies from exhaustion after only five days. It took the undertaker three days to get the smile off his face.

Confusion and incompetence are illustrated in this joke: *Grandpa visits a house of ill repute. The madam greets him at the door. "Grandpa," says the madam, "what can I do for you?" "I want the prettiest blonde in this establishment," says Grandpa. "Mister," says the madam, "you have had it!" Grandpa pulls out his wallet. "How much do I owe you?" he asks.*

Jokes concerning the physical attributes of grandparents are also frequently told. Here is an example: *A woman was asked if she carried a memento of someone in her locket. "I carry a lock of my husband's hair,* she said. *"But your husband is still here." "I know," said she, "but his hair isn't."*

Jokes concerning the relationships between the generations also imply that old grandfathers, in particular, are fools: *Grandpa is a rich widower and has a young girlfriend who plans to marry him. "What can May possibly find in December?" she is asked. "Christmas," replies the gold digger.*

Finally, it is instructive to consider the view of grandparents exhibited to children in cartoons, which are popular on Saturday mornings but can also be seen at other times on television and in newspapers and magazines. There can be no doubt that the number of grandparents appearing in such cartoons is exceedingly small, amounting to about 5 percent of all cartoon characters, and that they are almost always depicted in a negative fashion. Psychologist D. Dwayne Smith, one of the few who has made an effort to study the portrayal of grandparents in magazine cartoons, found that only 21 percent of such cartoons promote a positive image of grandparents.[50]

SUMMARY

Ageism permeates movies, television, and other popular forms of entertainment. Generally, the media recycle the same stereotypes concerning grandparents again and again. Contempt for aging leads movie characters to fear becoming grandfathers and induces others to use cosmetics to "cover up" their age.

Grandmothers are depicted as meddling fools who unnerve other people by their constant interference in matters that don't concern them. They are usually shown as domineering old women.

Grandparents are shown as ill and dying, rarely as healthy, working, and contributing adults. Grandparents are also shown as victims of all kinds of misfortunes, seldom as women and men in control of their own lives. Grandparents in movies and television portrayals talk too much but have no substance. They are superficial and superfluous.

Because old age is viewed with so much fear and contempt in America, grandparents in television advertisements are shown with young faces and gray hair. This ignores the fact that Americans over sixty-five constitute a $7-billion market that advertisers, in their prejudice, refuse to recognize.

Grandparents in TV advertisements are seen as endlessly needing all kinds of medication in order to function. Except for John Glenn and a few other superheroes, grandparents are depicted as incompetent and concerned with childish issues.

Grandparents fare somewhat better in adult novels by such foreign authors as Dickens, Proust, and Maeterlinck and American authors Adams, Westcott, Richter, and Gerney. In children's literature, however, grandparents are mostly sick, childish, rural simpletons.

Likewise, jokes concerning grandparents ridicule the infirmities of old age and the confusion old age reputedly brings.

In sum, the picture of grandparents drawn by the media is negative and unreal because it seldom corresponds to actual experience.

8

Grandparents

The Supporting Generation

INTERGENERATIONAL EMPATHY
AND THE KONDRATIEFF WAVE

Numerous investigations into the relationship between grandparents and grandchildren have revealed that these "skipped" generations are more likely to develop positive relationships than is portrayed in the media, which seek to portray grandparents as obsolescent and useless. The evidence is that although "old age" as a generic concept is disdained in American culture, grandchildren view their grandparents in a different light than that normally accorded "the old."

The concept of "modernization" and the ever-increasing longevity of the American population has led to the belief that "the old" cannot keep up with the rapid changes in our technological society and are therefore justly discarded by "the young." This situation, it is widely believed, leads to an insurmountable "generation gap."

While this hypothesis may have been true fifty years ago, at the start of the postindustrial age in the United States, it is hardly defensible now, because parents and grandparents at the beginning of this century are generally so well educated in technological matters that those now in high school are no longer dealing with matters utterly unknown to their elders. Those in earlier generations who learned about computers may have felt an immense gap between themselves and their elders, who had never heard of—or even seen—a computer. They may have felt greatly superior to those who, although older, knew nothing about such things. That day, however, is long gone, because so many parents and grandparents have a good education, which has given them access to technological advances and scientific knowledge. It is therefore more difficult for the young to "lord it over" the old on the grounds that their elders don't know anything. In fact, it is our argument that there is often more consensus between grandparents and grandchildren than between grandparents and their own children.[1]

It is naive to believe that age differences are merely biological and psychological. Aging also involves social stratification and, most important, social history. This means that grandparents who lived through the Great Depression of the 1930s are quite different from grandparents who did not experience the same hardships. Grandparents who lived through the depression may well feel that their children and grandchildren do not appreciate the value of a dollar. Furthermore, grandparents who were involved in the First World War may have more affinity for grandchildren who fought in Vietnam than for their own children, who were raised in peacetime and without combat experience. Likewise, grandparents who are themselves the product of a peaceful and strong economy may be much better able to understand current grandchildren, who have never seen a depression or a war. One argument is, therefore, that the affinity of cohorts to one another can be far more binding than a mere life cycle relationship.[2]

Therefore, value differences between generations may well be the result of cohort experiences, not of age. It is fairly certain that there are defining events in the lives of every cohort that lead that group to evaluate subsequent events in the light of those occurrences that most influenced their thinking. This is well illustrated by the worldview of World War II veterans as compared to those who never saw a shot fired in anger. Likewise, a 1974 study at Dartmouth College showed that those who graduated from there in 1940 revealed hardly any changes in social, economic, or political values over the course of three decades, because they were already the sons of privilege when they graduated and remained so throughout their adult lives. This illustrates once more that the experience of cohorts is more important than age in influencing their views.[3]

This argument assumes, then, that each member of a cohort moves along his life span in a manner similar to that of others in that cohort, and that this determines similarity in outlook and values.

Whatever strength this theory may have, Kalish and Johnson showed in their study that there was a greater degree of value similarities between grandmothers and granddaughters than between grandmothers and their own children. Likewise, the gerontologists Samuel Payne, David Summers, and Thomas R. Stewart found greater similarities between grandchildren and grandparents concerning their attitudes about personal failures than between either group and the generation between them. Additionally, greater similarity was found to exist between grandchildren and grandparents concerning attitudes toward the powerless and dependent citizens within our social structure.[4]

In 1926, during the dictatorship of Joseph Stalin (1879–1953), the Russian economist Nikolai Kondratieff was exiled to Siberia because he published his finding that capitalism is self-correcting every half century. This well-known phenomenon, called the "Kondratieff Wave," posits that for a period of twenty-five years there is a rise in wholesale prices, interest rates, and money supply, followed by a decline in the same phenomena— as well as increases in birth rates and declines in the homicide rate.

It is evident that the approximate age difference between grandparents and grandchildren is fifty years, the same as the Kondratieff Wave. The fact that grandparents have greater empathy for their grandchildren than parents and have more of a value consensus with them than with their own children can be traced to the fact that grandparents are likely to have spent their youth in the portion of the Kondratieff Wave that resembles the portion their grandchildren meet in their youth.[5]

In sum, we argue here that, at least in part, the lives of grandparents and grandchildren are formed by similar social, political, economic, and demographic events.[6]

ECONOMIC SUPPORT— HELPING WHERE IT COUNTS

Emotional support and support for values is by no means the only support that grandchildren derive from their grandparents. To some extent such support accrues to grandchildren indirectly as it is dispensed to their parents. In addition, economic support through the transfer of assets is very common. This has become so because of the increase in longevity over the past century. This longevity has permitted grandparenthood to continue through several epochs in the lives of grandchildren, from earliest childhood to marriage and beyond.

For most Americans, family finances are most strained during the period when there are dependent children in the house. It is at this stage that most families need financial assistance. Because so many grandmothers are now in the workforce, they are now more capable of assisting than was the case when women did not work outside the home and life expectancy was short.

Andrea is a sixty-year-old secretary who is always buying things for her four grandchildren. Her daughter and son-in-law are working hard to make ends meet. Andrea has purchased all of the young ones bicycles, additional clothing that they need, and shoes, which they outgrew too rapidly. Because Andrea's husband still works, she is able to put aside some money with which to purchase the "extras" that the youngsters would otherwise not be able to have.

The sociologist Gail Wilson has shown that normal events of the life cycle are usually reason enough to transfer assets from grandparents to grandchildren. Hence, births, birthdays, graduations, confirmations, and weddings are all occasions for such transfers.

Lucy gives her three grandchildren savings bonds for every birthday and Christmas. This is their college fund.

Then there is the transfer of assets from grandparents to their own children, which benefits the grandchildren as well. Surely the arrival of children leads to a strain on the financial condition of most American families—and to an increase of support given by grandparents particularly, because very few mothers return to work directly after the birth of a baby. According to Wilson's study, the presence of grandchildren not only increases the contributions parents will make to their daughters' financial situation, it also increases the willingness of their adult children to accept such help.[7]

When her first grandchild was born, Mabel opened a bank account for the child. She promised herself she would do the same for each subsequent birth. She is very open about expressing her feelings, stating that she looks back and wishes she had been fortunate enough to have a parent or grandparent who could have afforded to do that for her.

Wilson found that both grandfathers and grandmothers make contributions to the welfare of grandchildren, but that adults and children alike often overlook the contributions of grandfathers. Such help may consist of driving members of the family about, paying for entertainment, or helping a son or son-in-law with a physical task. These activities on the part of grandfathers were generally underestimated in the Wilson study.

When Michael bought an old house for his family, his Dad was there to help him with renovations and repairs. He worked hard, adding a bedroom for one of the grandsons so that he could have his own space. He spent much of his time plastering and painting the walls of the rooms that needed repair. This was a great savings for the young couple, who could not have afforded to pay to make the house livable. There was an additional benefit derived from this man's work: He felt capable and worthwhile, able to look at his accomplishments in a concrete way.

Several other investigators found similar responses concerning the support given grandchildren by grandfathers. Louis Moss and Harvey Goldstein found that help given by grandfathers is much more sporadic than support given by grandmothers. Therefore, grandfathers' help is often forgotten.[8]

There are, of course, some grandparents whose finances are far better than those of their children and who lend a great deal of support to their grandchildren. There are grandfathers who pay for furniture or even houses for their children and make such huge contributions to them that it becomes an embarrassment to the adult parents.

Lionel is an extremely wealthy man who owns a large factory. He is the father of four sons and a daughter. He established a trust for each of his five children and six grandchildren. He recalls how he "pulled himself up by his bootstraps," first as a construction worker, then as the "boss" of the company, and ultimately, through his wits and hard work, he built up a sizable fortune. He is determined not to have his children ever "go without."

Both the grandparents and their adult children express the view that all this is for the grandchildren. Such a view reduces the anxiety that so large a transfer of assets can produce, particularly in the middle class.[9]

Widowed grandfathers sometimes take on the "grandmother" role in that they give continuous support to grandchildren, including child care and supervision. Such continuous support is particularly common among single grandfathers who live in their adult children's homes.

Kenneth—"Doc Ken," as he is lovingly called—is a retired college professor. He is a widower whose only child, Thomas, is the father of twins. Both Thomas and his spouse work full-time in order to make ends meet. Doc Ken has offered to take care of the twins until the family is out of the woods. It isn't always easy for this man to spend his days at his son's house, when he would rather be at home reading and relaxing. The twins are very lively and demand a great deal of attention. He sometimes wonders how he ever got himself into this. He recalls that he did not diaper or take care of his own son when he was young. He also at times resents that he does not get enough recognition for his sacrifice. But other times he looks at his grandchildren and finds them so interesting and challenging. He promises himself that as soon as the couple can manage on their own he will do his own thing—although he is not quite certain what that is at the moment. At this time he is very much occupied and has no time to be bored.

The assumption that grandmothers must be supportive is so common that such support is hardly mentioned by adult children. However, lack of support by grandmothers is often a cause for complaint, while that is not true regarding grandfathers. Since most women earn less than men, few grandmothers are able to make large financial contributions to their grandchildren, directly or indirectly. So grandmothers are expected to give labor—baby-sitting, making dinners, having the kids for the night at Grandma's house, or being available in emergencies.

Judy Taylor expects a great deal from her mother. Judy is a second-year student at a local college and the single mother of a three-year-old boy. Judy lives in her parents' home and resents not being in total control of her child. She is not anxious to spend much time with him, since her college work takes a great deal of her time and effort. In addition to this she has a part-time job. She never hesitates to ask her mom to baby-sit in the evening so that she can go out "to find a life for herself." She gets angry

when her parents do things differently than she would have done, and is
critical of her mother's way of correcting the little boy. She dislikes that
her mother is not eager to have hosts of children in the house to play with
the child, and says that "other grandmothers are more giving." It does
not occur to Judy that she is imposing on her mother and father and
infringing on their privacy and space. She also complains often that her
parents should be willing to furnish a separate bathroom for herself and
her child.

There are also many grandmothers who will regularly pay for grandchildren's shoes or haircuts, not because of need but because they want to
make a contribution. Some grandmothers buy washing machines for their
daughters once a baby has arrived. This kind of contribution is seldom
delivered by grandfathers, because men do not often think of such needs.

There is an additional contribution grandparents make to their grandchildren, although it is seldom understood or even noticed. This contribution is related to grandchildren's academic success. Children who live
in wealthier homes, who do not have to face poverty, and who have space
for study, recreation, and other life amenities achieve higher scores in
their schoolwork than the children of the poor. Mark Rosenzweig and
Kenneth Wolpin have shown that there is a significant relationship
between the achievement of children and the contribution of grandparents
to households of the poor and the near-poor.[10]

Although Jane and Gilbert, grandparents of four, are not wealthy them-
selves, they are still employed and can afford more than their son, who is
struggling on one income. They have purchased a computer for their
nine-year-old grandson so that he can finish his homework with ease.
They have also been known to take one or another of their grandchildren
out for a snack or to a fast-food restaurant to give the child a little
"boost." They give a grandchild who gets a good grade a couple of
bucks—some incentive to do well.

It is intriguing to consider the economic value of grandparent assistance
to the families of their children. This is particularly important because the
common stereotype indicates that the old in our society are dependent,
self-indulgent, unproductive, and greedy. This can hardly be the case,

because at least 76 percent of Americans over fifty-five have grandchildren who are frequently the recipients of a good deal of help from their grandparents. The Commonwealth Fund Productive Aging Study has analyzed the value of the help grandparents give grandchildren and found that the typical older person who has grandchildren provides assistance to them for 7 hours a week. Those who provided help taking care of grandchildren and great-grandchildren did so, on average, for 13.6 hours per week. The Commonwealth study also found that 9 percent of all grandparents provided help for 20 hours or more per week.[11]

These percentages translate into 14.1 million older Americans helping grandchildren every week. The average of 13.7 hours of service rendered grandchildren represents the equivalent effort of 4.2 million full-time workers per year.

If we assume that child care costs a minimum of $2 per hour and rises to $3 or $3.35 in some regions of the country, then the number of hours provided equates to between $17.4 billion and $29.1 billion per year. Obviously then, grandparents provide a substantial amount of service to their grandchildren. The middle-aged parents of these children would have to spend a great deal to gain access to so much service, even if it were available.[12]

Sociologists have used the term "wealth span" to deal with the financial implications of aging within a multigenerational context. Two distinct age groups are represented in such a wealth span. These are young adults who live in the accumulative stage, beginning with first employment and ending with retirement, and older adults who live in the expenditure stage, which begins with retirement and continues until death.

There are, of course, grandparents whose wealth is such that they can take care of themselves and contribute to the financial condition of their children and grandchildren. Nevertheless, it is an axiom in current American family life that many middle-aged people must now find the financial resources to support both their children and their parents. That is the consequence of the increases in life expectancy that occurred during the second fifty years of the twentieth century.

For some time now, this trend in longevity has led commentators to use the so-called dependency ratio to argue that the "old" are getting far too expensive for the "young." The purpose of this calculation is to show that those young and middle-aged persons working now must support an ever-increasing number of nonworking old pensioners.

However, such a calculation overlooks the fact that there has been a steady decline in the birth rate in this country. The number of teenagers aged fourteen to seventeen declined from 7.8 percent of all Americans in 1970 to 5.7 percent in 2000. This constitutes a decline of 27 percent. Meanwhile, the American population sixty-five years old and over increased from 9.8 percent of all Americans in 1970 to 12.6 percent in 2000. That constitutes an increase of 22 percent. Therefore, there is really no evidence that middle-aged adults carry a greater financial burden now than their counterparts did thirty years ago. The difference lies only in the fact that grandparents may now be more often the recipients of financial aid, while the number of children and grandchildren has declined. Moreover, it is also evident that while all small children and adolescents need support, many grandparents *do not* need support, but instead provide it. We hold that the so-called dependency ratio argument is faulty and suspect. We can say with confidence that the financial burden on working Americans has not and will not increase, but that the age range has and will continue to increase so that the distribution of our resources is now quite different than it was thirty years ago.[13]

One consequence of increased life expectancy is the possibility that many grandchildren and their parents will inherit a good deal less, in terms of money and property, than they anticipated. This is so because a longer life also means higher costs for health maintenance, hospitalizations, and nursing homes. Nursing home residency now costs an average of about $45,000 or more per year. Indeed, government programs pay for 58 percent of these costs. Nevertheless, the patient must pay 42 percent, or an average of $19,000, each year. Many nursing homes charge a great deal more than that, exhausting the finances of the patient and his family quickly. Therefore, as longevity increases, the inheritance of children and grandchildren will decrease. In addition inheritance taxes are so enormous that a great deal of money which would otherwise have been inherited is now consumed by the government. Middle-class families are also affected as their elders' savings are consumed by nursing facility and health-care fees.

Economic support is not the only help grandparents give grandchildren. Social support is also very important in the grandparent-grandchild relationship, particularly when a child suffers from a physical disability. Research has shown that such support is related to a rank-order scheme.

Considering four grandparents, it appears that there is a hierarchy in the support given by grandparents and accepted by children.

Generally, grandparents are the most stable support available to mothers with disabled children. Mothers with disabled children rank the support given them by their mothers first, followed by the support given by their fathers, then support given by their mothers-in-law, and last support given by their fathers-in-law. This ranking confirms that the family of origin is generally more meaningful to us than the family adopted through marriage. To quote a mother with a handicapped child: "With my mother I don't have to play any games; she accepts me and my child at any time and in any mood." Mothers-in-law are seen in a different light and may in fact have a different attitude toward the handicapped child. "This child is ruining my son's career" is a comment attributed to a mother-in-law in a recent study of these relationships.

Thomas and Hilda are the paternal grandparents of Mallory, a hydroencephalic twelve-year-old who cannot speak clearly and who makes motions and grunting sounds to attempt to make his needs known. The two grandparents have made it clear that they have neither the time nor the patience to supervise Mallory. They say that they appreciate the enormity of the child's problems, but that it is the mother's "job" to take care of her son. They do call their son, however, and symphathize with his "misfortune."

Michelle and Gregory are the parents of Jonathan, a severely disabled boy. He is not ambulatory, cannot speak, and is incontinent. He needs total care on a twenty-four-hour basis. His maternal grandmother and great-grandmother take turns caring for him while his mother, an occupational therapist, works. Jonathan is not an easy child to handle. At age eight he is very difficult to lift, since he is a fairly chubby child. The older of the two women especially has an extremely difficult time changing his diapers and maneuvering his "buggy." Her arthritic hands do not help the situation. She never complains and is frequently heard saying, "God only gives you as much as you can handle." She and the child's grandmother are very caring women who accept the young boy completely and show him a great deal of attention and love.

Jennifer is the divorced mother of a twelve-year-old hydroencephalic son. She is a professional woman who has to work on a full-time basis. Her mother is very much involved in caring for her only grandson. She often stands at the bus stop waiting for him to return from school. She prepares his dinner when his mom can't be there, and she emotionally supports not only her grandson but her daughter as well. There is never a complaint from this gentle woman, who offers so much of herself to her family.

In situations involving handicapped children, the support needed by parents of such children may well be emotional rather than instrumental. Instrumental support may consist of financial aid, transportation, babysitting, or help with domestic chores. Grandparents, however, play a meaningful role in the lives of grandchildren with or without disability.

DIVORCE, SEPARATION, AND DEATH— GRANDPARENTS AS THE BACKSTOP

There are, of course, other family problems besides disabilities. Divorce is the most common of these, and here, too, grandparents can play an important role.[14]

Voorhees's parents were divorced before the boy was a year old. His father left town and has not seen the boy since. The child is now ten years old. His maternal grandparents, who live "right around the corner," have taken a great deal of interest in V.H., as they call him. He goes to their house after school, during vacation, and whenever his mother works. His grandfather takes him along on construction jobs, teaching him how to work and what is important. He instills in him the good qualities that he values, teaching him right from wrong, showing him how to handle money, and stressing the necessity of a good education. The child respects his grandfather and emulates him in many ways. His work ethic is strong, just like Grandpa's, and his manner of walking and talking are much like the older man's. The child is frequently mistaken for his grandfather's son. Whenever this happens a wide smile comes over the man's face. These grandparents, especially the grandfather, are strong role models for this child.

The support grandparents can and do give to grandchildren becomes particularly crucial when divorce breaks up a family. There is a wealth of evidence suggesting that grandparents have a great deal of influence on the development of their grandchildren, both directly and indirectly. Direct influence is, of course, the product of face-to-face interaction. This includes direct financial and emotional support as well as the transmission of family values and providing advice and information. Indirect influence involves the transmission of family values, and so on.

Divorce alters the relationship between grandparents and grandchildren. Animosity toward one in-law or another causes problems for the grandchildren, who may not feel free to visit their grandparents—who, in most cases, have little or no knowledge of the circumstances. Grandparents usually do not know the details of the relationships between their married children and their spouses, so many grandparents are shocked to hear that their son or daughter is contemplating divorce.

Steward and Laura appeared to be a very happy couple. They were the parents of three young children ranging in age from three to seven. They were married for nine years, had a very attractive home, good jobs, and what appeared to be a comfortable life. One weekend Steward asked his parents whether he could spend the night with them. After a brief pause he informed his folks that he was getting a divorce. Both his mother and father were shocked. They liked Laura and considered her a daughter. At first, Steward told them very little about the circumstances surrounding this situation. It was only after much prodding that a number of days later, he revealed his secret. He suspected and later confirmed that his wife was having an affair, with a man she worked with. He had suspected it for a long time, but was uncertain. When questioned, she adamantly denied any connection with John, the man in question. Steward's convictions were so strong that he wired the telephone and learned that the two "lovers" were meeting after work and "celebrating" their relationship. Steward was so devastated that he decided to end his marriage.

Several studies have shown that only about a third of all children discuss their marital problems with their parents, so the older generation is often amazed at the dissolution of a child's marriage. When asked about it, the reasons parents give for the dissolution of their children's marriage include money and other issues, but sexual problems are seldom mentioned. It may well be that parents do not want to mention that topic, but it is also quite possible that their children have never discussed their sex life with them. American puritanism makes that possibility likely. This fits in with the notion that "real men" do not weep or discuss their problems—especially not with their mothers.

In a good number of cases, grandparents are confronted with the dissolution of the marriages of two or more children, so they are suddenly burdened with the worry about the future of a number of grandchildren and their relationship with them.[15]

After divorce, this relationship is threatened because it is the parents who either facilitate or prevent contact between grandparents and grandchildren. Such contact is, of course, partly dependent on proximity. However, the most prominent influence on grandparent-grandchild relationships after divorce is lineage. Generally, contact between grandchildren and grandparents is most frequent between maternal grandmothers and their grandchildren, and least frequent for paternal grandfathers. This hierarchy is undoubtedly most stringently affected by the custody of children. Because mothers are far more likely to have custody of children, maternal grandparents are more likely to have contact with their grandchildren. Therefore, paternal grandparents are far more likely to lose contact with their grandchildren, particularly when a divorced person places some of the blame for the divorce on the parents of the former spouse.

After Jim and Denise divorced, Jim's parents rarely had the opportunity to see their three grandchildren. Denise held them largely responsible for their breakup, in spite of the fact that the paternal grandparents never interfered in the couple's life and were very careful to stay within the parameters of their daughter-in-law's dictates. Denise alleged that "these people" should have given more appropriate gifts (more toys and less clothing), visited more, baby-sat without being asked, and so on. She also alleged that they had undue influence over their son, who visited them too frequently. (He would visit for half an hour once a week after work.) She insisted that it would be harmful to her children to see these grandparents, and she wanted no contact between them.

Some divorced mothers move away from the father, thereby denying access to their children both to the father and his parents. In these cases, contact between paternal grandparents and their grandchildren is dependent on the relationship between the father and his former wife. It has been estimated that one-half of all noncustodial fathers lose all contact with their children, so paternal grandparents are at a much higher risk of losing sight of their grandchildren than is true for maternal grandparents. Therefore, court-ordered contact is often the only means paternal grandparents have to maintain any relationship with their grandchildren.

Jessica went to court because her former daughter-in-law refused to allow her grandson, Bertram, to visit with her. Jessica's son had moved out of town after the divorce, so the paternal grandmother was the only family nearby on Bertram's father's side. After much pain and expense, Jessica succeeded in getting visitation rights. She was given permission to see her grandchild one weekend per month. There were strained feelings in the beginning when Bert came to visit. His mother had told the young boy how much she disliked his father's entire family. She was irrational in her anger and vituperations. Bertram's misgivings were soon allayed when Jessica wholeheartedly welcomed him during his monthly visits. She never belittled his mother, nor did she ever speak even one word against her. This grandmother was a very wise woman who knew just how to create an atmosphere of comfort and tranquility for her young grandson.

This method may not work and can even backfire, because some mothers will ask the court to prohibit the paternal grandparents from visiting the grandchildren. Many times, mothers remarry and their second husbands adopt the children and change the children's last names. In such cases, the children have no connection to their paternal grandparents whatever and frequently do not know who they are. Courts generally side with parents and not grandparents in any disputes about visitation, so paternal grandparents have little chance of succeeding through legal action.[16]

Nancy, a registered nurse with two boys, ages nine and eleven, wanted neither her divorced husband nor her former in-laws to have any contact with her sons. She tried diligently to cut off contact with all three. When she was unsuccessful in her many attempts, she visited an attorney who suggested she have the children interviewed by a psychotherapist. She convinced herself that she would end this turmoil in this fashion. Lawyers choose therapists who will advocate for their paid clients, right or wrong, and this attorney chose accordingly. The therapist was informed by the lawyer what she must do and she proceeded with her task. The boys came to her and she spoke with each boy separately and then with both boys together. Bobby, the eleven-year-old, spoke lovingly of his father and of his paternal grandparents. He told of the happy times they had and how enjoyable his visits with Dad and Grandpa and Grandma were. He said he missed them and wished he could see them more often. He alleged that he had never been abused by his father (as the mother alleged in court) and that the grandparents were "much fun." Bill, the younger of the two children, wept when he spoke of missing his father. He related that his mother had told him that neither his father nor his grandparents wanted to see him anymore. He had begged to call his dad, but his mother forbade it. He also said that one evening when the mother was not at home he managed to reach his grandparents. They were delighted to speak to him and invited him to visit. When he hesitantly related his experience to his mother, she scolded him for doing something that she had forbidden. He stated that he hoped that the situation would change and that his mother would understand how much he missed a very important part of his family. To please the attorney, her employer, the psychotherapist did not advocate on behalf of the boys but wrote in her report in such a fashion that the father's side of this family were not a good influence and should only have supervised visits with the children. The judge unfortunately granted this request, and the two preteen children lost a very important part of their childhood and the normalcy of their emotional growth and upbringing.

Grandparenting can, of course, play an important part in the mental health of older people. Therefore, it is important for grandparents to have a functional relationship with their grandchildren. Such a relationship depends on the ability of grandparents to communicate openly and freely with their grandchildren and with the parents of the grandchildren. This also means that altruism is the most important characteristic of functional grandparents.

But there also are dysfunctional grandparents. The psychiatrist Arthur

Kornhaber has identified such dysfunctional grandparents and classified them in three groups. Those who exhibit "grandparent identity disorder" do not involve themselves with grandchildren if they can help it. Those who communicate a "grandparent activity disorder" do involve themselves with grandchildren, but create conflict and alienation because of their involvement. Those who have a "grandparent communication disorder," according to Kornhaber, have an inability to communicate feelings or actions concerning their grandchildren.[17]

Whatever the causes of a loss of contact with grandchildren, consequences can be severe and even devastating for older adults. The main reasons for such a loss of contact include divorce, the death of one or both of the grandchildren's parents, conflict with one or both parents, and adoption of the grandchild by someone else. In all these situations the grandchild is still alive, but the sense of loss and the grief is intense for grandparents cut off from their grandchildren. Some grandparents use the courts to overcome their loss of contact and demand their legal right to see their grandchildren. This may well succeed de jure but fail de facto.

Normally, there is a generational boundary between grandparents, their children, and their grandchildren. This boundary functions to permit privacy on the part of both the grandparents and their married children. Such privacy permits generations to live with one another, because it ensures the autonomy of both married couples. After a divorce, however, that privacy is lost because the married state no longer exists and the privacy of the nuclear unit has weakened. When an adult child is married, reasonable people agree that the role of spouse and parent takes precedence over the role of adult child. But because a divorced adult child has abandoned the spouse role, both the parents and the divorced child can more easily move across the privacy boundary. So there are those whose bonds with grandchildren are strengthened by divorce particularly because grandparents often hear about a failing marriage from their grandchildren before they hear it from their children.

Seven-year-old Megan seemed unusually talkative when visiting her grandparents. She told her Nana that her Daddy had a big fight, that her Mom has a boyfriend now, and that Daddy said that he is moving out. This was the first inkling the grandmother had that a problem existed in their son's marriage.

This is, of course, not true of everyone. There are indeed grandparents who remain aloof and distant from their grandchildren even after the children's parents have divorced.

INHERITANCE—THE LAST CONTRIBUTION

There is one more form of support grandparents can give to grandchildren: the financial and property inheritance the old must perforce leave to those who survive them. The inheritance grandparents leave to grandchildren is usually indirect in that the children of the grandparents are more likely to inherit than the grandchildren. Nevertheless, there are some grandparents who leave all or some of their property and money directly to their grandchildren. They may have had serious problems with the behavior of their adult children and feel that the next generation is much more deserving than the neglectful son or daughter who has emotionally injured them. This is often a way in which grandparents can retaliate for the hurts that have been inflicted on them. Leaving all of one's property to children and or grandchildren has become more difficult, as the tax policies of the United States require that a portion—sometimes significant—of the inheritance be paid to the Internal Revenue Service. This scheme is as old as the republic. In 1797 Congress imposed the first temporary estate tax, which was repeated in 1862 and in 1898. In all three instances, the purpose of the tax was to raise money for the national defense. Then, in 1917, the estate tax was levied again, this time permanently. The tax seizes up to 37 percent and in some cases up to 60 percent of stocks, family businesses, family farms, and other assets left by the deceased in their wills. Thirteen states also impose an inheritance tax. Because these taxes are so high, more than ten thousand farms and other family businesses have to be sold for taxes each year, substantially reducing the amount left to children and grandchildren.[18]

There was a time when the estate tax applied only to a very few of the superrich. The purpose of this tax was the redistribution of income, because the estate tax prevented the very rich to pass on their entire fortunes to their heirs. The theory here is that such a tax allows equal economic opportunity to everyone. That theory is hard to believe, since money collected by the government is surely not shared with the average

American, nor does it accrue to his benefit. Evidently, then, the estate tax now affects the average American grandparents because it prevents them from leaving anything to their children and grandchildren. Since grandparents have paid income taxes, capital gains taxes, property taxes, sales taxes, and a host of other taxes, an estate tax now seizes the assets left at death. This penalizes the very hardworking folk who have accumulated money and property whereas others who have put out very little effort in life and in addition those who spend their money benefit from the former's labor and ambition. The Beatles sang: "Now my advice for those who die,/declare the pennies on your eyes/ . . . 'cause I'm the tax man . . . /and you're working for no one but me."

Two percent of Americans pay the estate tax. The extremely clever and wealthy do escape some of these taxes through "loopholes" that allow them to buy tax-free municipal bonds and other tax-free investments. They have ways of protecting their assets by hiring costly tax attorneys who are experts in divesting assets. So it is, for the most part, the "lower class" of wealthy who pay these taxes.

To avoid the estate tax, the older taxpayer can give $10,000 per year to each child or grandchild while still alive. This can, however, impoverish the parent/grandparent, who needs his assets to provide for his own existence.

There are some few people who advocate for the continuation of the estate tax. These are generally the poor or near-poor, who resent the wealthy. There are also those who support the estate tax on the grounds that the deceased should pay the same taxes they would have paid if they had lived. Supporters also point to the exclusion provided by the tax law. It is claimed that the estate tax touches only a few billionaires. That is hardly the case, since many upper-middle-class people are subject to the estate tax. Because this tax reduces the incentive to work and build resources for retirement, old age, and the next generation, Congress has partially to repealed the so-called death tax. This effort received the support of both parties in Congress and was signed by President Bush. It is also claimed by the supporters of the estate tax that that tax stimulates charitable contributions.[19]

DEVALUING GRANDPARENTS IN A GERONTOPHOBIC SOCIETY

We have seen that grandparents can be and often are very supportive of their children and grandchildren, and that such support saves the family a great deal of money.

For the grandparents themselves, a relationship with their grandchildren can be of the greatest importance because such relationships can defeat the ageism to which so many grandparents have to accede.

Because ageism is so entrenched in the United States, it follows that those older Americans who are also grandparents have a better opportunity to fend off the consequences of these prejudices than those who are not grandparents. Surely the most painful experience for the old in American society is the status change that old age brings with it, relegating many old people to the status of "nonperson." A "nonperson" is here defined as someone who is indeed alive but receives no recognition in the most ordinary meaning of that word. This problem can be overcome, at least in part, by those who have good relationships with their grandchildren.

Social recognition is the very content of life because we are a "looking-glass self," as Charles Horton Cooley demonstrated years ago. The concept "looking-glass self" is, of course, also dependent on the work of Sigmund Freud, Margaret Mead, William James, Jean Piaget, and others. In any event, Cooley understood that our self-image is based on how others respond to us. Therefore, it is evident to those who are ignored, rejected, and treated as if they were not present, that they are devalued and are without meaning. There are many old people who have accepted that view of themselves, who regard themselves without value because they encounter these attitudes every day. Grandchildren can, therefore, be most important in contradicting this devaluation by their frequently enthusiastic and unreserved affection for otherwise discarded grandparents.[20]

It is our contention here that devaluation of the self is a life-threatening experience. This devaluation of grandparents became particularly acute with the advent of the twentieth century and has continued for more than a hundred years. The principal source of this devaluation has been the change from the extended family to the nuclear family system, as discussed in the first chapter.

Another reason for devaluing grandparents is the common belief that the old are a burden on the young. We have shown that the relationship between grandparents and their children and grandchildren are at least reciprocal. Grandparents provide a great deal of help in many ways. Some of that help consists of advice derived from a lifetime of experience. Such advice can involve both family and work situations. Help can range from buying minor food items at the grocery store to paying for large and substantial equipment such as a refrigerator for the children and grandchildren. Support can also mean doing household chores involving grandchildren, supporting children in case of illness or other crises, and helping grandchildren with their homework.[21]

Grandchildren can also be a source of reassurance and support for grandparents who are retired. Many retired people are shocked to find that upon retirement they have lost almost all their social contacts. This is frequently the case because so many working people participate in the recreational and social functions that employment offers. Here, again, we find that grandparents are better off than those who have no grandchildren, because the former can involve themselves at least some of the time in the activities of their grandchildren.

Therein lies another danger, however. It is a common prejudice in America to associate the old with children in the sense that those no longer in the labor market are defunct, senile, incompetent, and living a "second childhood." It is not necessary to refute all these beliefs here. It suffices to recognize that the popular association of grandparents with the limited abilities of little children can easily be reinforced by visible proof that this is indeed taking place.

The most important means of assessing social standing in the United States is occupation. Therefore, grandparents who are not employed run the risk of being viewed as superfluous. The presumption that the old are incapable of thinking and must therefore be told how to conduct themselves has been called "role reversal." This refers to the gradual assumption of near-parental supervision of grandparents by their own children, who make decisions for them, speak about them in the third person, fail to introduce them to friends and associates, control their money, and segregate them in the course of the day.

As this role reversal continues, it arouses anger and resentment among many grandparents and also among their children, who view the dependency of their parents and grandparents as obnoxious. This sense that the old adult is a child once more is related to the inactivity of retired people. Therefore, those who are able to work or otherwise keep from becoming bored—and boring—in their old age are far more likely to be appealing to their family and friends than those who take up the time of middle-aged working people with constant complaints and hostilities.

The family has traditionally been the caregiver of grandparents, whose dependency required this. Two social forces have altered this situation during the past fifty years. One of these is the greater affluence of grandparents. Because today's grandparents have more money than their counterparts in any previous generation, there are now many grandparents who can take care of their own needs without involving the family financially. Therefore, the chances of basing grandparent-grandchildren relationships on pure sentiment are far better than ever before.

The government has also taken on a much more active role concerning the needs of grandparents than was true prior to the Franklin D. Roosevelt administration. The role of government in promoting the interests of the old, and grandparents in particular, has expanded during the past sixty years. In one sense, this government support has relieved the family of many burdens old age would have imposed on them in prior years. Now, however, the family—including grandchildren—have become mediators between the government bureaucracy and grandparents who need help. In fact, there are still some older people in the United States who believe in the Puritan tradition that any money given by government is charity or a "handout," and constitutes an embarrassment for the recipient and the family. Grandchildren, no longer part of that tradition, can act as mediators between their grandparents and the government agencies to bring about the support to which the old are entitled by law.

Grandchildren can also facilitate the ability for grandparents to conduct a life review. The purpose of a life review is *existential validation*. This refers to our need to tell ourselves that we have not lived in vain, but have done worthwhile things, that we have achieved something and have been of benefit to others. Grandchildren can help immensely in that task because in one fashion they are the living representatives of an accomplished life. Whatever the role of grandparents may be, the thought that grandchildren will live after us and perpetuate our memory is one of the great consolations of old age in a world that sometimes seems all too impersonal and uncaring.

SUMMARY

Grandparents are viewed by grandchildren in a light other than just being old. This has become true in the current generation because the latest grandparent generation includes many who have a college education and many more who are well-off financially. In addition, there is an affinity between grandparents and grandchildren resulting from value congruence associated with the Kondratieff Wave.

Grandparents are of help to grandchildren in several ways. One of these is the financial aid many parents can furnish young married couples who face a good deal of financial hardship when their children are small. It is remarkable that the contributions of grandfathers are often overlooked, while those of grandmothers are taken for granted. Yet these financial and other contributions by grandparents have a positive, indirect effect on many aspects of the grandchildren's lives, including academic success.

There is a "wealth span" in three generations that is affected by increasing longevity and the need to pay for medical costs in old age, which has a bearing on the inheritance available to grandchildren. The tax laws pertaining to inheritance also reduce the opportunity grandparents have to leave some of their money to the next generation.

Grandparents can give a great deal of support to grandchildren in case of parental divorce and when grandchildren are physically handicapped. Divorce, in particular, raises the issue of visitation rights of grandparents. While most grandparents are supportive of their children and grandchildren there are also some "dysfunctional" grandparents.

Grandchildren are of great help in conducting a "life review," which is an almost universal experience for those old enough to have grandchildren. Grandparents are a blessing; they enrich the lives of children as well as their own lives.

Appendix

The Legal Rights
of Grandparents

Children of divorce experience feelings of rejection, abandonment, fear, insecurity, guilt, and resentment, because they don't understand why they have been abandoned by one or even both of their parents. Of course, the vast majority of abandoned children are abandoned by only one parent, and therefore live with the "custodial parent." In 5 percent of the cases, that parent is the father. Usually, however, it is the mother. In 2000, one out of every five American children lived in a household without a father.

The custodial parent is likely to voice constant derision and resentment toward the absent parent, which the children have to hear day in and day out. In most such cases, the children are torn between the anger of both parents toward each other, because almost all divorce situations involve visitation rights by the noncustodial parent. These are generally the fathers, who have custody on weekends or holidays or during vacations. The constant conflict to which children of divorce are therefore exposed can be alleviated by grandparents. This can be done, first and foremost, by giving single parents the love and support they need from their own parents, which is then passed on to the grandchildren. In short, a caring grandparent can, to some extent, restore the confidence of the child. Yet this cannot take place unless grandparents have access to their grandchildren—a particular problem if they are the parents of the noncustodial parent. It is common that the custodial parent, acting on resentment of the former spouse, seeks to prevent the parents of the former spouse from visiting their grandchildren.

This is where the law can be of help. Laws in all fifty states provide for visitation rights of grandparents "in the best interest of the child." What are these "best interests"? At least this much: Grandparents have lived through injustices in life and know a great deal about facing all kinds of pain and disappointment. They are, therefore, in a unique position to help their grandchildren face the crisis of divorce. They are perhaps the only people in the child's life who can explain the situation. All of us suffer all kinds of pain as we progress through life. If we survive our obstacles, we learn how to deal with them, and we learn that any crisis, no matter how awful, can be overcome. Inexperienced youngsters don't know that. To them, abandonment in particular is devastating. Therefore, it is in the best interest of the child for his grandparents to gain visitation.

Grandparents in loco parentis are far more important to children than the grandparents know. Many grandparents are not aware of the role they play in the lives of their grandchildren. Of course, this is generally possible only if the grandparents live in the same geographical area as their children. Yet even those who are prevented from visiting often because of distance are of significance to their grandchildren, for they represent continuity and stability, particularly among those children who have been abandoned by a parent. This is, of course, even more true when the grandparents become in loco parentis, in the absence of both parents. Here the law provides for custodial rights for grandparents who, in most cases, are the closest many abandoned children will ever come to having parents of any kind.

Of course, high mobility prevents many children from knowing their grandparents. Therefore, some children who have been abandoned by their parents must learn to know and understand the grandparents in whose custody they now devolve. This is still easier for children than having to face total strangers, unrelated to them. Children are forever hoping that their parents will yet come to claim them. In the hands of grandparents, that hope seems always within reach, because the parents will be more likely to visit their own parents than a stranger. So the law is once again reaching out to children by requiring that decisions concerning them be made in their best interest.

There are, of course, some grandparents who "write off" their grandchildren after a divorce. These grandparents may believe that they cannot give money, or that they are interfering. The belief that money is the cure for abandonment is hardly supportable. Children need love and emotional support that money cannot buy. The evidence for this is, of course, the great effort on the part of divorced parents to buy the affection of their children by spending great sums on toys, candy, entertainment, travel, and so on. These tactics are mostly used by absentee fathers, with little success.

Many grandparents do not know what their rights are following the divorce of their child. Many grandparents must engage in court battles to gain custody or visitation rights allowing them to see their grandchildren. The parents of the noncustodial parent, usually the father, often face this problem when the custodial parent seeks to exclude them. Every state has, therefore, passed legislation concerning the rights of grandparents. In the case of *Troxel* v. *Granville*, these rights were limited by a decision of the U.S. Supreme Court, which upheld the right of the mother to guard against unjustified interference by the state of Washington in her family life.

Some grandparents escalate the hostility toward the "other side," that is, the former spouse of their child. Such an attitude increases the devastation abandoned children feel. It is therefore vital that grandparents have good relationships with their adult children and children-in-law, to protect grandchildren from the pain of such alienation.

Today, at the beginning of the twenty-first century, the young-old (those between the ages of fifty-five and seventy-five) are wealthier, healthier, and better educated than ever before. This age group is most often involved in gaining visitation rights or custodial rights over grandchildren. Unlike their predecessors in earlier generations, these grandparents are financially well-off. Therefore, many grandparents can afford to take care of their grandchildren without the help of the children's parents. This, of course, is not true of the poor, who may face terrible financial burdens when suddenly confronted with the need to raise abandoned grandchildren.

With so many children left behind by one or both parents, it is legitimate to ask: Can our grandparents save a "lost generation"?

ALABAMA

Section 30-3-4. Visitation rights for grandparents

At the discretion of the court, visitation privileges for grandparents of minor grandchildren shall be granted in any of the following situations:

(1) When the parents of the child have filed for a dissolution of their marriage or when they are divorced. A grandparent may intervene in any dissolution action solely on the issue of visitation privileges or may file a petition to modify an original decree of dissolution to seek visitation rights when those rights have not been previously established by the court. A grandparent may file a motion for contempt when visitation rights granted by the court have been unreasonably denied.

(2) When the parent related by blood to the grandparents is deceased and the surviving parent denies reasonable visitation privileges to the grandparents, or when the surviving parent relinquishes custody, or when the rights of the surviving parent are terminated voluntarily or by any order of the court. A grandparent may intervene in any legal action solely on the issue of visitation privileges or may file a petition to modify an original decree in any court when visitation privileges have not been previously established by the court.

(Acts 1983, 2nd Ex. Sess., No. 83-176, p. 345, §1; Acts 1989, No. 89-864, p. 1731, §1; Acts 1995, No. 95-584, p. 1242, §1.)

ALASKA

Sec. 25.24.150. Judgments for custody

(a) In an action for divorce or for legal separation or for placement of a child when one or both parents have died, the court may, if it has jurisdiction under AS 25.30.300–25.30.320, and is an appropriate forum under AS 25.30.350 and 25.30.360, during the pendency of the action, or at the final hearing or at any time thereafter during the minority of a child of the marriage, make, modify, or vacate an order for the custody of or visitation with the minor child that may seem necessary or proper, including an order that provides for visitation by a grandparent or other person if that is in the best interests of the child.

(b) If a guardian ad litem for a child is appointed, the appointment shall be made under the terms of AS 25.24.310 (c).

(c) The court shall determine custody in accordance with the best interests of the child under AS 25.20.060 - 25.20.130. In determining the best interests of the child the court shall consider (1) the physical, emotional, mental, religious, and social needs of the child; (2) the capability and desire of each parent to meet these needs; (3) the child's preference if the child is of sufficient age and capacity to form a preference; (4) the love and affection existing between the child and each parent; (5) the length of time the child has lived in a stable, satisfactory environment and the desirability of maintaining continuity; (6) the desire and ability of each parent to allow an open and loving frequent relationship between the child and the other parent; (7) any evidence of domestic violence, child abuse, or child neglect in the proposed custodial household or a history of violence between the parents; (8) evidence that substance abuse by either parent or other members of the household directly affects the emotional or physical well-being of the child; (9) other factors that the court considers pertinent.

(d) In awarding custody the court may consider only those facts that directly affect the well-being of the child.

(e) Notwithstanding the provisions of (d) of this section, in awarding custody the court shall comply with the provisions of 25 U.S.C. 1901–1963 (P.L. 95-608, the Indian Child Welfare Act of 1978).

(f) If the issue of child custody is before the court at the time it issues a judgment under AS 25.24.160, the court shall concurrently issue a judgment for custody under this section unless, subject to AS 25.24.155, the court delays the custody decision for a later time.

ARIZONA

25-409. Visitation rights of grandparents and great-grandparents

A. The superior court may grant the grandparents of the child reasonable visitation rights to the child during his minority on a finding that the visitation rights would be in the best interests of the child and any of the following are true:

1. The marriage of the parents of the child has been dissolved for at least three months.

2. A parent of the child has been deceased or has been missing for at least three months. For the purposes of this paragraph, a parent is considered to be missing if the parent's location has not been determined and the parent has been reported as missing to a law enforcement agency.

3. The child was born out of wedlock.

B. The superior court may grant the great-grandparents of the child reasonable visitation rights on a finding that the great-grandparents would be entitled to such rights under subsection A if the great-grandparents were grandparents of the child.

C. In determining the child's best interests the court shall consider all relevant factors, including:

1. The historical relationship, if any, between the child and the person seeking visitation.

2. The motivation of the requesting party in seeking visitation.

3. The motivation of the person denying visitation.

4. The quantity of visitation time requested and the potential adverse impact that visitation will have on the child's customary activities.

5. If one or both of the child's parents are dead, the benefit in maintaining an extended family relationship.

D. If logistically possible and appropriate the court shall order visitation by a grandparent or great-grandparent to occur when the child is residing or spending time with the parent through whom the grandparent or great-grandparent claims a right of access to the child. If a parent is unable to have the child reside or spend time with that parent, the court shall order visitation by a grandparent or great-grandparent to occur when that parent would have had that opportunity.

E. A grandparent or great-grandparent seeking to obtain visitation rights under this section shall petition for these rights in the same action in which the parents had their marriage dissolved or by a separate action in the county where the child resides if no action for dissolution has been filed or the court entering the decree of dissolution no longer has jurisdiction.

F. All visitation rights granted under this section automatically terminate if the child has been adopted or placed for adoption. If the child is removed from an adoptive placement, the court may reinstate the visitation rights. This subsection does not apply to the adoption of the child by the spouse of a natural parent if the natural parent remarries.

25-401. Jurisdiction; commencement of proceedings

A. Jurisdiction for child custody proceedings is governed by chapter 4, article 2 of this title.

B. A child custody proceeding is commenced in the superior court:
  1. By a parent, by filing a petition for either of the following:
     (a) Dissolution or legal separation.
     (b) Custody of the child in the county in which the child is permanently resident or found.
  2. By a person other than a parent, by filing a petition for custody of the child in the county in which he is permanently resident or found, but only if he is not in the physical custody of one of his parents.

C. The provisions of subsection B, paragraph 1, subdivision (b) of this section do not apply if a child is born out of wedlock and there has not been a prior adjudication of maternity or paternity.

25-414. Violation of visitation rights; penalties

A. If the court, based on a verified petition and after it gives reasonable notice to an alleged violating parent and an opportunity for that person to be heard, finds that a parent has refused without good cause to comply with a visitation order, the court shall do at least one of the following:
  1. Find the violating parent in contempt of court.
  2. Order visitation time to make up for the missed sessions.
  3. Order parent education at the violating parent's expense.
  4. Order family counseling at the violating parent's expense.

    5. Order civil penalties of not to exceed one hundred dollars for each violation. The court shall transmit monies collected pursuant to this paragraph each month to the county treasurer. The county treasurer shall transmit these monies monthly to the state treasurer for deposit into the alternative dispute resolution fund established by section 12-135.

    6. Order both parents to participate in mediation or some other appropriate form of alternative dispute resolution at the violating parent's expense.

    7. Make any other order that may promote the best interests of the child or children involved.

B. Within twenty-five days of service of the petition the court shall hold a hearing or conference before a judge, commissioner or person appointed by the court to review noncompliance with a visitation order.

C. Court costs and attorney fees incurred by the nonviolating parent associated with the review of noncompliance with a visitation order shall be paid by the violating parent. In the event the custodial parent prevails, the court in its discretion may award court costs and attorney fees to the custodial parent.

ARKANSAS

§ 9-13-103. *Visitation rights of grandparents*

(a)(1) Upon petition by a person properly before it, a chancery court of this state may grant grandparents and great-grandparents reasonable visitation rights with respect to their grandchild or grandchildren or great-grandchild or great-grandchildren at any time if: (A) The marital relationship between the parents of the child has been severed by death, divorce, or legal separation; or (B) The child is in the custody or under the guardianship of a person other than one (1) or both of his natural or adoptive parents; or (C) The child is illegitimate, and the person is a maternal grandparent of the illegitimate child; or (D) The child is illegitimate, and the person is a paternal grandparent of the illegitimate child, and paternity has been established by a court of competent jurisdiction.

(2) The visitation rights may only be granted when the court determines that such an order would be in the best interest and welfare of the minor. (3)(A) An order denying visitation rights to grandparents and great-grandparents shall be in writing and shall state the reasons for denial. (B) An order denying visitation rights is a final order for purposes of appeal.

(b) If the court denies the petition requesting grandparent visitation rights and determines that the petition for grandparent visitation rights is not well-founded, was filed with malicious intent or purpose, or is not in the best interest and welfare of the child, the court may, upon motion of the respondent, order the petitioner to pay reasonable attorney's fees and court costs to the attorney of the respondent, after taking into consideration the financial ability of the petitioner and the circumstances involved.

(c) The provisions of subsections (a) and (b) of this section shall only be applicable in situations: (1) In which there is a severed marital relationship between the parents of the natural or adoptive children by either death, divorce, or legal separation; or (2) In which the child is in the custody or under the guardianship of a person other than one (1) or both of his natural or adoptive parents; or (3) If the child is illegitimate.

§ 9-13-101. Award of custody

(a) In an action for divorce, the award of custody of the children of the marriage shall be made without regard to the sex of the parent, but solely in accordance with the welfare and best interests of the children.

(b)(1) When in the best interests of a child, custody shall be awarded in such a way so as to assure the frequent and continuing contact of the child with both parents. (2) To this effect, in making an order for custody to either parent, the court may consider, among other facts, which parent is more likely to allow the child or children frequent and continuing contact with the noncustodial parent.

(c) Where a party to an action concerning custody of or a right to visitation with a child has committed an act of domestic violence against the party making the allegation or a family or household member of either party, and such allegations are proven by a preponderance of the evidence, the court must consider the effect of such domestic violence upon the best interests of the child, whether or not the child was physically injured or personally witnessed the abuse, together with such other facts and circumstances as the court deems relevant in making a direction pursuant to this section.

(d) Child custody representation. (1)(A) The Director of the Administrative Office of the Courts is authorized to establish an attorney ad litem program to represent children in chancery court cases where custody is an issue. (B) When a chancellor determines that the appointment of an attorney ad litem would facilitate a case in which custody is an issue and further protect the rights of the child, the chancellor may appoint a private attorney to represent the child. (C)(i) The Arkansas Supreme Court, with advice of the chancellors, shall adopt standards of practice and qualifications for service for attorneys who seek to be appointed to provide legal representation for children in custody cases.

CALIFORNIA

3100. (a) In making an order pursuant to Chapter 4 (commencing with Section 3080), the court shall grant reasonable visitation rights to a parent unless it is shown that the visitation would be detrimental to the best interest of the child. In the discretion of the court, reasonable visitation rights may be granted to any other person having an interest in the welfare of the child.

(b) If a protective order, as defined in Section 6218, has been directed to a parent, the court shall consider whether the best interest of the child requires that any visitation by that parent shall be limited to situations in which a third person, specified by the court, is present, or whether visitation shall be suspended or denied. The court shall include in its deliberations a consideration of the nature of the acts from which the parent was enjoined and the period of time that has elapsed since that order. A parent may submit to the court the name of a person that the parent deems suitable to be present during visitation.

(c) Whenever visitation is ordered in a case in which domestic violence is alleged and an emergency protective order, protective order, or other restraining order has been issued, the visitation order shall specify the time, day, place, and manner of transfer of the child, so as to limit the child's exposure to potential domestic conflict or violence and to ensure the safety of all family members.

(d) Where the court finds a party is staying in a place designated as a shelter for victims of domestic violence or other confidential location, the court's order for time, day, place, and manner of transfer of the child for visitation shall be designed to prevent disclosure of the location of the shelter or other confidential location.

3101. (a) Notwithstanding any other provision of law, the court may grant reasonable visitation to a stepparent, i. visitation by the stepparent is determined to be in the best interest of the minor child.

(b) If a protective order, as defined in Section 6218, has been directed to a stepparent to whom visitation may be granted pursuant to this section, the court shall consider whether the best interest of the child requires that any visitation by the stepparent be denied.

(c) Visitation rights may not be ordered under this section that would conflict with a right of custody or visitation of a birth parent who is not a party to the proceeding.

(d) As used in this section: (1) "Birth parent" means "birth parent" as defined in Section 8512. (2) "Stepparent" means a person who is a party to the marriage that is the subject of the proceeding, with respect to a minor child of the other party to the marriage.

3102. (a) If either parent of an unemancipated minor child is deceased, the children, siblings, parents, and grandparents of the deceased parent may be granted reasonable visitation with the child during the child's minority upon a finding that the visitation would be in the best interest of the minor child.

(b) In granting visitation pursuant to this section to a person other than a grandparent of the child, the court shall consider the amount of personal contact between the person and the child before the application for the visitation order.

(c) This section does not apply if the child has been adopted by a person other than a stepparent or grandparent of the child. Any visitation rights granted pursuant to this section before the adoption of the child automatically terminate if the child is adopted by a person other han a stepparent or grandparent of the child.

3103. (a) Notwithstanding any other provision of law, in a proceeding described in Section 3021, the court may grant reasonable visitation to a grandparent of a minor child of a party to the proceeding if the court determines that visitation by the grandparent is in the best interest of the child.

(b) If a protective order as defined in Section 6218 has been directed to the grandparent during the dependency of the proceeding, the court shall consider whether the best interest of the child requires that visitation by the grandparent be denied.

(c) The petitioner shall give notice of the petition to each of the parents of the child, any stepparent, and any person who has physical custody of the child, by certified mail, return receipt requested, postage prepaid, to the person's last known address, or to the attorneys of record of the parties to the proceeding.

(d) There is a rebuttable presumption affecting the burden of proof that the visitation of a grandparent is not in the best interest of a minor child if the child's parents agree that the grandparent should not be granted visitation rights.

(e) Visitation rights may not be ordered under this section if that would conflict with a right of custody or visitation of a birth parent who is not a party to the proceeding.

(f) Visitation ordered pursuant to this section shall not create a basis for or against a change of residence of the child, but shall be one of the factors for the court to consider in ordering a change of esidence.

(g) When a court orders grandparental visitation pursuant to this section, the court in its discretion may, based upon the relevant circumstances of the case: (1) Allocate the percentage of grandparental visitation between the parents for purposes of the calculation of child support pursuant to the statewide uniform guideline (Article 2 (commencing with Section 4050) of Chapter 2 of Part 2 of Division 9). (2) Notwithstanding Sections 3930 and 3951, order a parent or grandparent to pay to the other, an amount for the support of the child or grandchild. For purposes of this paragraph, "support" means costs related to visitation such as any of the following: (A) Transportation. (B) Provision of basic expenses for the child or grandchild, such as medical expenses, day care costs, and other necessities.

(h) As used in this section, "birth parent" means "birth parent" as defined in Section 8512.

3104. (a) On petition to the court by a grandparent of a minor child, the court may grant reasonable visitation rights to the grandparent if the court does both of the following: (1) Finds that there is a preexisting relationship between the grandparent and the grandchild that has engendered a bond such that visitation is in the best interest of the child. (2) Balances the interest of the child in having visitation with the grandparent against the right of the parents to exercise their parental authority.

(b) A petition for visitation under this section may not be filed while the natural or adoptive parents are married, unless one or more of the following circumstances exist: (1) The parents are currently living separately and apart on a permanent or indefinite basis. (2) One of the parents has been absent for more than one month without the other spouse knowing the whereabouts of the absent spouse. (3) One of the parents joins in the petition with the grandparents. (4) The child is not residing with either parent. At any time that a change of circumstances occurs such that none of these circumstances exist, the parent or parents may move the court to terminate grandparental visitation and the court shall grant the termination.

(c) The petitioner shall give notice of the petition to each of the parents of the child, any stepparent, and any person who has physical custody of the child, by personal service pursuant to Section 415.10 of the Code of Civil Procedure.

(d) If a protective order as defined in Section 6218 has been directed to the grandparent during the pendency of the proceeding, the court shall consider whether the best interest of the child requires that any visitation by that grandparent should be denied.

(e) There is a rebuttable presumption that the visitation of a grandparent is not in the best interest of a minor child if the natural or adoptive parents agree that the grandparent should not be granted visitation rights.

(f) There is a rebuttable presumption affecting the burden of proof that the visitation of a grandparent is not in the best interest of a minor child if the parent who has been awarded sole legal and physical custody of the child in another proceeding or with whom the child resides if there is currently no operative custody order objects to visitation by the grandparent.

(g) Visitation rights may not be ordered under this section if that would conflict with a right of custody or visitation of a birth parent who is not a party to the proceeding.

(h) Visitation ordered pursuant to this section shall not create a basis for or against a change of residence of the child, but shall be one of the factors for the court to consider in ordering a change of residence.

(i) When a court orders grandparental visitation pursuant to this section, the court in its discretion may, based upon the relevant circumstances of the case: (1) Allocate the percentage of grandparental visitation between the parents for purposes of the calculation of child support pursuant to the statewide uniform guideline (Article 2 [commencing with Section 4050] of Chapter 2 of Part 2 of Division 9). (2) Notwithstanding Sections 3930 and 3951, order a parent or grandparent to pay to the other, an amount for the support of the child or grandchild. For purposes of this paragraph, "support" means costs related to visitation such as any of the following: (A) Transportation. (B) Provision of basic expenses for the child or grandchild, such as medical expenses, day care costs, and other necessities.

(j) As used in this section, "birth parent" means "birth parent" as defined in Section 8512.

COLORADO

19-1-117. Visitation rights of grandparents

(1) Any grandparent of a child may, in the manner set forth in this section, seek a court order granting the grandparent reasonable grandchild visitation rights when there is or has been a child custody case or a case concerning the allocation of parental responsibilities relating to that child. Because cases arise that do not directly deal with child custody or the allocation of parental responsibilities but nonetheless have an impact on the custody of or parental responsibilities with respect to a child, for the purposes of this section, a "case concerning the allocation of parental responsibilities with respect to a child" includes any of the following, whether or not child custody was or parental responsibilities were specifically an issue: (a)That the marriage of the child's parents has been declared invalid or has been dissolved by a court or that a court has entered a decree of legal separation with regard to such marriage; (b) That legal custody of or parental responsibilities with respect to the child have been given or allocated to a party other than the child's parent or that the child has been placed outside of and does not reside in the home of the child's parent, excluding any child who has been placed for adoption or

whose adoption has been legally finalized; or (c) That the child's parent, who is the child of the grandparent, has died.

(2) A party seeking a grandchild visitation order shall submit, together with his or her motion for visitation, to the district court for the district in which the child resides an affidavit setting forth facts supporting the requested order and shall give notice, together with a copy of his or her affidavit, to the party who has legal custody of the child or to the party with parental responsibilities as determined by a court pursuant to article 10 of title 14, C.R.S. The party with legal custody or parental responsibilities as determined by a court pursuant to article 10 of title 14, C.R.S., may file opposing affidavits. If neither party requests a hearing, the court shall enter an order granting grandchild visitation rights to the petitioning grandparent only upon a finding that the visitation is in the best interests of the child. A hearing shall be held if either party so requests or if it appears to the court that it is in the best interests of the child that a hearing be held. At the hearing, parties submitting affidavits shall be allowed an opportunity to be heard. If, at the conclusion of the hearing, the court finds it is in the best interests of the child to grant grandchild visitation rights to the petitioning grandparent, the court shall enter an order granting such rights.

(3) No grandparent may file an affidavit seeking an order granting grandchild visitation rights more than once every two years absent a showing of good cause. If the court finds there is good cause to file more than one such affidavit, it shall allow such additional affidavit to be filed and shall consider it. The court may order reasonable attorney fees to the prevailing party. The court may not make any order restricting the movement of the child if such restriction is solely for the purpose of allowing the grandparent the opportunity to exercise his grandchild visitation rights.

(4) The court may make an order modifying or terminating grandchild visitation rights whenever such order would serve the best interests of the child.

(5) Any order granting or denying parenting time rights to the parent of a child shall not affect visitation rights granted to a grandparent pursuant to this section.

Requests for placement—legal custody by grandparents

Whenever a grandparent seeks the placement of his or her grandchild in the grandparent's home or seeks the legal custody of his or her grandchild pursuant to the provisions of this title, the court entering such order shall consider any credible evidence of the grandparent's past conduct of child abuse or neglect. Such evidence may include, but shall not be limited to, medical records, school records, police reports, records of the state central registry of child protection, and court records.

CONNECTICUT

Sec. 46b-56 (formerly Sec. 46-42)

Superior Court orders re custody and care of minor children in actions for dissolution of marriage, legal separation and annulment. Access to records of minor children by noncustodial parent. Parenting education program.

(a) In any controversy before the Superior Court as to the custody or care of minor children, and at any time after the return day of any complaint under section 46b-45, the court may at any time make or modify any proper order regarding the education and support of the children and of care, custody and visitation if it has jurisdiction under the provisions of chapter 815o. Subject to the provisions of section 46b-56a, the court may assign the custody of any child to the parents jointly, to either parent or to a third party, according to its best judgment upon the facts of the case and subject to such conditions and limitations as it deems equitable. The court may also make any order granting the right of visitation of any child to a third party, including but not limited to, grandparents.

(b) In making or modifying any order with respect to custody or visitation, the court shall (1) be guided by the best interests of the child, giving consideration to the wishes of the child if the child is of sufficient age and capable of forming an intelligent preference, provided in making the initial order the court may take into consideration the causes for dissolution of the marriage or legal separation if such causes are relevant in a determination of the best interests of the child and (2) consider whether the party satisfactorily completed participation in a parenting education program established pursuant to section 46b-69b.

(c) In determining whether a child is in need of support and, if in need, the respective abilities of the parents to provide support, the court shall take into consideration all the factors enumerated in section 46b-84.

(d) When the court is not sitting, any judge of the court may make any order in the cause which the court might make under subsection (a) of this section, including orders of injunction, prior to any action in the cause by the court.

(e) A parent not granted custody of a minor child shall not be denied the right of access to the academic, medical, hospital or other health records of such minor child unless otherwise ordered by the court for good cause shown.

DELAWARE

§ 728. Residence; visitation; sanctions

(a) The Court shall determine, whether the parents have joint legal custody of the child or one of them has sole legal custody of the child, with which parent the child shall primarily reside and a schedule of visitation with the other parent, consistent with the child's best interests and maturity, which is designed to permit and encourage the child to have frequent and meaningful contact with both parents unless the Court finds, after a hearing, that contact of the child with 1 parent would endanger the child's physical health or significantly impair his or her emotional development. The Court shall specifically state in any order denying or restricting a parent's access to a child the facts and conclusions in support of such a denial or restriction.

(b) The Court shall encourage all parents and other persons to foster the exercise of a parent's joint or sole custodial authority and the maintenance of frequent and meaningful contact, in person, by mail and by telephone, between parents and children unless an order has been entered pursuant to subsection (a) of this section denying or restricting such contact. If the Court finds, after a hearing, that a parent or any other person has violated, interfered with, impaired or impeded the rights of a parent or a child with respect to the exercise of joint or sole custodial authority, residence, visitation or other contact with the child, the Court shall order such person to pay the costs and reasonable counsel fees of the parent applying for relief under this section. The Court shall also impose 1 or more of the following remedies or sanctions: (1) Extra visitation with the child to enable the child to make up any wrongfully denied visitation with a parent; (2) A temporary transfer of custody or primary residence or both of the child to a parent applying for relief under this section for up to 30 days without regard to the factors set forth in § 729 of this title; (3) A surcharge to be assessed against the parent with rights of visitation with the child or children for his or her unilateral failure, without just cause and/or without sufficient notice, to comply with the visitation schedule. Failure to comply consists of more than minimal violations, such as, but not limited to, slight alterations in the times for visitation. The amount of the surcharge shall be up to 10 percent of the visiting parent's monthly child support obligation for each violation and shall be payable to the parent with whom the child or children reside(s); (4) A fine in the discretion of the Court; or (5) A term of imprisonment if a person is found to be in contempt of prior orders of the Court. In addition, the Court may impose such other sanctions or remedies as the Court deems just and proper to ensure the maintenance in the future of frequent and meaningful contact between parent and child and participation by both parents in the child's upbringing if the parents have joint legal custody.

(c) A parent or custodian of a child who believes it to be in the best interests of a child for the custodial authority, visitation or communication between a parent and a child as established by a prior Court order or written agreement of the parties to be modified may apply to the Court for such modification, and the Court may grant such an application if it finds after application of the standards set forth in subsection (a) of this section that the best interests of the child would be served by ordering such a modification. The filing of an application under this subsection by any person shall not be a defense in an action brought against any person under subsection (b) of this section unless the Court has entered an appropriate order allowing such conduct prior to the occurrence of the conduct complained of in the action brought under subsection (b).

(d) If a child is conceived and subsequently born as the result of an act of rape of any degree or unlawful sexual intercourse, in either the first or second degree with the mother, the biological father of said child shall not be permitted visitation privileges under this section. This subsection shall apply only where the father pleads guilty or nolo contendre, or is convicted of any degree of rape or unlawful sexual intercourse, in either the first or second degree.

§ 727. Custody

(a) Whether the parents have joint legal custody or 1 parent has sole legal custody of a child, each parent has the right to receive, on request, from the other parent, whenever practicable in advance, all material information concerning the child's progress in school, medical treatment, significant developments in the child's life, and school activities and conferences, special religious events and other activities in which parents may wish to participate and each parent and child has a right to reasonable access to the other by telephone or mail. The Court shall not restrict the rights of a child or a parent under this subsection unless it finds, after a hearing, that the exercise of such rights would endanger a child's physical health or significantly impair his or her emotional development.

(b) Any custody order entered by the Court may include the following provisions: (1) Granting temporary joint or sole custody for a period of time not to exceed 6 months in duration to give the parents the opportunity of demonstrating to the satisfaction of the Court their ability and willingness to cooperate with the custodial arrangement ordered. Following a timely review of this temporary order by the Court either at the end of this temporary period or sooner upon the application of any party to the proceeding, the Court shall have the authority to continue or modify the temporary order on a permanent basis. (2) Counseling of the parents, and their child if appropriate, by a public or private agency approved by the Court to help the parents develop the necessary skills to deal effectively with the major as well as daily decisions involving their child under the custodial arrangement ordered, to continue until such time as the Court is advised in writing by the agency that such counseling is no longer required. Counseling expenses may be assessed by the Court as a cost of the proceeding.

(c) Any custody order entered by the Court shall include a contact schedule by the child with both parents which shall control absent parental modification by written agreement.

DISTRICT OF COLUMBIA

No provisions for grandparents' visitiation rights or custody rights.

FLORIDA

The 1999 Florida statutes

Action by grandparent for right of visitation; when petition shall be granted.

(1) The court shall, upon petition filed by a grandparent of a minor child, award reasonable rights of visitation to the grandparent with respect to the child when it is in the best interest of the minor child if: (a) One or both parents of the child are deceased; (b) The marriage of the parents of the child has been dissolved; (c) A parent of the child has deserted the child; (d) The minor child was born out of wedlock and not later determined to be a child born within wedlock as provided in s. 742.091; or (e) The minor is living with both natural parents who are still married to each other whether or not there is a broken relationship between either or both parents of the minor child and the grandparents, and either or both parents have used their parental authority to prohibit a relationship between the minor child and the grandparents.

(2) In determining the best interest of the minor child, the court shall consider: (a) The willingness of the grandparent or grandparents to encourage a close relationship between the child and the parent or parents. (b) The length and quality of the prior relationship between the child and the grandparent or grandparents. (c) The preference of the child if the child is determined to be of sufficient maturity to express a preference. (d) The mental and physical health of the child. (e) The mental and physical health of the grandparent or grandparents. (f) Such other factors as are necessary in the particular circumstances.

(3) This act does not provide for grandparental visitation rights for children placed for adoption under chapter 63 except as provided in s. 752.07 with respect to adoption by a stepparent.

61.13 Custody and support of children; visitation rights; power of court in making orders

(1)(a) In a proceeding for dissolution of marriage, the court may at any time order either or both parents who owe a duty of support to a child to pay support in accordance with the guidelines in s. 61.30. The court initially entering an order requiring one or both parents to make child support payments shall have continuing jurisdiction after the entry of the initial order to modify the amount and terms and conditions of the child support payments when the modification is found necessary by the court in the best interests of the child, when the child reaches majority, or when there is a substantial change in the circumstances of the parties. The court initially entering a child support order shall also have continuing jurisdiction to require the obligee to report to the court on terms prescribed by the court regarding the disposition of the child support payments.

GEORGIA

19-9-3

(a)(1) In all cases in which the custody of any minor child or children is at issue between the parents, there shall be no prima-facie right to the custody of the child or children in the father or mother. (2) The court hearing the issue of custody, in exercise of its sound discretion, may take into consideration all the circumstances of the case, including the improvement of the health of the party seeking a change in custody provisions, in determining to whom custody of the child or children should be awarded. The duty of the court in all such cases shall be to exercise its discretion to look to and determine solely what is for the best interest of the child or children and what will best promote their welfare and happiness and to make its award accordingly. (3) In addition to other factors that a court may consider in a proceeding in which the custody of a child or visitation by a parent is at issue and in which the court has made a finding of family violence: (A) The court shall consider as primary the safety and well-being of the child and of the parent who is the victim of family violence; (B) The court shall consider the perpetrator's history of causing physical harm, bodily injury, assault, or causing reasonable fear of physical harm, bodily injury, or assault to another person; (C) If a parent is absent or relocates because of an act of domestic violence by the other parent, such absence or relocation for a reasonable period of time in the circumstances shall not be deemed an abandonment of the child or children for the purposes of custody determination; and (D) The court shall not refuse to consider relevant or otherwise admissible evidence of acts of family violence merely because there has been no previous finding of family violence. The court may, in addition to other appropriate actions, order supervised visitation pursuant to Code Section 19-9-7. (4) In all custody cases in which the child has reached the age of 14 years, the child shall have the right to select the parent with whom he or she desires to live. The child's selection shall be controlling unless the parent so selected is determined not to be a fit and proper person to have the custody of the child. (5) Joint custody, as defined by Code Section 19-9-6, may be considered as an alternative form of custody by the court. This provision allows a court at any temporary or permanent hearing to grant sole custody, joint custody, joint legal custody, or joint physical custody where appropriate. (6) The court is authorized to order a psychological custody evaluation of the family or an independent medical evaluation.

(b) In any case in which a judgment awarding the custody of a minor has been entered, on the motion of any party or on the motion of the court, that portion of the judgment effecting visitation rights between the parties and their minor children may be subject to review and modification or alteration without the necessity of any showing of a change in any material conditions and circumstances of either party or the minor, provided that the review and modification or alteration shall not be had more often than once in each two-year period following the date of entry of the judgment. However, this subsection shall not limit or restrict the power of the court to enter a judgment relating to the custody of a minor in any new proceeding based upon a showing of a change in any material conditions or circumstances of a party or the minor.

(c) In the event of any conflict between this Code section and any provision of Article 3 of this chapter, Article 3 shall apply.

(d) It is the express policy of this state to encourage that a minor child has continuing contact with parents and *grandparents* who have shown the ability to act in the best interest of the child and to encourage parents to share in the rights and responsibilities of raising their children after such parents have separated or dissolved their marriage.

(e) Upon the filing of an action for a change of child custody, the court may in its discretion change the terms of custody on a temporary basis pending final judgment on such issue. Any such award of temporary custody shall not constitute an adjudication of the rights of the parties.

HAWAII

§571-46.3. Grandparents' visitation rights; petition; notice; order

A grandparent or the grandparents of a minor child may file a petition with the court for an order of reasonable visitation rights. The court may award reasonable visitation rights provided that the following criteria are met: (1) This State is the home state of the child at the time of the commencement of the proceeding; and (2) Reasonable visitation rights are in the best interests of the child. No hearing for an order of reasonable visitation rights under this section shall be had unless each of the living parents and the child's custodians shall have had due notice, actual or constructive, of the allegations of the petition and of the time and place of the hearing thereof. An order made pursuant to this section shall be enforceable by the court, and the court may issue other orders to carry out these enforcement powers if in the best interests of the child. [L 1993, c 166, §1; am L 1998, c 20, §2]

IDAHO

Visitation rights of grandparents and great-grandparents

The district court may grant reasonable visitation rights to grandparents or great-grandparents upon a proper showing that the visitation would be in the best interests of the child.

Custody of children—best interest

A. In an action for divorce the court may, before and after judgment, give such direction for the custody, care and education of the children of the marriage as may seem necessary or proper in the best interests of the children. The court shall consider all relevant factors which may include: 1. The wishes of the child's parent or parents as to his or her custody; 2. The wishes of the child as to his or her custodian; 3. The interaction and interrelationship of the child with his or her parent or parents, and his or her siblings; 4. The child's adjustment to his or her home, school, and community; 5. The mental and physical health and integrity of all individuals involved; 6. The need to promote continuity and stability in the life of the child; and 7. Domestic violence as defined in section 39-6303, Idaho Code, whether or not in the presence of the child.

B. In any case where the child is actually residing with a grandparent in a stable relationship, the court may recognize the grandparent as having the same standing as a parent for evaluating what custody arrangements are in the best interests of the child.

ILLINOIS

750 ILCS 5/ Illinois Marriage and Dissolution of Marriage Act

Part VI Custody (750 ILCS 5/601) Sec. 601. Jurisdiction; commencement of proceeding

(a) A court of this State competent to decide child custody matters has jurisdiction to make a child custody determination in original or modification proceedings as provided in Section 4 of the Uniform Child Custody Jurisdiction Act as adopted by this State.

(b) A child custody proceeding is commenced in the court: (1) by a parent, by filing a petition: (i) for dissolution of marriage or legal separation or declaration of invalidity of marriage; or (ii) for custody of the child, in the county in which he is permanently resident or found; (2) by a person other than a parent, by filing a petition for custody of the child in the county in which he is permanently resident or found, but only if he is not in the physical custody of one of his parents; or (3) by a stepparent, by filing a petition, if all of the following circumstances are met: (A) the child is at least 12 years old; (B) the custodial parent and stepparent were married for at least 5 years during which the child resided with the parent and stepparent; (C) the custodial parent is deceased or is disabled and cannot perform the duties of a parent to the child; (D) the stepparent provided for the care, control, and welfare to the child prior to the initiation of custody proceedings; (E) the child wishes to live with the stepparent; and (F) it is alleged to be in the best interests and welfare of the child to live with the stepparent as provided in Section 602 of this Act.

(c) Notice of a child custody proceeding, including an action for modification of a previous custody order, shall be given to the child's parents, guardian and custodian, who may appear, be heard, and file a responsive pleading. The court, upon showing of good cause, may permit intervention of other interested parties.

(d) Proceedings for modification of a previous custody order commenced more than 30 days following the entry of a previous custody order must be initiated by serving a written notice and a copy of the petition for modification upon the child's parent, guardian and custodian at least 30 days prior to hearing on the petition. Nothing in this Section shall preclude a party in custody modification proceedings from moving for a temporary order under Section 603 of this Act.

(e) In a custody proceeding involving an out-of-state party, the court, prior to granting or modifying a custody judgment, shall consult the registry of out-of-state judgments to determine whether there exists any communications or documents alleging that the child who is the subject of custody proceedings may have been improperly removed from the physical custody of the person entitled to custody or may have been improperly retained after a visit or other temporary relinquishment of physical custody. Where, on the basis of such documents or communications contained in the registry of out-of-state judgments, the court determines that the child who is the subject of custody may have been improperly removed or retained, the court shall notify the person or agency who submitted such communications as to the location of the child, as soon as is practicable. (Source: P.A. 90-782, eff. 8-14-98.)

(750 ILCS 5/602) Sec. 602. Best interest of the child

(a) The court shall determine custody in accordance with the best interest of the child. The court shall consider all relevant factors including: (1) the wishes of the child's parent or parents as to his custody; (2) the wishes of the child as to his custodian; (3) the interaction and interrelationship of the child with his parent or parents, his siblings and any other person who may significantly affect the child's best interest; (4) the child's adjustment to his home, school and community; (5) the mental and physical health of all individuals involved; (6) the physical violence or threat of physical violence by the child's potential custodian, whether directed against the child or directed against another person; (7) the occurrence of ongoing abuse as defined in Section 103 of the Illinois Domestic Violence Act of 1986, whether directed against the child or directed against another person; and (8) the willingness and ability of each parent to facilitate and encourage a close and continuing relationship between the other parent and the child. In the case of a custody proceeding in which a stepparent has standing under Section 601, it is presumed to be in the best interest of the minor child that the natural parent have the custody of the minor child unless the presumption is rebutted by the stepparent.

(b) The court shall not consider conduct of a present or proposed custodian that does not affect his relationship to the child.

(c) Unless the court finds the occurrence of ongoing abuse as defined in Section 103 of the Illinois Domestic Violence Act of 1986, the court shall presume that the maximum involvement and cooperation of both parents regarding the physical, mental, moral, and emotional well-being of their child is in the best interest of the child. There shall be no presumption in favor of or against joint custody. (Source: P.A. 90-782, eff. 8-14-98.)

(750 ILCS 5/602.1) Sec. 602.1

(a) The dissolution of marriage, the declaration of invalidity of marriage, the legal separation of the parents, or the parents living separate and apart shall not diminish parental powers, rights, and responsibilities except as the court for good reason may determine under the standards of Section 602.

(b) Upon the application of either or both parents, or upon its own motion, the court shall consider an award of joint custody. Joint custody means custody determined pursuant to a Joint Parenting Agreement or a Joint Parenting Order. In such cases, the court shall initially request the parents to produce a Joint Parenting Agreement. Such Agreement shall specify each parent's powers, rights and responsibilities for the personal care of the child and for major decisions such as education, health care, and religious training. The Agreement shall further specify a procedure by which proposed changes, disputes and alleged breaches may be mediated or otherwise resolved and shall provide for a periodic review of its terms by the parents. In producing a Joint Parenting Agreement, the parents shall be flexible in arriving at resolutions which further the policy of this State as expressed in Sections 102 and 602. For the purpose of assisting the court in making a determination whether an award of joint custody is appropriate, the court may order mediation and may direct that an investigation be conducted pursuant to the provisions of Section 605. In the event the parents fail to produce a Joint Parenting Agreement, the court may enter an appropriate Joint Parenting Order under the standards of Section 602 which shall specify and contain the same elements as a Joint Parenting Agreement, or it may award sole custody under the standards of Sections 602, 607, and 608.

(c) The court may enter an order of joint custody if it determines that joint custody would be in the best interests of the child, taking into account the following: (1) the ability of the parents to cooperate effectively and consistently in matters that directly affect the joint parenting of the child. "Ability of the parents to cooperate" means the parents' capacity to substantially comply with a Joint Parenting Order. The court shall not consider the inability of the parents to cooperate effectively and consistently in matters that do not directly affect the joint parenting of the child; (2) The residential circumstances of each parent; and (3) all other factors which may be relevant to the best interest of the child.

(d) Nothing within this section shall imply or presume that joint custody shall necessarily mean equal parenting time. The physical residence of the child in joint custodial situations shall be determined by: (1) express agreement of the parties; or (2) order of the court under the standards of this Section.

(e) Notwithstanding any other provision of law, access to records and information pertaining to a child, including but not limited to medical, dental, child care and school records, shall not be denied to a parent for the reason that such parent is not the child's custodial parent; however, no parent shall have access to the school records of a child if the parent is prohibited by an order of protection from inspecting or obtaining such records pursuant to the Illinois Domestic Violence Act of 1986, as now or hereafter amended. (Source: P.A. 88-409.)

(750 ILCS 5/603) Sec. 603. Temporary orders

(a) A party to a custody proceeding, including a proceeding to modify custody, may move for a temporary custody order. The court may award temporary custody under the standards of Section 602 and the standards and procedures of Section 602.1, after a hearing, or, if there is no objection, solely on the basis of the affidavits.

(b) If a proceeding for dissolution of marriage or legal separation or declaration of invalidity of marriage is dismissed, any temporary custody order is vacated unless a parent or the child's custodian moves that the proceeding continue as a custody proceeding and the court finds, after a hearing, that the circumstances of the parents and the best interest of the child requires that a custody judgment be issued.

(c) If a custody proceeding commenced in the absence of a petition for dissolution of marriage or legal separation, under either subparagraph (ii) of paragraph (1), or paragraph (2), of subsection (d) of Section 601, is dismissed, any temporary custody order is vacated. (Source: P.A. 86-530; 87-1255.)

(750 ILCS 5/604) Sec. 604. Interviews

(a) The court may interview the child in chambers to ascertain the child's wishes as to his custodian and as to visitation. Counsel shall be present at the interview unless otherwise agreed upon by the parties. The court shall cause a court reporter to be present who shall make a complete record of the interview instantaneously to be part of the record in the case.

(b) The court may seek the advice of professional personnel, whether or not employed by the court on a regular basis. The advice given shall be in writing and made available by the court to counsel. Counsel may examine, as a witness, any professional personnel consulted by the court, designated as a court's witness. (Source: P.A. 80-923.)

(750 ILCS 5/605) Sec. 605. Investigations and reports

(a) In contested custody proceedings, and in other custody proceedings if a parent or the child's custodian so requests, the court may order an investigation and report concerning custodial arrangements for the child. The investigation and report may be made by a child welfare agency approved by the Department of Children and Family Services, but shall not be made by that Department unless the court determines either that there is no child welfare agency available or that the parent or the child's custodian is financially unable to pay for the investigation or report.

(b) In preparing his report concerning a child, the investigator may consult any person who may have information about the child and his potential custodial arrangements. Under order of the court, the investigator may refer the child to professional personnel for diagnosis. The investigator may consult with and obtain information from medical, psychiatric or other expert persons who have served the child in the past, without obtaining the consent of the parent or the child's custodian. The child's consent must be obtained if he has reached the age of 16, unless the court finds that he lacks mental capacity to consent.

(c) The investigator shall mail the report to counsel, and to any party not represented by counsel, at least 10 days prior to the hearing. The court may examine and consider the investigator's report in determining custody. The investigator shall make available to counsel, and to any party not represented by counsel, the investigator's file of underlying data, reports, and the complete texts of diagnostic reports made to the investigator pursuant to the provisions of subsection (b) of this Section, and the names and addresses of all persons whom the investigator has consulted. Any party to the proceeding may call the investigator, or any person whom he has consulted, as a court's witness, for cross-examination. A party may not waive his right of cross-examination prior to the hearing. (Source: P.A. 86-659.)

(750 ILCS 5/606) Sec. 606. Hearings

(a) Custody proceedings shall receive priority in being set for hearing.

(b) The court may tax as costs the payment of necessary travel and other expenses incurred by any person whose presence at the hearing the court deems necessary to determine the best interest of the child.

(c) The court, without a jury, shall determine questions of law and fact. If it finds that a public hearing may be detrimental to the child's best interest, the court may exclude the public from a custody hearing, but may admit any person who has a direct and legitimate interest in the particular case or a legitimate educational or research interest in the work of the court.

(d) If the court finds it necessary, in order to protect the child's welfare, that the record of any interview, report, investigation, or testimony in a custody proceeding be kept secret, the court may make an appropriate order sealing the record.

(e) Previous statements made by the child relating to any allegations that the child is an abused or neglected child within the meaning of the Abused and Neglected Child Reporting Act, or an abused or neglected minor within the meaning of the Juvenile Court Act of 1987, shall be admissible in evidence in a hearing concerning custody of or visitation with the child. No such statement, however, if uncorroborated and not subject to cross-examination, shall be sufficient in itself to support a finding of abuse or neglect. (Source: P.A. 87-1081.)

(750 ILCS5/607) Sec. 607. Visitation

(a) A parent not granted custody of the child is entitled to reasonable visitation rights unless the court finds, after a hearing, that visitation would endanger seriously the child's physical, mental, moral or emotional health. If the custodian's street address is not identified, pursuant to Section 708, the court shall require the parties to identify reasonable alternative arrangements for visitation by a non-custodial parent, including but not limited to visitation of the minor child at the residence of another person or at a local public or private facility.

(b) (1) The court may grant reasonable visitation privileges to a grandparent, great-grandparent, or sibling of any minor child upon petition to the court by the grandparents or great-grandparents or on behalf of the sibling, with notice to the parties required to be notified under Section 601 of this Act, if the court determines that it is in the best interests and welfare of the child, and may issue any necessary orders to enforce such visitation privileges. Except as provided in paragraph (2) of this subsection (b), a petition for visitation privileges may be filed under this paragraph (1) whether or not a petition pursuant to this Act has been previously filed or is currently pending if one or more of the following circumstances exist: (A) the parents are not currently cohabiting on a permanent or an indefinite basis; (B) one of the parents has been absent from the marital abode for more than one month without the spouse knowing his or her whereabouts; (C) one of the parents is deceased; (D) one of the parents joins in the petition with the grandparents, great-grandparents, or sibling; or (E) a sibling is in State custody. (1.5) The Court may grant reasonable visitation privileges to a stepparent upon petition to the court by the stepparent, with notice to the parties required to be notified under Section 601 of this Act, if the court determines that it is in the best interests and welfare of the child, and may issue any necessary orders to enforce those visitation privileges. A petition for visitation privileges may be filed under this paragraph (1.5) whether or not a petition pursuant to this Act has been previously filed or is currently pending if the following circumstances are met: (A) the child is at least 12 years old; (B) the child resided continuously with the parent and stepparent for at least 5 years; (C) the parent is deceased or is disabled and is unable to care for the child; (D) the child wishes to have reasonable visitation with the stepparent; and (E) the stepparent was providing for the care, control, and welfare to the child prior to the initiation of the petition for visitation. (2)(A) A petition for visitation privileges shall not be filed pursuant to this subsection (b) by the parents or grandparents of a putative father if the paternity of the putative father has not been legally established. (B) A petition for visitation privileges may not be filed under this subsection (b) if the child who is the subject of the grandparents' or great-grandparents' petition has been voluntarily surrendered by the parent or parents, except for a surrender to the Illinois Department of Children and Family Services or a foster care facility, or has been previously adopted by an individual or individuals who are not related to the biological parents of the child or is the subject of a pending adoption petition by an individual or individuals who are not related to the biological parents of the child. (3) When one parent is deceased, the surviving parent shall not interfere with the visitation rights of the grandparents.

(c) The court may modify an order granting or denying visitation rights of a parent whenever modification would serve the best interest of the child; but the court shall not restrict a parent's visitation rights unless it finds that the visitation would endanger seriously the child's physical, mental, moral or emotional health. The court may modify an order granting, denying, or limiting visitation rights of a grandparent, great-grandparent, or sibling of any minor child whenever a change of circumstances has occurred based on facts occurring subsequent to the judgment and the court finds by clear and convincing evidence that the modification is in the best interest of the minor child.

(d) If any court has entered an order prohibiting a non-custodial parent of a child from any contact with a child or restricting the non-custodial parent's contact with the child, the following provisions shall apply: (1) If an order has been entered granting visitation privileges with the child to a grandparent or great-grandparent who is related to the child through the non-custodial parent, the visitation privileges of the grandparent or great-grandparent may be revoked if: (i) a court has entered an order prohibiting the non-custodial parent from any contact with the child, and the grandparent or great-grandparent is found to have used his or her visitation privileges to facilitate contact between the child and the non-custodial parent; or (ii) a court has entered an order restricting the non-custodial parent's contact with the child, and the grandparent or great-grandparent is found to have used his or her visitation privileges to facilitate contact between the child and the non-custodial parent in a manner that violates the terms of the order restricting the non-custodial parent's contact with the child. Nothing in this subdivision (1) limits the authority of the court to enforce its orders in any manner permitted by law. (2) Any order granting visitation privileges with the child to a grandparent or great-grandparent who is related to the child through the non-custodial parent shall contain the following provision: "If the (grandparent or great-grandparent, whichever is applicable) who has been granted visitation privileges under this order uses the visitation privileges to facilitate contact between the child and the child's non-custodial parent, the visitation privileges granted under this order shall be permanently revoked."

(e) No parent, not granted custody of the child, or grandparent, or great-grandparent, or stepparent, or sibling of any minor child, convicted of any offense involving an illegal sex act perpetrated upon a victim less than 18 years of age including but not limited to offenses for violations of Article 12 of the Criminal Code of 1961, is entitled to visitation rights while incarcerated or while on parole, probation, conditional discharge, periodic imprisonment, or mandatory supervised release for that offense, and upon discharge from incarceration for a misdemeanor offense or upon discharge from parole, probation, conditional discharge, periodic imprisonment, or mandatory supervised release for a felony offense, visitation shall be denied until the person successfully completes a treatment program approved by the court.

(f) Unless the court determines, after considering all relevant factors, including but not limited to those set forth in Section 602(a), that it would be in the best interests of the child to allow visitation, the court shall not enter an order providing visitation rights and pursuant to a motion to modify visitation shall revoke visitation rights previously granted to any person who would otherwise be entitled to petition for visitation rights under this Section who has been convicted of first degree murder of the parent, grandparent, great-grandparent, or sibling of the child who is the subject of the order. Until an order is entered pursuant to this subsection, no person shall visit, with the child present, a person who has been convicted of first degree murder of the parent, grandparent, great-grandparent, or sibling of the child without the consent of the child's parent, other than a parent convicted of first degree murder as set forth herein, or legal guardian.

(g) If an order has been entered limiting, for cause, a minor child's contact or visitation with a grandparent, great-grandparent, or sibling on the grounds that it was in the best interest of the child to do so, that order may be modified only upon a showing of a substantial change in circumstances occurring subsequent to the entry of the order with proof by clear and convincing evidence that modification is in the best interest of the minor child. (Source: P.A. 90-782, eff. 8-14-98; 90-801, eff. 6-1-99; 91-357, eff. 7-29-99; 91-610, eff. 8-19-99.)

(750 ILCS 5/607.1) Sec. 607.1. Enforcement of visitation orders; visitation abuse

(a) The circuit court shall provide an expedited procedure for enforcement of court ordered visitation in cases of visitation abuse. Visitation abuse occurs when a party has willfully and without justification: (1) denied another party visitation as set forth by the court; or (2) exercised his or her visitation rights in a manner that is harmful to the child or child's custodian.

(b) An Action may be commenced by filing a petition setting forth: (i) the petitioner's name, residence address or mailing address, and telephone number; (ii) respondent's name and place of residence, place of employment, or mailing address; (iii) the nature of the visitation abuse, giving dates and other relevant information; (iv) that a reasonable attempt was made to resolve the dispute; and (v) the relief sought. Notice of the filing of the petitions shall be given as provided in Section 511.

(c) After hearing all of the evidence, the court may order one or more of the following: (1) Modification of the visitation order to specifically outline periods of visitation or restrict visitation as provided by law. (2) Supervised visitation with a third party or public agency. (3) Make up visitation of the same time period, such as weekend for weekend, holiday for holiday. (4) Counseling or mediation, except in cases where there is evidence of domestic violence, as defined in Section 1 of the Domestic Violence Shelters Act, occurring between the parties. (5) Other appropriate relief deemed equitable.

(d) Nothing contained in this Section shall be construed to limit the court's contempt power, except as provided in subsection (g) of this Section.

(e) When the court issues an order holding a party in contempt of court for violation of a visitation order, the clerk shall transmit a copy of the contempt order to the sheriff of the county. The sheriff shall furnish a copy of each contempt order to the Department of State Police on a daily basis in the form and manner required by the Department. The Department shall maintain a complete record and index of the contempt orders and make this data available to all local law enforcement agencies.

(f) Attorney fees and costs shall be assessed against a party if the court finds that the enforcement action is vexatious and constitutes harassment.

(g) A person convicted of unlawful visitation interference under Section 10-5.5 of the Criminal Code of 1961 shall not be subject to the provisions of this Section and the court may not enter a contempt order for visitation abuse against any person for the same conduct for which the person was convicted of unlawful visitation interference or subject that person to the sanctions provided for in this Section. (Source: P.A. 87-895; 88-96.)

(750 ILCS 5/608) Sec. 608. Judicial supervision

(a) Except as otherwise agreed by the parties in writing at the time of the custody judgment or as otherwise ordered by the court, the custodian may determine the child's upbringing, including but not limited to, his education, health care and religious training, unless the court, after hearing, finds, upon motion by the noncustodial parent, that the absence of a specific limitation of the custodian's authority would clearly be contrary to the best interests of the child.

(b) If both parents or all contestants agree to the order, or if the court finds that in the absence of agreement the child's physical health would be endangered or his emotional development significantly impaired, the court may order the Department of Children and Family Services to exercise continuing supervision over the case to assure that the custodial or visitation terms of the judgment are carried out. Supervision shall be carried out under the provisions of Section 5 of the Children and Family Services Act. (Source: P.A. 87-824.)

(750 ILCS 5/609) Sec. 609. Leave to remove children

(a) The court may grant leave, before or after judgment, to any party having custody of any minor child or children to remove such child or children from Illinois whenever such approval is in the best interests of such child or children. The burden of proving that such removal is in the best interests of such child or children is on the party seeking the removal. When such removal is permitted, the court may require the party removing such child or children from Illinois to give reasonable security guaranteeing the return of such children.

(b) Before a minor child is temporarily removed from Illinois, the parent responsible for the removal shall inform the other parent, or the other parent's attorney, of the address and telephone number where the child may be reached during the period of temporary removal, and the date on which the child shall return to Illinois. The State of Illinois retains jurisdiction when the minor child is absent from the State pursuant to this subsection. (Source: P.A. 85-768.)

INDIANA

Chapter 5. Grandparent's visitation IC 31-17-5-1

Sec. 1. (a) A child's grandparent may seek visitation rights if: (1) the child's parent is deceased; (2) the marriage of the child's parents has been dissolved in Indiana; or (3) subject to subsection (b), the child was born out of wedlock. (b) A court may not grant visitation rights to a paternal grandparent of a child who is born out of wedlock under subsection (a)(3) if the child's father has not established paternity in relation to the child. As added by P.L.1-1997, SEC.9. IC 31-17-5-2

Sec. 2. (a) The court may grant visitation rights if the court determines that visitation rights are in the best interests of the child. (b) In determining the best interests of the child under this section, the court may consider whether a grandparent has had or has attempted to have meaningful contact with the child. As added by P.L.1-1997, SEC.9.IC 31-17-5-3

Sec. 3. A proceeding for grandparent's visitation must be commenced by the filing of a petition entitled, "In Re the visitation of _____." The petition must: (1) be filed by a grandparent entitled to receive visitation rights under this chapter; (2) be verified; and (3) set forth the following: (A) The names and relationship of: (i) the petitioning grandparent or grandparents; (ii) each child with whom visitation is sought; and (iii) the custodial parent or guardian of each child. (B) The present address of each person named in clause (A). (C) The date of birth of each child with whom visitation is sought. (D) The status under section 1 of this chapter upon which the grandparent seeks visitation. (E) The relief sought. As added by P.L.1-1997, SEC.9.IC 31-17-5-4

Sec. 4. A grandparent seeking visitation rights shall file a petition requesting reasonable visitation rights: (1) in a circuit or superior court of the county in which the child resides in a case described in section 1(a)(1), 1(a)(3), or 10 of this chapter; or (2) in the court having jurisdiction over the dissolution of the parents' marriage in a case described in section 1(a)(2) of this chapter. As added by P.L.1-1997, SEC.9.IC 31-17-5-5

Sec. 5. Whenever a petition is filed, a copy of the petition, together with a copy of a summons, shall be served upon the custodial and noncustodial parent or guardian of each child with whom visitation is sought in the same manner as service of summons in civil actions generally. As added by P.L.1-1997, SEC.9. IC 31-17-5-6

Sec. 6. Upon hearing evidence in support of and opposition to a petition filed under this chapter, the court shall enter a decree setting forth the court's findings and conclusions. As added by P.L.1-1997, SEC.9.IC 31-17-5-7

Sec. 7. The court may modify an order granting or denying visitation rights whenever modification would serve the best interests of the child. As added by P.L.1-1997, SEC.9.IC 31-17-5-8

Sec. 8. (a) This section applies to a child born out of wedlock. (b) Visitation rights provided for in section 1 or 10 of this chapter survive the establishment of paternity of a child by a court proceeding other than an adoption proceeding. As added by P.L.1-1997, SEC.9. IC 31-17-5-9

Sec. 9. Visitation rights provided for in section 1 or 10 of this chapter survive the adoption of the child by any of the following: (1) A stepparent. (2) A person who is biologically related to the child as: (A) a grandparent; (B) a sibling; (C) an aunt; (D) an uncle; (E) a niece; or (F) a nephew. As added by P.L.1-1997, SEC.9.IC 31-17-5-10

Sec. 10. If the marriage of the child's parents has been dissolved in another state, the child's maternal or paternal grandparent may seek visitation rights if: (1) the custody decree entered in the action for dissolution of marriage does not bind the grandparent under IC 31-17-3-12; and (2) an Indiana court would have jurisdiction under IC 31-17-3-3 or IC 31-17-3-14 to grant visitation rights to the grandparent in a modification decree. As added by P.L.1-1997, Sec. 9.

Grandparent visitation rights

Expands grandparent visitation rights to allow a grandparent to petition a court for visitation rights with a grandchild regardless of the marital status of the child's parents, unless a paternal grandparent is seeking visitation with a child born out of wedlock and the child's father has not established paternity. Expands the factors that the court may consider when determining whether the grandparent visitation is in the best interests of the child. Provides for appointment by the court of a guardian ad litem or court appointed special advocate for a child who is the subject of a proceeding for grandparent visitation.

IOWA

Grandparent—great-grandparent—visitation rights

The grandparent or great-grandparent of a child may petition the district court for grandchild or great-grand child visitation rights when any of the following circumstances occur: 1. The parents of the child are divorced. 2. A petition for dissolution of marriage has been filed by one of the parents of the child. 3. The parent of the child, who is the child of the grandparent, or who is the grandchild of the great-grandparent, has died. 4. The child has been placed in a foster home. 5. The parents of the child are divorced, and the parent who is not the child of the grandparent or who is not the grandchild of the great-grandparent has legal custody of the child, and the spouse of the child's custodial parent has been issued a final adoption decree pursuant to section 600.13. 6. The paternity of a child born out of wedlock is judicially established and the grandparent of the child is the parent of the mother or father of the child or the great-grandparent of the child is the grandparent of the mother or father of the child and the mother of the child has custody of the child, or the grandparent of a child born out of wedlock is the parent of the mother or father of the child or the great-grandparent of the child is the grandparent of the mother or father of the child and custody has been awarded to the father of the child. 7. A parent of the child unreasonably refuses to allow visitation by the grandparent or great-grandparent or unreasonably restricts visitation. This subsection applies tobut is not limited in application to a situation in which the parents of the child are divorced and the parent who is the child of the grandparent or who is the grandchild of the great-grandparent has legal custody of the child. A petition for grandchild or great-grandchild visitation rights shall be granted only upon a finding that the visitation is in the best interests of the child and that the grandparent or great-grandparent had established a substantial relationship with the child prior to the filing of the petition.

598.21. Orders for disposition and support

Upon every judgment of annulment, dissolution or separate maintenance the court shall divide the property of the parties and transfer the title of the property accordingly. The court may protect and promote the best interests of children of the parties by setting aside a portion of the property of the parties in a separate fund or conservatorship for the support, maintenance, education and general welfare of the minor children. The court shall divide all property, except inherited property or gifts received by one party, equitably between the parties.

KANSAS

Chapter 60.—Procedure, civil divorce and maintenance

60-1616. Visitation orders; enforcement

(a) Parents. A parent not granted custody or residency of the child is entitled to reasonable visitation rights unless the court finds, after a hearing, that visitation would endanger seriously the child's physical, mental, moral or emotional health.

(b) Grandparents and stepparents. Grandparents and stepparents may be granted visitation rights.

(c) Modification. The court may modify an order granting or denying visitation rights whenever modification would serve the best interests of the child.

d) Enforcement of rights. An order granting visitation rights to a parent pursuant to this section may be enforced in accordance with K.S.A. 23-701, and amendments thereto.

(e) Repeated denial of rights, effect. Repeated unreasonable denial of or interference with visitation rights granted to a parent pursuant to this section may be considered a material change of circumstances which justifies modification of a prior order of child custody.

(f) Repeated child support misuse, effect. Repeated child support misuse may be considered a material change of circumstances which justifies modification of a prior order of child custody.

(g) Court ordered exchange or visitation at a child exchange and visitation center. (1) The court may order exchange or visitation to take place at a child exchange and visitation center, as established in K.S.A. 75-720. (2) A parent may petition the court to modify an order granting visitation rights to require that the exchange or transfer of children for visitation or visitation take place at a child exchange and visitation center, as established in K.S.A. 75-720. The court may modify an order granting visitation rights whenever modification would serve the best interests of the child.

Nonparental custody

If during the proceedings the court determines that there is probable cause to believe that: (i) The child is a child in need of care as defined by subsections (a)(1), (2) or (3) of K.S.A. 38-1502 and amendments thereto; (ii) neither parent is fit to have custody; or (iii) the child is currently residing with such child's grandparent, grandparents, aunt or uncle and such relative has had actual physical custody of such child for a significant length of time, the court may award temporary custody of the child to such relative, another person or agency if the court finds the award of custody to such relative, another person or agency is in the best interests of the child. In making such a custody order, the court shall give preference, to the extent that the court finds it is in the best interests of the child, first to awarding such custody to a relative of the child by blood, marriage or adoption and second to awarding such custody to another person with whom the child has close emotional ties. The court may make temporary orders for care, support, education and visitation that it considers appropriate. Temporary custody orders are to be entered in lieu of temporary orders provided for in K.S.A. 38-1542 and 38-1543, and amendments thereto, and shall remain in effect until there is a final determination under the Kansas code for care of children. An award of temporary custody under this paragraph shall not terminate parental rights nor give the court the authority to consent to the adoption of the child. When the court enters orders awarding temporary custody of the child to an agency or a person other than the parent but not a relative as described in subpart (iii), the court shall refer a transcript of the proceedings to the county or district attorney. The county or district attorney shall file a petition as provided in K.S.A. 38-1531 and amendments thereto and may request termination of parental rights pursuant to K.S.A. 38-1581 and amendments thereto. The costs of the proceedings shall be paid from the general fund of the county. When a final determination is made that the child is not a child in need of care, the county or district attorney shall notify the court in writing and the court, after a hearing, shall enter appropriate custody orders pursuant to this section. If the same judge presides over both proceedings, the notice is not required. Any disposition pursuant to the Kansas code for care of children shall be binding and shall supersede any order under this section. When the court enters orders awarding temporary custody of the child to a relative as described in subpart (iii), the court shall annually review the temporary custody to evaluate whether such custody is still in the best interests of the child. If the court finds such custody is in the best interests of the child, such custody shall continue. If the court finds such custody is not in the best interests of the child, the court shall determine the custody pursuant to this section.

KENTUCKY

405.021

The Circuit Court may grant reasonable visitation rights to either the paternal of maternal grandparents of a child and issue any necessary orders to enforce the decree if it determines that it is in the best interest of the child to do so. Once a grandparent has been granted visitation rights under this subsection, those rights shall not be adversely affected by the termination of parental rights belonging to the grandparent's son or daughter who is the father or mother of the child visited by the grandparent, unless the circuit court determines that it is in the best interest of the child to do so.

405.020

Notwithstanding the provisions of subsections (1) and (2) of this section, a person claiming to be a de facto custodian, as defined in KRS 403.270, may petition court for legal custody of a child. The court shall grant legal custody to the person if the court determines that the person meets the definition of de facto custodian and that the best interests of the child will be served by awarding custody to the de facto custodian.

LOUISIANA

Chapter 14. Visitation rights of grandparents

Art. 1264. Post-adoption visitation rights of grandparents

Notwithstanding any provision of law to the contrary, the natural parents of a deceased party to a marriage dissolved by death whose child is thereafter adopted, and the parents of a party who has forfeited the right to object to the adoption of his child pursuant to Article 1245 may have limited visitation rights to the minor child so adopted. Acts 1991, No. 235,§ 12, eff. Jan. 1, 1992.

Section 3. Child Custody Art. 131. Court to determine custody

In a proceeding for divorce or thereafter, the court shall award custody of a child in accordance with the best interest of the child. Amended by Acts 1888, No. 124; Acts 1979, No. 718,§ 1; Acts 1981, No. 283,§ 1; Acts 1982, No. 307,§ 1, eff. Jan. 1,1983; Acts 1983, No. 695,§ 1; Acts 1984, No. 133,§ 1; Acts 1984, No. 786,§ 1; Acts 1986, No. 950,§ 1, eff. July 14, 1986; Acts 1989, No. 188,§ 1; Acts 1993, No. 261,§ 1, eff. Jan. 1, 1994.

MAINE

Title 19-A: Domestic relations (Heading: PL 1995, c. 694, Pt. B), Chapter 59: Visitation rights of grandparents (Heading: PL 1995, c. 694, Pt. B, @2 (new); Pt. E, @2)

Standing to petition for visitation rights

1. A grandparent of a minor child may petition the court for reasonable rights of visitation or access if: A. At least one of the child's parents or legal guardians has died; [1995, c. 694, Pt. B, §2 (new); Pt. E, §2 (aff)]. B. There is a sufficient existing relationship between the grandparent and the child; or [1995, c. 694, Pt. B, §2 (new); Pt. E, §2 (aff)]. C. When a suffi-

cient existing relationship between the grandparent and the child does not exist, a sufficient effort to establish one has been made. [1995, c. 694, Pt. B, §2 (new); Pt. E, §2 (aff).] [1995, c. 694, Pt. B, §2 (new); Pt. E, §2 (aff).]

2. Procedure. The following procedures apply to petitions for rights of visitation or access under subsection 1, paragraph B or C. A. The grandparent must file with the petition for rights of visitation or access an affidavit alleging a sufficient existing relationship with the child, or that sufficient efforts have been made to establish a relationship with the child. When the petition and accompanying affidavit are filed with the court, the grandparent shall serve a copy of both on at least one of the parents or legal guardians of the child. [1995, c. 694, Pt. B, §2 (new); Pt. E, §2 (aff).] B. The parent or legal guardian of the child may file an affidavit in response to the grandparent's petition and accompanying affidavit. When the affidavit in response is filed with the court, the parent or legal guardian shall deliver a copy to the grandparent. [1995, c. 694, Pt. B, §2 (new); Pt. E, §2 (aff).] C. The court shall determine on the basis of the petition and the affidavit whether it is more likely than not that there is a sufficient existing relationship or, if a sufficient relationship does not exist, that a sufficient effort to establish one has been made. [1995, c. 694, Pt. B, §2 (new); Pt. E, §2 (aff).] D. If the court's determination under paragraph C is in the affirmative, the court shall hold a hearing on the grandparent's petition for reasonable rights of visitation or access and shall consider any objections the parents or legal guardians may have concerning the award of rights of visitation or access to the grandparent. The standard for the award of reasonable rights of visitation or access is provided in subsection 3. [1995, c. 694, Pt. B, §2 (new); Pt. E, §2 (aff).] [1995, c. 694, Pt. B, §2 (new); Pt. E, §2 (aff).]

3. Best interest of the child. The court may grant a grandparent reasonable rights of visitation or access to a minor child upon finding that rights of visitation or access are in the best interest of the child and would not significantly interfere with any parent-child relationship or with the parent's rightful authority over the child. In applying this standard, the court shall consider the following factors: A. The age of the child; [1995, c. 694, Pt. B, §2 (new); Pt. E, §2 (aff).] B. The relationship of the child with the child's grandparents, including the amount of previous contact; [1995, c. 694, Pt. B, §2 (new); Pt. E, §2 (aff).] C. The preference of the

child, if old enough to express a meaningful preference; [1995, c. 694, Pt. B, §2 (new); Pt. E, §2 (aff).] D. The duration and adequacy of the child's current living arrangements and the desirability of maintaining continuity; [1995, c. 694, Pt. B, §2 (new); Pt. E, §2 (aff).] E. The stability of any proposed living arrangements for the child; [1995, c. 694, Pt. B, §2 (new); Pt. E, §2 (aff).] F. The motivation of the parties involved and their capacities to give the child love, affection and guidance; [1995, c. 694, Pt. B, §2 (new); Pt. E, §2 (aff).] G. The child's adjustment to the child's present home, school and community; [1995, c. 694, Pt. B, §2 (new); Pt. E, §2 (aff).] H. The capacity of the parent and grandparent to cooperate or to learn to cooperate in child care; [1995, c. 694, Pt. B, §2 (new); Pt. E, §2 (aff).] . Methods of assisting cooperation and resolving disputes and each person's willingness to use those methods; and [1995, c. 694, Pt. B, §2 (new); Pt. E, §2 (aff).] J. Any other factor having a reasonable bearing on the physical and psychological well-being of the child. [1995, c. 694, Pt. B, §2 (new); Pt. E, §2 (aff).]

Chapter 58: Uniform Child Custody Jurisdiction and Enforcement Act (Heading: PL 1999, c.§ 1745)

Initial child custody jurisdiction

1. Jurisdiction over initial determination. Except as otherwise provided in section 1748, a court of this State has jurisdiction to make an initial child custody determination only if: A. This State is the home state of the child on the date of the commencement of the proceeding or was the home state of the child within 6 months before the commencement of the proceeding and the child is absent from this State but a parent or person acting as a parent continues to live in this State; [1999, c. 486, §3 (new); §6 (aff).] B. A court of another state does not have jurisdiction under paragraph A or a court of the home state of the child has declined to exercise jurisdiction on the ground that this State is the more appropriate forum under section 1751 or 1752 and:(1) The child and the child's parents, or the child and at least one parent or a person acting as a parent, have a significant connection with this State other than mere physical presence; and (2) Substantial evidence is available in this State concerning the child's care, protection, training and personal relationships; [1999, c. 486, §3 (new); §6

(aff).] C. All courts having jurisdiction under paragraph A or B have declined to exercise jurisdiction on the ground that a court of this State is the more appropriate forum to determine the custody of the child under section 1751 or 1752; or [1999, c. 486, §3 (new); §6 (aff).] D. No court of any other state would have jurisdiction under the criteria specified in paragraph A, B or C. [1999, c. 486, §3 (new); §6 (aff).]

2. Exclusive jurisdictional basis. Subsection 1 is the exclusive jurisdictional basis for making a child custody determination by a court of this State.

3. Physical presence or personal jurisdiction not necessary or sufficient. Physical presence of or personal jurisdiction over a party or a child is not necessary or sufficient to make a child custody determination.

MARYLAND

Article Family Law § 9-102

An equity court may: (1) consider a petition for reasonable visitation of a grandchild by a grandparent; and (2) if the court finds it to be in the best interests of the child, grant visitation rights to the grandparent.

Custody: No statutory factors

MASSACHUSETTS

General Laws of Massachusetts

Chapter 119: Section 39D. Visitation rights to certain grandparents of unmarried minor children

If the parents of an unmarried minor child are divorced, married but living apart, under a temporary order or judgment of separate support, or if either or both parents are deceased, or if said unmarried minor child was born out of wedlock whose paternity has been adjudicated by a court of competent jurisdiction or whose father has signed an acknowledgement of paternity, and the parents do not reside together, the grandparents of such minor child may be granted reasonable visitation rights to the minor child during his minority by the probate and family court department of the trial court upon a written finding that such visitation rights would be in the best interest of the said minor child; provided, however, that such adjudication of paternity or acknowledgment of paternity shall not be required in order to proceed under this section where maternal grandparents are seeking such visitation rights. No such visitation rights shall be granted if said minor child has been adopted by a person other than a stepparent of such child and any visitation rights granted pursuant to this section prior to such adoption of the said minor child shall be terminated upon such adoption without any further action of the court. A petition for grandparents visitation authorized under this section shall, where applicable, be filed in the county within the commonwealth in which the divorce or separate support complaint or the complaint to establish paternity was filed. If the divorce, separate support or paternity judgment was entered without the commonwealth but the child presently resides within the commonwealth, said petition may be filed in the county where the child resides.

Chapter 208: Section 31. Custody of children; shared custody plans

For the purposes of this section, the following words shall have the following meaning unless the context requires otherwise: "Sole legal custody," one parent shall have the right and responsibility to make major decisions regarding the child's welfare including matters of education, medical care and emotional, moral and religious development. "Shared legal custody," continued mutual responsibility and involvement by both parents in major decisions regarding the child's welfare including matters of education, medical care and emotional, moral and religious development. "Sole physical custody," a child shall reside with and be under the supervision of one parent, subject to reasonable visitation by the other parent, unless the court determines that such visitation would not be in the best interest of the child. "Shared physical custody," a child shall have periods of residing with and being under the supervision of each parent; provided, however, that physical custody shall be shared by the parents in such a way as to assure a child frequent and continued contact with both parents. In making an order or judgment relative to the custody of children, the rights of the parents shall, in the absence of misconduct, be held to be equal, and the happiness and welfare of the children shall determine their custody. When considering the happiness and welfare of the child, the court shall consider whether or not the child's present or past living conditions adversely affect his physical, mental, moral or emotional health. Upon the filing of an action in accordance with the provisions of this section, section twenty-eight of this chapter, or section thirty-two of chapter two hundred and nine and until a judgment on the merits is rendered, absent emergency conditions, abuse or neglect, the parents shall have temporary shared legal custody of any minor child of the marriage; provided, however, that the judge may enter an order for temporary sole legal custody for one parent if written findings are made that such shared custody would not be in the best interest of the child. Nothing herein shall be construed to create any presumption of temporary shared physical custody. In determining whether temporary shared legal custody would not be in the best interest of the child, the court shall consider all relevant facts including, but not limited to, whether any member of the family has been the perpetrator of domestic violence, abuses alcohol or other drugs or has deserted the child and whether the parties have a history of being able and willing to cooperate in matters concerning the child. If, despite the prior or current issuance of a restraining order against one parent pursuant to chapter two hundred and nine A, the court orders shared legal or physical custody either as a temporary order or at a trial on the merits, the court shall provide written findings to support such shared custody order. There shall be no presumption either in favor of or against shared legal or physical custody at the time of the trial on the merits. At the trial on the merits, if the issue of custody is contested and either party seeks shared legal or physical custody, the parties, jointly or individually, shall submit to the court at the trial a shared custody implementation plan setting forth the details of shared custody including, but not limited to, the child's education; the child's health care; procedures for resolving disputes between the parties with respect to child-raising decisions and duties; and the periods of time during which each party will have the child reside or visit with him, including holidays and vacations, or the procedure by which such periods of time shall be determined. At the trial on the merits, the court shall consider the shared custody implementation plans submitted by the parties. The court may issue a shared legal and physical custody order and, in conjunction therewith, may accept the shared custody implementation plan submitted by either party or by the parties jointly or may issue a plan modifying the plan or plans submitted by the parties. The court may also reject the plan and issue a sole legal and physical custody award to either parent. A shared custody implementation plan issued or accepted by the court shall become part of the judgment in the action, together with any other appropriate custody orders and orders regarding the responsibility of the parties for the support of the child. Provisions regarding shared custody contained in an agreement executed by the parties and submitted to the court for its approval that addresses the details of shared custody shall be deemed to constitute a shared custody implementation plan for purposes of this section An award of shared legal or physical custody shall not affect a parent's responsibility for child support. An order of shared custody shall not constitute grounds for modifying a support order absent demonstrated economic impact that is an otherwise sufficient basis warranting modification. The entry of an order or judgment relative to the custody of minor children shall not negate or impede the ability of the non-custodial parent to have access to the academic, medical, hospital or other health records of the child, as he would have had if the custody order or judgment had not been entered; provided, however, that if a court has issued an order to vacate against the non-custodial parent or an order prohibiting the non-custodial parent from imposing any restraint upon the personal liberty of the other parent or if nondisclosure of the present or prior address of the child or a party is necessary to ensure the health, safety or welfare of such child or party, the court may order that any part of such record pertaining to such address shall not be disclosed to such non-custodial parent. Where the parents have reached an agreement providing for the custody of the children, the court may enter an order in accordance with such agreement, unless specific findings are made by the court indicating that such an order would not be in the best interests of the children. (Amended by 1989, 689 eff. 4-10-90.)

MICHIGAN

Michigan Compiled Laws Main Functions 722.27b

Child Custody Act of 1970 (excerpt)

722.27b. Order for grandparenting time in child custody dispute; action for grandparenting time by parent of deceased natural parent of unmarried child; effect of adoption by stepparent; commencement of action in circuit court; affidavit; notice; opposing affidavit; hearing; basis for entry of order; entry of order for parents of putative father; condition; record; frequency of filing complaint or motion seeking order; attorney fees; order restricting movement of grandchild; effect of entry of order; modifying or terminating order. [M.S.A. 25.312(7b)]

Sec. 7b. (1) Except as provided in this subsection, a grandparent of the child may seek an order for grandparenting time in the manner set forth in this section only if a child custody dispute with respect to that child is pending before the court. If a natural parent of an unmarried child is deceased, a parent of the deceased person may commence an action for grandparenting time. Adoption of the child by a stepparent under chapter X of Act No. 288 of the Public Acts of 1939, being sections 710.21 to 710.70 of the Michigan Compiled Laws, does not terminate the right of a parent of the deceased person to commence an action for grandparenting time.

(2) As used in this section, "child custody dispute" includes a proceeding in which any of the following occurs: (a) The marriage of the child's parents is declared invalid or is dissolved by the court, or a court enters a decree of legal separation with regard to the marriage. (b) Legal custody of the child is given to a party other than the child's parent, or the child is placed outside of and does not reside in the home of a parent, excluding any child who has been placed for adoption with other than a stepparent, or whose adoption by other than a stepparent has been legally finalized.

(3) A grandparent seeking a grandparenting time order may commence an action for grandparenting time, by complaint or complaint and motion for an order to show cause, in the circuit court in the county in which the grandchild resides. If a child custody dispute is pending, the order shall be sought by motion for an order to show cause. The com-

plaint or motion shall be accompanied by an affidavit setting forth facts supporting the requested order. The grandparent shall give notice of the filing to each party who has legal custody of the grandchild. A party having legal custody may file an opposing affidavit. A hearing shall be held by the court on its own motion or if a party so requests. At the hearing, parties submitting affidavits shall be allowed an opportunity to be heard. At the conclusion of the hearing, if the court finds that it is in the best interests of the child to enter a grandparenting time order, the court shall enter an order providing for reasonable grandparenting time of the child by the grandparent by general or specific terms and conditions. If a hearing is not held, the court shall enter a grandparenting time order only upon a finding that grandparenting time is in the best interests of the child. A grandparenting time order shall not be entered for the parents of a putative father unless the father has acknowledged paternity in writing, has been adjudicated to be the father by a court of competent jurisdiction, or has contributed regularly to the support of the child or children. The court shall make a record of the reasons for a denial of a requested grandparenting time order.

(4) A grandparent may not file more than once every 2 years, absent a showing of good cause, a complaint or motion seeking a grandparenting time order. If the court finds there is good cause to allow a grandparent to file more than 1 complaint or motion under this section in a 2-year period, the court shall allow the filing and shall consider the complaint or motion. The court may order reasonable attorney fees to the prevailing party.

(5) The court shall not enter an order restricting the movement of the grandchild if the restriction is solely for the purpose of allowing the grandparent to exercise the rights conferred in a grandparenting time order.

(6) A grandparenting time order entered in accordance with this section shall not be considered to have created parental rights in the person or persons to whom grandparenting time rights are granted. The entry of a grandparenting time order shall not prevent a court of competent jurisdiction from acting upon the custody of the child, the parental rights of the child, or the adoption of the child.

(7) The court may enter an order modifying or terminating a grandparenting time order whenever such a modification or termination is in the best interests of the child.

MINNESOTA

257.022. Rights of visitation to unmarried persons

Subd. 1. When parent is deceased

If a parent of an unmarried minor child is deceased, the parents and grandparents of the deceased parent may be granted reasonable visitation rights to the unmarried minor child during minority by the district court upon finding that visitation rights would be in the best interests of the child and would not interfere with the parent child relationship. The court shall consider the amount of personal contact between the parents or grandparents of the deceased parent and the child prior to the application.

Subd. 2. Family court proceedings

(a) In all proceedings for dissolution, custody, legal separation, annulment, or parentage, after the commencement of the proceeding, or at any time after completion of the proceedings, and continuing during the minority of the child, the court may, upon the request of the parent or grandparent of a party, grant reasonable visitation rights to the unmarried minor child, after dissolution of marriage, legal separation, annulment, or determination of parentage during minority if it finds that: (1) visitation rights would be in the best interests of the child; and (2) such visitation would not interfere with the parent-child relationship. The court shall consider the amount of personal contact between the parents or grandparents of the party and the child prior to the application.

(b) If a motion for grandparent visitation has been heard and denied, unless agreed to in writing by the parties, no subsequent motion may be filed within six months after disposition of a prior motion on its merits.

Subd. 2a. When child has resided with grandparents

If an unmarried minor has resided with grandparents or great-grandparents for a period of 12 months or more, and is subsequently removed from the home by the minor's parents, the grandparents or great-grandparents may petition the district court for an order granting them reasonable visitation rights to the child during minority. The court shall grant the petition if it finds that visitation rights would be in the best interests of the child and would not interfere with the parent and child relationship. Subd. 2b. When child has resided with other person. If an unmarried minor has resided in a household with a person, other than a foster parent, for two years or more and no longer resides with the person, the person may petition the district court for an order granting the person reasonable visitation rights to the child during the child's minority. The court shall grant the petition if it finds that: (1) visitation rights would be in the best interests of the child; (2) the petitioner and child had established emotional ties creating a parent and child relationship; and (3) visitation rights would not interfere with the relationship between the custodial parent and the child. The court shall consider the reasonable preference of the child, if the court considers the child to be of sufficient age to express a preference.

Subd. 3. Exception for adopted children

This section shall not apply if the child has been adopted by a person other than a stepparent or grandparent. Any visitation rights granted pursuant to this section prior to the adoption of the child shall be automatically terminated upon such adoption.

Subd. 3a. Grandparent visitation with an adopted child

(a) A grandparent of a child adopted by a stepparent may petition and a court may grant an order setting visitation with the child if: (1) the grandparent is the parent of: (i) a deceased parent of the child; or (ii) a parent of the child whose parental relationship was terminated by a decree of adoption according to section 259.57, subdivision 1; and (2) the court determines that the requested visitation: (i) is in the best interests of the child; and (ii) would not interfere with the parent and child relationship.

(b) Failure to comply with the terms of an order for visitation granted under this subdivision is not a basis for revoking, setting aside, or otherwise challenging the validity of a consent, relinquishment, or adoption of a child.

Subd. 4. Establishment of interference with parent and child relationship

The court may not deny visitation rights under this section based on allegations that the visitation rights would interfere with the relationship between the *custodial parent and the child unless after a hearing the court determines by a preponderance of the evidence that interference would occur.*

Subd. 5. Visitation proceeding may not be combined with proceeding under chapter 518b

Proceedings under this section may not be combined with a proceeding under chapter 518B.

MISSISSIPPI

Grandparents' visitation rights

§93-16-1. Jurisdiction of court to grant grandparents visitation rights with minor child

Any court of this state which is competent to decide child custody matters shall have jurisdiction to grant visitation rights with a minor child or children to the grandparents of such minor child or children as provided in this chapter. Sources: Laws, 1983, ch. 497, § 1; Laws, 1990, ch. 537, § 1, eff from and after July 1, 1990.

§ 93-16-3. Who may petition for visitation rights; when; court in which to file petition

(1) Whenever a court of this state enters a decree or order awarding custody of a minor child to one (1) of the parents of the child or terminating the parental rights of one (1) of the parents of a minor child, or whenever one (1) of the parents of a minor child dies, either parent of the child's parents who was not awarded custody or whose parental rights have been terminated or who has died may petition the court in which the decree or

order was rendered or, in the case of the death of a parent, petition the chancery court in the county in which the child resides, and seek visitation rights with such child.

(2) Any grandparent who is not authorized to petition for visitation rights pursuant to subsection (1) of this section may petition the chancery court and seek visitation rights with his or her grandchild, and the court may grant visitation rights to the grandparent, provided the court finds: (a) That the grandparent of the child had established a viable relationship with the child and the parent or custodian of the child unreasonably denied the grandparent visitation rights with the child; and (b) That visitation rights of the grandparent with the child would be in the best interests of the child.

(3) For purposes of subsection (3) of this section, the term "viable relationship" means a relationship in which the grandparents or either of them have voluntarily and in good faith supported the child financially in whole or in part for a period of not less than six (6) months before filing any petition for visitation rights with the child or the grandparents have had frequent visitation including occasional overnight visitation with said child for a period of not less than one (1) year.

(4) Any petition for visitation rights under subsection (2) of this section shall be filed in the county where an order of custody as to such child has previously been entered. If no such custody order has been entered, then the grandparents' petition shall be filed in the county where the child resides or may be found. The court shall on motion of the parent or parents direct the grandparents to pay reasonable attorney's fees to the parent or parents in advance and prior to any hearing, except in cases in which the court finds that no financial hardship will be imposed upon the parents. The court may also direct the grandparents to pay reasonable attorney's fees to the parent or parents of the child and court costs regardless of the outcome of the petition.

§ 93-16-5. Parties to proceeding; discretion of court in granting, enforcing, modifying or terminating rights

All persons required to be made parties in child custody proceedings or proceedings for the termination of parental rights shall be made parties to any proceeding in which a grandparent of a minor child or children seeks to obtain visitation rights with such minor child or children; and the court may, in its discretion, if it finds that such visitation rights would be in the best interest of the child, grant to a grandparent reasonable visitation rights with the child. Whenever visitation rights are granted to a grandparent, the court may issue such orders as shall be necessary to enforce such rights and may modify or terminate such visitation rights for cause at any time. This chapter shall not apply to the granting of visitation rights to the natural grandparents of any child who has been adopted by order or decree of any court unless: (a) one (1) of the legal parents of such child is also a natural parent of such child; or (b) one (1) of the legal parents of such child was related to the child by blood or marriage prior to the adoption. This chapter shall apply to persons who become grandparents of a child by virtue of adoption. Sources: Laws, 1983, ch. 497, § 2; Laws, 1986, ch. 421, § 2; Laws, 1990, ch. 537, § 3, eff from and after July 1, 1990.

MISSOURI

Missouri Revised Statutes Chapter 452. Dissolution of marriage, divorce, alimony and separate maintenance

Section 452.402. Grandparent's visitation rights granted, when, terminated, when—guardian ad litem appointed, when—attorney fees and costs assessed, when

1. The court may grant reasonable visitation rights to the grandparents of the child and issue any necessary orders to enforce the decree. The court may grant grandparent visitation when: (1) The parents of the child have filed for a dissolution of their marriage. A grandparent shall have the right to intervene in any dissolution action solely on the issue of visitation rights. Grandparents shall also have the right to file a motion to modify the original decree of dissolution to seek visitation rights when such rights have been denied to them; (2) One parent of the child is deceased and the surviving parent denies reasonable visitation rights; (3) A grandparent is unreasonably denied visitation with the child for a period exceeding ninety days; or (4) The child is adopted by a stepparent, another grandparent or other blood relative.

2. The court shall determine if the visitation by the grandparent would be in the child's best interest or if it would danger the child's physical health or impair the child's emotional development. Visitation may only be ordered when the court finds such visitation to be in the best interests of the child. The court may order reasonable conditions or restrictions on grandparent visitation.

3. If the court finds it to be in the best interests of the child, the court may appoint a guardian ad litem for the child. The guardian ad litem shall be an attorney licensed to practice law in Missouri. The guardian ad litem may, for the purpose of determining the question of grandparent visitation rights, participate in the proceedings as if such guardian ad litem were a party.The court shall enter judgment allowing a reasonable fee to the guardian ad litem.

4. A home study, as described by section 452.390, may be ordered by the court to assist in determining the best interests of the child.

5. The court may, in its discretion, consult with the child regarding the child's wishes in determining the best interest of the child.

6. The right of a grandparent to seek or maintain visitation rights pursuant to this section may terminate upon the adoption of the child.

7. The court may award reasonable attorneys fees and expenses to the prevailing party. (1990) Although father of child born out of wedlock did not acknowledge paternity, pay support or otherwise establish a relationship with the child, parent of father could seek grandparent's visitation under statute. In the Matter of C.E.R., 796 S.W. 2d 423 (Mo.App. 1990). (1993) Statute granting grandparent's visitation rights held to be constitutional. *Herndon v. Tuhey*, No. 75184, Mo. S. Ct., June 29, 1993. (1993) Although parents have constitutional right to make decisions affecting family, statute is constitutional as court considers magnitude of infringement by state as significant factor and whether there is substantial infringement by state on family relationship. Statute granting grandparents right to petition court for visitation with grandchildren is reasonable both because it contemplates only minimal intrusion on family relationship and because it is narrowly tailored to adequately protect interests of parents and children. *Herndon v. Tuhey*, 857 S.W. 2d 203 (Mo. en banc).

MONTANA

40-4-212. Best interest of child

(1) The court shall determine the parenting plan in accordance with the best interest of the child. The court shall consider all relevant parenting factors, which may include but are not limited to: (a) the wishes of the child's parent or parents; (b) the wishes of the child; (c) the interaction and interrelationship of the child with the child's parent or parents and siblings and with any other person who significantly affects the child's best interest; (d) the child's adjustment to home, school, and community; (e) the mental and physical health of all individuals involved; (f) physical abuse or threat of physical abuse by one parent against the other parent or the child; (g) chemical dependency, as defined in 53-24-103, or chemical abuse on the part of either parent; (h) continuity and stability of care; (i) developmental needs of the child; (j) whether a parent has knowingly failed to pay birth-related costs that the parent is able to pay, which is considered to be not in the child's best interests; (k) whether a parent has knowingly failed to financially support a child that the parent is able to support, which is considered to be not in the child's best interests;

40-9-102. Grandparent-grandchild contact

(1) Except as provided in subsection (5), the district court may grant to a grandparent of a child reasonable rights to contact with the child, including but not limited to rights regarding a child who is the subject of, or as to whom a disposition has been made during, an administrative or court proceeding under Title 41 or this title. The department of public health and human services must be given notice of a petition for grandparent-grandchild contact regarding a child who is the subject of, or as to whom a disposition has been made during, an administrative or court proceeding under Title 41 or this title.

(2) Grandparent-grandchild contact granted under this section may be granted only upon a finding by the court, after a hearing, that the contact would be in the best interest of the child.

(3) A person may not petition the court under this section more often

than once every 2 years unless there has been a significant change in the circumstances of: (a) the child; (b) the child's parent, guardian, or custodian; or (c) the child's grandparent.

(4) The court may appoint an attorney to represent the interests of a child with respect to grandparent-grandchild contact when the interests are not adequately represented by the parties to the proceeding. . . .

(5) This section does not apply if the child has been adopted by a person other than a stepparent or a grandparent. Grandparent-grandchild contact granted under this section terminates upon the adoption of the child by a person other than a grandparent.

NEBRASKA

Visitation; conditions; order; modification

(1) A grandparent may seek visitation with his or her minor grandchild if: (a) The child's parent or parents are deceased; (b) The marriage of the child's parents has been dissolved or petition for the dissolution of such marriage has been filed, is still pending, but no decree has been entered; or (c) The parents of the minor child have never been married but paternity has been legally established.

(2) In determining whether a grandparent shall be granted visitation, the court shall require evidence concerning the beneficial nature of the relationship of the grandparent to the child. The evidence may be presented by affidavit and shall demonstrate that a significant beneficial relationship exists, or has existed in the past, between the grandparent and the child and that it would be in the best interests of the child to allow such relationship to continue. Reasonable rights of visitation may be granted when the court determines by clear and convincing evidence that there is, or has been, a significant beneficial relationship between the grandparent and the child, that it is in the best interests of the child that such relationship continue, and that such visitation will not adversely interfere with the parent-child relationship.

(3) The court may modify an order granting or denying such visitation upon a showing that there has been a material change in circumstances which justifies such modification and that the modification would serve the best interests of the child.

This section sets out criteria for awarding grandparent visitation which must be proved by clear and convincing evidence before a court may exercise its discretionary authority to grant grandparent visitation rights. *Eberspacher* v. *Hulme*, 248 Neb. 202, 533 N.W.2d 103 (1995).

After the deaths of the minor child's biological parents, the child's maternal biological grandparents became his parents by adopting him. Therefore, the child's parents are not deceased within the meaning of this statute, and the paternal biological grandparents cannot seek court ordered visitation under subsection (1)(a) of this section. *Rust* v. *Buckler*, 247 Neb. 852, 530 N.W.2d 630 (1995).

The grandparent visitation statutes do not provide for an award of attorney fees, nor is there a uniform course of procedure in these cases which would allow recovery of attorney fees. A grandparent visitation action may be initiated either during the dissolution proceeding or after the marriage of the parents has been dissolved. *Rosse* v. *Rosse*, 244 Neb. 967, 510 N.W.2d 73 (1994).

The overriding and paramount consideration in determining grandparent visitation rights is the best interests of the children. The disruption to the lives of the grandchildren, including the distance of travel to exercise visitation rights, is clearly an appropriate consideration in the award of grandparent visitation privileges. *Beal* v. *Endsley*, 3 Neb. App. 589, 529 N.W.2d 125 (1995).

The standard of review in cases involving visitation by grandparents is the same as the standard of review in other custody and visitation cases. *Dice* v. *Dice*, 1 Neb. App. 241, 493 N.W.2d 207 (1992).

NEVADA

Chapter 125C–Custody and visitation

NRS 125C.010 1. Order awarding visitation rights must define rights with particularity and specify habitual residence of child. Any order awarding a party a right of visitation of a minor child must: (a) Define that right with sufficient particularity to ensure that the rights of the parties can be properly enforced and that the best interest of the child is achieved; and (b) Specify that the State of Nevada or the state where the child resides within the United States of America is the habitual residence of the child. The order must include all specific times and other terms of the right of visitation.

2. As used in this section, "sufficient particularity" means a statement of the rights in absolute terms and not by the use of the term "reasonable" or other similar term which is susceptible to different interpretations by the parties. (Added to NRS by 1993, 2137; A 1995, 1493, 2289)-(Substituted in revision for NRS 125A.290)

INS 125C.020 1. Rights of noncustodial parent: Additional visits to compensate for wrongful deprivation of right to visit. Court may, if it finds that the noncustodial parent is being wrongfully deprived of his right to visit, enter a judgment ordering the custodial parent to permit additional visits to compensate for the visit of which he was deprived.

2. An additional visit must be: (a) Of the same type and duration as the wrongfully denied visit; (b) Taken within 1 year after the wrongfully denied visit; and (c) At a time chosen by the noncustodial parent.

3. The noncustodial parent must give the court and the custodial parent written notice of his intention to make the additional visit at least 7 days before the proposed visit if it is to be on a weekday or weekend and at least 30 days before the proposed visit if it is to be on a holiday or vacation. (Added to NRS by 1985, 1892)-(Substituted in revision for NRS 125A.300)

NRS 125C.030 Imprisonment for contempt for failure to comply with judgment ordering additional visit. 1. Custodial parent who fails to comply with a judgment ordering an additional visit may, upon a judgment of the court, be found guilty of contempt and sentenced to imprisonment in the county jail. During the period of imprisonment, the court may authorize his temporary release from confinement during such hours and under such supervision as the court determines are necessary to allow him to go to and return from his place of employment.

2. A custodial parent imprisoned for contempt pursuant to subsection 1 must be released from the jail if the court has reasonable cause to believe that he will comply with the order for the additional visit.

NEW HAMPSHIRE

Title 43 Chapter 458, Uniform Child Custody Jurisdiction Act

Section 458-A:3 Jurisdiction to make child custody determinations

I. A court of this state which is competent to decide child custody matters has jurisdiction to make a child custody determination by initial or modification decree only when: (a) This state (1) is the home state of the child at the time of commencement of the custody proceeding; or (2) has been the child's home state within 6 months before commencement of such proceeding and the child is absent from this state because of his removal or retention by a person claiming his custody or for other reasons, and a parent or person acting as parent continues to live in this state; or (b) It is in the best interest of the child that a court of this state assume jurisdiction because (1) the child and his parents, or the child and at least one contestant, have a significant connection with this state, and (2) there is within the jurisdiction of the court substantial evidence concerning the child's present or future care, protection, training, and personal relationships; or (c) The child is physically present in this state and (1) the child has been abandoned or (2) it is necessary in an emergency to protect the child; or (d) (1) It appears that no other state would have jurisdiction under prerequisites substantially in accordance with subparagraph (a), (b), or (c), or another state has declined to exercise jurisdiction on the ground that this state is the more appropriate forum to determine the custody of the child, and (2) it is in the best interest of the child that this court assume jurisdiction.

II. Except under subparagraphs I(c) and (d), physical presence in this state of the child, or of the child and one of the contestants, is not alone sufficient to confer jurisdiction on a court of this state to make a child custody determination.

III. Physical presence of the child, while desirable, is not a prerequisite for jurisdiction to determine his custody.

Section 458:17-d Grandparents' visitation rights

I. Grandparents, whether adoptive or natural, may petition the court for reasonable rights of visitation with the minor child as provided in paragraph III. The provisions of this section shall not apply in cases where access by the grandparent or grandparents to the minor child has been restricted for any reason prior to or contemporaneous with the divorce, death, relinquishment or termination of parental rights, or other cause of the absence of a nuclear family.

II. The court shall consider the following criteria in making an order relative to a grandparent's visitation rights to the minor child: (a) Whether such visitation would be in the best interest of the child. (b) Whether such visitation would interfere with any parent-child relationship or with a parent's authority over the child. (c) The nature of the relationship between the grandparent and the minor child, including but not limited to, the frequency of contact, and whether the child has lived with the grandparent and length of time of such residence, and when there is no reasonable cause to believe that the child's physical and emotional health would be endangered by such visitation or lack of it. (d) The nature of the relationship between the grandparent and the parent of the minor child, including friction between the grandparent and the parent, and the effect such friction would have on the child. (e) The circumstances which resulted in the absence of a nuclear family, whether divorce, death, relinquishment or termination of parental rights, or other cause. (f) The recommendation regarding visitation made by any guardian ad litem appointed for the child pursuant to RSA 458:17-a. (g) Any preference or wishes expressed by the child. (h) Any such other factors as the court may find appropriate or relevant to the petition for visitation.

III. The petition for visitation shall be entered in the superior court which has jurisdiction over the divorce, legal separation or other proceeding brought under RSA 458; in the case of death of a parent, step-parent adoption, or unwed parents, subject to paragraph IV, the petition shall be entered in the superior court located in the county where the child resides.

IV. If the parent of the minor child is unwed, then any grandparent filing a petition under this section shall attach with the petition proof of legitimation by the parent pursuant to RSA 460:29 or establishment of paternity pursuant to RSA 168-A.

V. Upon the motion of any original party, the court may modify or terminate any order made pursuant to this section to reflect changed circumstances of the parties involved.

VI. Nothing contained in this section shall be construed to affect the rights of a child or natural parent or guardian under RSA 463 or adoptive parent under RSA 170-B:20.

NEW JERSEY

9:2-7.1. Visitation rights for grandparents, siblings

1.a. A grandparent or any sibling of a child residing in this State may make application before the Superior Court, in accordance with the Rules of Court, for an order for visitation. It shall be the burden of the applicant to prove by a preponderance of the evidence that the granting of visitation is in the best interests of the child.

b. In making a determination on an application filed pursuant to this section, the court shall consider the following factors: (1) The relationship between the child and the applicant; (2) The relationship between each of the child's parents or the person with whom the child is residing and the applicant; (3) The time which has elapsed since the child last had contact with the applicant; (4) The effect that such visitation will have on the relationship between the child and the child's parents or the person with whom the child is residing; (5) If the parents are divorced or separated, the time sharing arrangement which exists between the parents with regard to the child; (6) The good faith of the applicant in filing the application; (7) Any history of physical, emotional or sexual abuse or neglect by the applicant; and (8) Any other factor relevant to the best interests of the child.

c. With regard to any application made pursuant to this section, it shall be prima facie evidence that visitation is in the child's best interest if the applicant had, in the past, been a full-time caretaker for the child.

NEW MEXICO

40-9-2. Children; visitation by grandparent

A. In rendering a judgment of dissolution of marriage, legal separation or the existence of the parent and child relationship pursuant to the provisions of the

Uniform Parentage Act [40-11-1 to 40-11-23 NMSA 1978], or at any time after the entry of the judgment, the district court may grant reasonable visitation privileges to a grandparent of a minor child, not in conflict with the child's education or prior established visitation or time-sharing privileges.

B. If one or both parents of a minor child are deceased, any grandparent of the minor child may petition the district court for visitation privileges with respect to the minor. The district court may order temporary visitation privileges until a final order regarding visitation privileges is issued by the court.

C. If a minor child resided with a grandparent for a period of at least three months and the child was less than six years of age at the beginning of the three-month period and the child was subsequently removed from the grandparent's home by the child's parent or any other person, the grandparent may petition the district court for visitation privileges with respect to the child, if the child's home state is New Mexico, as provided in the Child Custody Jurisdiction Act [40-10-1 to 40-10-24 NMSA 1978].

D. If a minor child resided with a grandparent for a period of at least six months and the child was six years of age or older at the beginning of the six-month period and the child was subsequently removed from the grandparent's home by the child's parent or any other person, the grandparent may petition the district court for visitation privileges with respect to the child, if the child's home state is New Mexico, as provided in the Child Custody Jurisdiction Act.

E. A biological grandparent may petition the district court for visitation privileges with respect to a grandchild when the grandchild has been adopted or adoption is sought, pursuant to the provisions of the Adoption Act [32A-5-1 to 32A-5-45 NMSA 1978], by: (1) a stepparent; (2) a relative of the grandchild; (3) a person designated to care for the grandchild in the provisions of a deceased parent's will; or (4) a person who sponsored the grandchild at a baptism or confirmation conducted by a recognized religious organization.

F. When a minor child is adopted by a stepparent and the parental rights of the natural parent terminate or are relinquished, the biological grandparents are not precluded from attempting to establish visitation privileges. When a petition filed pursuant to the provisions of the Grandparent's Visitation Privileges Act [this article] is filed during the pendency of an adoption proceeding, the petition shall be filed as part of the adoption proceedings. The provisions of the Grandparent's Visitation Privileges Act shall have no application in the event of a relinquishment or termination of parental rights in cases of other statutory adoption proceedings.

G. When considering a grandparent's petition for visitation privileges with a child, the district court shall assess: (1) any factors relevant to the best interests of the child; (2) the prior interaction between the grandparent and the child; (3) the prior interaction between the grandparent and each parent of the child; (4) the present relationship between the grandparent and each parent of the child; (5) time-sharing or visitation arrangements that were in place prior to filing of the petition; (6) the effect the visitation with the grandparent will have on the child; (7) if the grandparent has any prior convictions for physical, emotional or sexual abuse or neglect; and (8) if the grandparent has previously been a full-time caretaker for the child for a significant period.

H. The district court may order mediation and evaluation in any matter when a grandparent's visitation privileges with respect to a minor child are at issue. When a judicial district has established a domestic relations mediation program pursuant to the provisions of the Domestic Relations Mediation Act [40-12-1 to 40-12-6 NMSA 1978], the mediation shall conform with the provisions of that act. Upon motion and hearing, the district court shall act promptly on the recommendations set forth in a mediation report and consider assessment of mediation and evaluation to the parties. The district court may order temporary visitation privileges until a final order regarding visitation privileges is issued by the court.

I. When the district court decides that visitation is not in the best interest of the child, the court may issue an order requiring other reasonable contact between the grandparent and the child, including regular communication by telephone.

J. The provisions of the Child Custody Jurisdiction Act and Section 30-4-4 NMSA 1978, regarding custodial interference, are applicable to the provisions of the Grandparent's Visitation Privileges Act.

40-9-3. Visitation; modification; restrictions

A. When the district court grants reasonable visitation privileges to a grandparent pursuant to the provisions of the Grandparent's Visitation Privileges Act [this article], the court shall issue any necessary order to enforce the visitation privileges and may modify the privileges or order upon a showing of good cause by any interested person.

B. Absent a showing of good cause, no grandparent or parent shall file a petition pursuant to the provisions of the Grandparent's Visitation Privileges Act more often than once a year.

C. When an action for enforcement of a court order allowing visitation privileges is brought pursuant to the Grandparent's Visitation Privileges Act by a grandparent, the court may award court costs and reasonable attorneys' fees to the prevailing party when a court order is violated.

40-9-4. Change of child's domicile; notice to grandparent

A. When a grandparent is granted visitation privileges with respect to a minor child pursuant to the provisions of the Act [this article] and the child's custodian intends to depart the state or to relocate within the state with the intention of changing that child's domicile, the custodian shall: (1) notify the grandparents of the minor child of the custodian's intent to change the child's domicile at least five days prior to the child's change of domicile; (2) provide the grandparent with an address and telephone number for the minor child; and (3) afford the grandparent of the minor child the opportunity to communicate with the child.

B. This state will recognize an order or act regarding grandparent visitation privileges issued by any state, district, Indian tribe or territory of the United States of America.

C. Grandparents and other relatives: We agree that the child(ren)'s relationship(s) with grandparents and other extended family members are important, and that it is beneficial for the child(ren) to spend time with our extended families as long as the members of those families do not try to alienate the child(ren) from one of us. In order to encourage the continuation of good relationships between our extended families and the child(ren), we agree to the following extended family visitation and communication: The child(ren)'s grandparents shall have reasonable rights of visitation. Normally, the paternal grandparent's visitation shall be expected to occur during the father's period of responsibility and the maternal grandparent's visitation shall be expected to occur during the mother's period of responsibility. If additional visitation with the grandparents is requested, the parties shall mutually agree to any additional visitation.

40-4-9. Standards for the determination of child custody; hearing

A. In any case in which a judgment or decree will be entered awarding the custody of a minor, the district court shall, if the minor is under the age of fourteen, determine custody in accordance with the best interests of the child. The court shall consider all relevant factors including, but not limited to: (1) the wishes of the child's parent or parents as to his custody; (2) the wishes of the child as to his custodian; (3) the interaction and interrelationship of the child with his parents, his siblings and any other person who may significantly affect the child's best interest; (4) the child's adjustment to his home, school and community; and (5) the mental and physical health of all individuals involved.

B. If the minor is fourteen years of age or older, the court shall consider the desires of the minor as to with whom he wishes to live before awarding custody of such minor.

C. Whenever testimony is taken from the minor concerning his choice of custodian, the court shall hold a private hearing in his chambers. The judge shall have a court reporter in his chambers who shall transcribe the hearing; however, the court reporter shall not file a transcript unless an appeal is taken.

History: 1953 Comp., § 22-7-7.1, enacted by Laws 1977, ch. 172, § 1.

40-4-9.1. Joint custody; standards for determination; parenting plan

A. There shall be a presumption that joint custody is in the best interests of a child in an initial custody determination. An award of joint custody does not imply an equal division of financial responsibility for the child. Joint custody shall not be awarded as a substitute for an existing custody arrangement unless there has been a substantial and material change in circumstances since the entry of the prior custody order or decree, which change affects the welfare of the child such that joint custody is presently in the best interests of the child. With respect to any proceeding in which it is proposed that joint custody be terminated, the court shall not terminate joint custody unless there has been a substantial and material change in circumstances affecting the welfare of the child, since entry of the joint custody order, such that joint custody is no longer in the best interests of the child.

B. In determining whether a joint custody order is in the best interests of the child, in addition to the factors provided in Section 40-4-9 NMSA 1978, the court shall consider the following factors: (1) whether the child has established a close relationship with each parent; (2) whether each parent is capable of providing adequate care for the child throughout each period of responsibility, including arranging for the child's care by others as needed; (3) whether each parent is willing to accept all responsibilities of parenting, including a willingness to accept care of the child at specified times and to relinquish care to the other parent at specified times; (4) whether the child can best maintain and strengthen a relationship with both parents through predictable, frequent contact and whether the child's development will profit from such involvement and influence from both parents; (5) whether each parent is able to allow the other to provide care without intrusion, that is, to respect the other's parental rights and responsibilities and right to privacy; (6) the suitability of a parenting plan for the implementation of joint custody, preferably, although not necessarily, one arrived at through parental agreement; (7) geographic distance between the parents' residences; (8) willingness or ability of the parents to communicate, cooperate or agree on issues regarding the child's needs; and (9) whether a judicial adjudication has been made in a prior or the present proceeding that either parent or other person seeking custody has engaged in one or more acts of domestic abuse against the child, a parent of the child or other household member. If a determination is made that domestic abuse has occurred, the court shall set forth findings that the custody or visitation ordered by the court adequately protects the child, the abused parent or other household member.

C. In any proceeding in which the custody of a child is at issue, the court shall not prefer one parent as a custodian solely because of gender.

D. In any case in which the parents agree to a form of custody, the court should award custody consistent with the agreement unless the court determines that such agreement is not in the best interests of the child.

E. In making an order of joint custody, the court may specify the circumstances, if any, under which the consent of both legal custodians is required to be obtained in order to exercise legal control of the child and the consequences of the failure to obtain mutual consent.

F. When joint custody is awarded, the court shall approve a parenting plan for the implementation of the prospective custody arrangement prior to the award of joint custody. The parenting plan shall include a division of a child's time and care into periods of responsibility for each parent. It may also include: (1) statements regarding the child's religion, education, child care, recreational activities and medical and dental care; (2) designation of specific decision-making responsibilities; (3) methods of communicating information about the child, transporting the child, exchanging care for the child and maintaining telephone and mail contact between parent and child; (4) procedures for future decision making, including procedures for dispute resolution; and the child or designed to clarify and facilitate parenting under joint custody arrangements. In a case where joint custody is not agreed to or necessary aspects of the parenting plan are contested, the parties shall each submit parenting plans. The court may accept the plan proposed by either party or it may combine or revise these plans as it deems necessary in the child's best interests. The time of filing of parenting plans shall be set by local rule. A plan adopted by the court shall be entered as an order of the court.

G. Where custody is contested, the court shall refer that issue to mediation if feasible. The court may also use auxiliary services such as professional evaluation by application of Rule 706 [Rule 11-706 NMRA] of the New Mexico Rules of Evidence or Rule 53 [Rule 1-053 NMRA] of the Rules of Civil Procedure for the District Courts.

H. Notwithstanding any other provisions of law, access to records and information pertaining to a minor child, including medical, dental and school records, shall not be denied to a parent because that parent is not the child's physical custodial parent or because that parent is not a joint custodial parent.

I. Whenever a request for joint custody is granted or denied, the court shall state in its decision its basis for granting or denying the request for joint custody. A statement that joint custody is or is not in the best interests of the child is not sufficient to meet the requirements of this subsection.

J. An award of joint custody means that: (1) each parent shall have significant, well-defined periods of responsibility for the child; (2) each parent shall have, and be allowed and expected to carry out, responsibility for the child's financial, physical, emotional and developmental needs during that parent's periods of responsibility; (3) the parents shall consult with each other on major decisions involving the child before implementing those decisions; that is, neither parent shall make a decision or take an action which results in a major change in a child's life until the matter has been discussed with the other parent and the parents agree. If the parents, after discussion, cannot agree and if one parent wishes to effect a major change while the other does not wish the major change to occur, then no change shall occur until the issue has been resolved as provided in this subsection; (4) the following guidelines apply to major changes in a child's life: (a) if either parent plans to change his home city or state of residence, he shall provide to the other parent thirty days' notice in writing stating the date and destination of move.

NEW YORK

Sec. 75-d. Jurisdiction to make child custody determinations

1. A court of this state which is competent to decide child custody matters has jurisdiction to make a child custody determination by initial or modification decree only when: (a) this state (i) is the home state of the child at the time of commencement of the custody proceeding, or (ii) had been the child's home state within six months before commencement of such proceeding and the child is absent from this state because of his removal or retention by a person claiming his custody or for other reasons, and a parent or person acting as parent continues; (b) it is in the best interest of the child that a court of this state assume jurisdiction because (i) the child and his parents, or the child and at least one contestant, have a significant connection with this state, and (ii) there is within the jurisdiction of the court substantial evidence concerning the child's present or future care, protection, training, and personal relationships; or (c) the child is physically present in this state and (i) the child has been abandoned or (ii) it is necessary in an emergency to protect the child.

    Sec. 72. Where either both of the parents of a minor child, residing within this state, is or are deceased, or where circumstances show that conditions exist which equity would see fit to intervene the court may make such directions as the best interest of the child may require for visitation rights for such grandparent or grandparents.

NORTH CAROLINA

§ 50-13.2. Who is entitled to custody; terms of custody; visitation rights of grandparents; taking child out of state

(b1) An order for custody of a minor child may provide visitation rights for any grandparent of the child as the court, in its discretion, deems appropriate. As used in this subsection, "grandparent" includes a biological grandparent of a child adopted by a stepparent or a relative of the child where a substantial relationship exists between the grandparent and the child. Under no circumstances shall a biological grandparent of a child adopted by adoptive parents, neither of whom is related to the child and where parental rights of both biological parents have been terminated, be entitled to visitation rights.

(c) An order for custody of a minor child may provide for such child to be taken outside of the State, but if the order contemplates the return of the child to this State, the judge may require the person, agency, organization or institution having custody out of this State to give bond or other security conditioned upon the return of the child to this State in accordance with the order of the court.

(d) If, within a reasonable time, one parent fails to consent to adoption pursuant to Chapter 48 of the General Statutes or parental rights have not been terminated, the consent of the other consenting parent shall not be effective in an action for custody of the child.

§50-13.2A. Action for visitation of an adopted grandchild

A biological grandparent may institute an action or proceeding for visitation rights with a child adopted by a stepparent or a relative of the child where a substantial relationship exists between the grandparent and the child. Under no circumstances shall a biological grandparent of a child adopted by adoptive parents, neither of whom is related to the child and where parental rights of both biological parents have been terminated, be entitled to visitation rights. A court may award visitation rights if it determines that visitation is in the best interest of the child. An order awarding visitation rights shall contain findings of fact which support the determination by the judge of the best interest of the child. Procedure, venue, and jurisdiction shall be as in an action for custody. (1985, c. 575, s. 2.)

NORTH DAKOTA

Sec. 14-09-05-1

The grandparents of an unmarried minor must be granted reasonable visitation rights by the district court upon application by the grandparents unless a finding is made that visitation is not in the best interests of the minor. Visitation rights of grandparents to an unmarried minor are presumed to be in the best interests of the minor.

OHIO

Title 31, Section 3109.051 B

(1) In a divorce, dissolution of marriage, legal separation, annulment, or child support proceeding that involves a child, the court may grant reasonable companionship or visitation rights to any grandparent, any person related to the child by consanguinity or affinity, or any other person other than a parent, if all of the following apply: (a) The grandparent, relative, or other person files a motion with the court seeking companionship or visitation rights. (b) The court determines that the grandparent, relative, or other person has an interest in the welfare of the child.(c) The court determines that the granting of the companionship or visitation rights is in the best interest of the child.

(2) A motion may be filed under division (B)(1) of this section during the pendency of the divorce, dissolution of marriage, legal separation, annulment, or child support proceeding or, if a motion was not filed at that time or was filed at that time and the circumstances in the case have changed, at any time after a decree or final order is issued in the case. "kinship caregiver" means any of the following who is eighteen years of age or older and is caring for a child in place of the child's parents:(A) The following individuals related by blood or adoption to the child: (1)

Grandparents, including grandparents with the prefix "great," "great-great," or "great-great-great"; (3) Aunts, uncles, nephews, and nieces, including such relatives with the prefix "great," "great-great," "grand," or "great-grand"; (4) First cousins and first cousins once removed. (B) Stepparents and stepsiblings of the child; (C) Spouses and former spouses of individuals named in divisions (A) and (B) of this section; (D) A legal guardian of the child; (E) A legal custodian of the child.

OKLAHOMA

§10-5

A. 1. Pursuant to the provisions of this section, each and every grandparent of an unmarried minor child shall have reasonable rights of visitation to the child if the district court deems it to be in the best interest of the child.

B. The right of visitation to any grandparent of an unmarried minor child shall be granted only so far as that right is authorized and provided by order of the district court.

C. The district courts are vested with jurisdiction to issue orders granting grandparental visitation rights and enforce such visitation rights, upon the filing of a verified application for such visitation rights or enforcement thereof. Notice as ordered by the court shall be given to the person or parent having custody of the child and the venue of such action shall be in the county of the residence of such person or parent.

9. a. When reunification of the family is not recommended or possible, the court may rder a child's permanent care and custody transferred to a kinship guardian. Kinship guardianship shall include, but not be limited to, the following parental responsibilities with respect to a child: (1) protection, (2) education, (3) care and control, (4) custody, and (5) decision making.

b. A kinship foster parent may file a petition with the court to be appointed as kinship guardian for a child. The petition shall allege that: (1) a child is placed with the Department, (2) more than twelve (12) months have passed since the date of the dispositional order placing such child with the Department, (3) the parents of the child are presently and for the foreseeable (4) the prospective kinship guardian consents to the appointment, (5) the child has resided with the kinship foster parent and there exists a loving and emotional tie between the child and the kinship foster parent, and (6) it would be in the best interests of the child for the petition to be granted.

c. Notice of the petition and a copy of the petition shall be served upon the parties, the Department, and the guardian ad litem of the child.

d. If the court finds that the elements of the petition have been proven based on clear and convincing evidence, or upon the consent of all parties, the court shall grant the petition.

e. An order appointing a person as a kinship guardian shall award custody of the child to the kinship guardian. A kinship guardian shall have the same authority as a parent to consent on behalf of a child, except that a kinship guardian shall not consent to the adoption or surrender of a child.

OREGON

109.121. Procedure whereby grandparents may establish visitation rights with grandchildren

(1)(a) A child's petition to the circuit court, be granted an order establishing reasonable rights of visitation between the grandparent and the child if: (A) The grandparent has established or has attempted to establish ongoing personal contact with the child; and (B) The custodian of the child has denied the grandparent reasonable opportunity to visit the child. (b) After the commencement of a domestic relations suit, as defined in ORS 107.510, or a proceeding under ORS 108.110, 109.100, 109.103, 109.125, 419B.400 or 419C.590, and before a decree or final order dissolving the marriage of the parties, any grandparent of the minor children of the parties therein may petition the court for an order providing for reasonable rights of visitation between the grandparent and the child. (c) After a decree or final order is entered dissolving the marriage of the child's parents, the grandparent may petition the court only if: (A) The grandparent did not file a petition during the pendency of the dissolution proceedings; or (B) There has been a change in circumstances relating to the custodial parent or the minor child such as is required to allow the court to reconsider the provisions of the decree that provide for the future custody, support and welfare of the minor child.

(2) A petition filed with a court under subsection (1) of this section shall state the following: (a) The names of the petitioners. (b) The names, addresses and dates of birth of all the minor children to whom the petitioners seek visitation rights. (c) The names and addresses of the parents or other custodians of the minor children. (d) When the petition is filed under subsection (1)(b) or (c) of this section, the relationship of the petitioners to the parties in the proceeding. (e) When the petition is filed under subsection (1)(c) of this section, if the petitioner is asserting a change in circumstances as justification for the petition, the facts constituting the asserted change in circumstances.

107.137. Factors considered in determining custody of minor child

(1) In determining custody of a minor child pursuant to ORS 107.105 or 107.135, the court shall give primary consideration to the best interests and welfare of the child. In determining the best interests and welfare of the child, the court shall consider the following relevant factors: (a) The emotional ties between the child and other family members; (b) The interest of the parties in and attitude toward the child; (c) The desirability of continuing an existing relationship; (d) The abuse of one parent by the other; and (e) The willingness and ability of each parent to facilitate and encourage a close and continuing relationship between the other parent and the child. However, the court may not consider such willingness and ability if one parent shows that the other parent has sexually assaulted or engaged in a pattern of behavior of abuse against the parent or a child and that a continuing relationship with the other parent will endanger the health or safety of either parent or the child.

(2) The best interests and welfare of the child in a custody matter shall not be determined by isolating any one of the relevant factors referred to in subsection (1) of this section, or any other relevant factor, and relying on it to the exclusion of other factors.

(3) In determining custody of a minor child pursuant to ORS 107.105 or 107.135, the court shall consider the conduct, marital status, income, social environment or life style of either party only if it is shown that any of these factors are causing or may cause emotional or physical damage to the child.

(4) No preference in custody shall be given to the mother over the father for the sole reason that she is the mother, nor shall any preference be given to the father over the mother for the sole reason that he is the father. [1975 c.722 s.2; 1987 c.795 s.14; 1997 c.707 s.35]

PENNSYLVANIA

Title 23, Section 204. Judicial appointment of guardian: Conditions for appointment

(a) The court may appoint a guardian for a minor if the court finds the appointment is in the minor's best interest, and: (i) the parents consent; (ii) all parental rights have been terminated; or (iii) the parents are unwilling or unable to exercise their parental rights. If a guardian is appointed by a parent pursuant to Section 202 and the appointment has not been prevented or terminated under Section 203, that appointee has priority for appointment. However, the court may proceed with another appointment upon a finding that the appointee under Section 202 has failed to accept the appointment within 30 days after notice of the guardianship proceeding.

(b) If necessary and on petition or motion and whether or not the conditions of subsection (a) have been established, the court may appoint a temporary guardian for a minor upon a showing that an immediate need exists and that the appointment would be in the best interest of the minor. Notice as provided in Section 113 must be given to the parents and to a minor who has attained 14 years of age. Except as otherwise ordered by the court, the temporary guardian has the authority of an unlimited guardian, but the duration of the temporary guardianship may not exceed six months. Within five days after the appointment, the temporary guardian o notice of hearing under Section 205.

Title 23, Section 5311. When a parent is deceased

Visitation may be granted when at least one of the parents of the child is deceased, when the parents marriage is dissolved or the parents have been separated for six months or more, or when the child has resided with the grandparents for twelve months or more and is subsequently removed from the home of his parents. The court must find that the visitation is in the best interests of the child and will not interfere with the parent-child relationship and must consider the amount of personal contact between the child and the grandparent prior to the application. If the visitation is based on a deceased parent, only the parents of the deceased parent qualify. If access is sought under the provision where the child has lived with the grandparents for twelve months the grandparents can seek partial custody.

RHODE ISLAND

§ 15-5-24.1. Visitation rights of grandparents

The court may, upon miscellaneous petition of a grandparent whose child is deceased, grant reasonable visitation rights of the grandchild or grandchildren to the grandparent, whether or not any divorce or custody proceedings were ever commenced, and may issue all necessary orders to enforce visitation rights.

Custody. No statutory factors

SOUTH CAROLINA

Title 20-7-420

The court can order periods of visitation for the grandparents of a minor child where either or both parents of the minor child is or are deceased, or are divorced, or are living separate and apart in different habitats regardless of the existence of a court order or agreement, and upon a written finding that the visitation rights would be in the best interests of the child and would not interfere with the parent/child relationship. In determining whether to order visitation for the grandparents, the court shall consider the nature of the relationship between the child and his grandparents prior to the filing of the petition or complaint.

Section 20-3-160. Care, custody and maintenance of children

In any action for divorce from the bonds of matrimony the court may at any stage of the cause, or from time to time after final judgment, make such orders touching the care, custody and maintenance of the children of the marriage and what, if any, security shall be given for the same as from the circumstances of the parties and the nature of the case and the best spiritual as well as other interests of the children may be fit, equitable and just.

SOUTH DAKOTA

§ 25-4-52. Visitation rights for grandparents— Authority of circuit court

The circuit court may grant grandparents reasonable rights of visitation with their grandchild, with or without petition by the grandparents, if it is in the best interests of the grandchild.

Custody Statutes 25-4-14

Only: "Custody is to be determined as may seem necessary and proper."

TENNESSEE

36-6-302. Grandparents' visitation rights

(c) (1) (A) If a child is removed from the custody of the child's parents, guardian or legal custodian; and (B) If a child is placed in a licensed foster home, a facility operated by a licensed child welfare agency, or other home or facility designated or operated by the court, whether such placement is by court order, voluntary placement agreement, surrender of parental rights, or otherwise; (2) Then, the grandparents of such child may be granted reasonable visitation rights to the child during such child's minority by the court of competent jurisdiction upon a finding that: (A) Such visitation rights would be in the best interest of the minor child; (B) The grandparents would adequately protect the child from further abuse or intimidation by the perpetrator or any other family member; (C) The grandparents were not implicated in the commission of any alleged act against such child or of their own children that under the law in effect prior to November 1, 1989.

(a) (1) In a suit for annulment, divorce or separate maintenance, where the custody of a minor child or minor children is a question, the court may, notwithstanding a decree for annulment, divorce or separate maintenance is denied, award the care, custody and control of such child or children to either of the parties to the suit or to both parties in the instance of joint custody or shared parenting, or to some suitable person, as the welfare and interest of the child or children may demand, and the court may decree that suitable support be made by the natural parents or those who stand in the place of the natural parents by adoption. Such decree shall remain within the control of the court and be subject to such changes or modification as the exigencies of the case may require.

TEXAS

Sec. 153.433. Possession of and Access to Grandchild

The court shall order reasonable access to a grandchild by a grandparent if: (1) at the time the relief is requested, at least one biological or adoptive parent of the child has not had that parent's parental rights terminated; and (2) access is in the best interest of the child, and at least one of the following facts is present: (A) the grandparent requesting access to the child is a parent of a parent of the child and that parent of the child has been incarcerated in jail or prison during the three-month period preceding the filing of the petition or has been found by a court to be incompetent or is dead; (B) the parents of the child are divorced or have been living apart for the three-month period preceding the filing of the petition or a suit for the dissolution of the (C) the child has been abused or neglected by a parent of the child; the child has been adjudicated to be a child in need of supervision or a delinquent child under Title 3; (E) the grandparent requesting access to the child is the parent of a person whose parent-child relationship with the child has been terminated by court order; or (F) the child has resided with the grandparent requesting access to the child for at least six months within the 24-month period preceding the filing of the petition.

Custody statutes Sec. 14-01

No mention of grandparents.

UTAH

30-5-2. Visitation rights of grandparents

(1) Grandparents have standing to bring an action in district court requesting visitation in accordance with the provisions and requirements of this section.

(2) The district court may grant grandparents reasonable rights of visitation, if it is in the best interest of the children, in cases where a grandparent's child has died or has become a noncustodial rent through divorce or legal separation.

(3) In cases other than those described in Subsection (2), a grandparent may petition the court for reasonable rights of visitation with a child. The court may enter an order granting the petitioner reasonable visitation rights in accordance with the provisions and requirements of this Subsection (3). There is a presumption that a parent's decision with regard to grandparent visitation is reasonable. The court may override the parent's decision and grant reasonable visitation rights to a grandparent if it finds that: (a) it is in the best interest of the grandchild; (b) the petitioner is a fit and proper person to have rights of visitation with the grandchild; (c) the petitioner has repeatedly attempted to visit the grandchild and has not been allowed to visit the grandchild as a direct result of the actions of the parent or parents; (d) there is no other way for the petitioner to visit the grandchild without court intervention; and (e) the petitioner has rebutted the presumption that the parent's decision to refuse or limit visitation with the grandchild was reasonable.

(4) (a) There is a presumption that adoption of a child, voluntary or

involuntary termination of parental rights, or relinquishment to a licensed child placing agency terminates all rights of a grandparent to petition for visitation under this section. That presumption may be rebutted if the court finds that a child has established a relationship with the grandparent, and that the child's continued contact with the grandparent will be in the best interest of the child. (b) Nothing in this subsection (4) affects visitation rights of a grandparent that have been ordered by a court pursuant to this section, if the grandchild is adopted by the grandchild's stepparent.

(5) Grandparents may petition the court as provided in Section 78-32-12.2 to remedy a parent's wrongful noncompliance with a visitation order.

VERMONT

Title 15, Sec. 101. Grandparent visitation

Visitation may be granted when an action for custody or visitation is or has been considered by the court . . . the court must find that the visitation is in the child's best interest after considering the statutory factors relating to the best interest.

§ 665. Rights and responsibilities order; best interests of the child

(a) In an action under this chapter the court shall make an order concerning parental rights and responsibilities of any minor child of the parties. The court may order parental rights and responsibilities to be divided or shared between the parents on such terms and conditions as serve the best interests of the child. When the parents cannot agree to divide or share parental rights and responsibilities, the court shall award parental rights and responsibilities primarily or solely to one parent. (b) In making an order under this section, the court shall be guided by the best interests of the child, and shall consider at least the following factors: (1) the relationship of the child with each parent and the ability and disposition of each parent to provide the child with love, affection and guidance; (2) the ability and disposition of each parent to assure that the child receives adequate clothing, medical care, other material needs and a safe environment; (3)

the ability and disposition of each parent to meet the child's present and future developmental needs; (4) the quality of the child's adjustment to the child's present housing, school and community and the potential effect of any change; (5) the ability and disposition of each parent to foster a positive relationship and frequent and continuing contact with the other parent, including physical contact, except where contact will result in harm to the child or to a parent; (6) the quality of the child's relationship with the primary care provider, if appropriate given the child's age and development; (7) the relationship of the child with any other person who may significantly affect the child; (8) the ability and disposition of the parents to communicate, cooperate with each other and make joint decisions concerning the children where parental rights and responsibilities are to be shared or divided. (9) In addition, the court shall consider evidence of abuse, as defined in section 1101 of this title, and the impact of the abuse on the child and on the relationship between the child and the abusing parent.

(c) The court shall not apply a preference for one parent over the other because of the sex of the child, the sex of a parent or the financial resources of a parent.

(d) The court may order a parent who is awarded responsibility for a certain matter involving a child's welfare to inform the other parent when a major change in that matter occurs.

VIRGINIA

§ 20-124.1. Grandparent visitation

Definitions as used in this chapter

"Joint custody" means (i) joint legal custody where both parents retain joint responsibility for the care and control of the child and joint authority to make decisions concerning the child even though the child's primary residence may be with only one parent, (ii) joint physical custody where both parents share physical and custodial care of the child or (iii) any combination of joint legal and joint physical custody which the court deems to be in the best interest of the child. "Person with a legitimate interest" shall be broadly construed and includes, but is not limited to grandparents, stepparents, former stepparents, blood relatives and family members provided any such party has intervened in the suit or is otherwise properly before the court. The term shall be broadly construed to accommodate the best interest of the child. A party with a legitimate interest shall not include any person (i) whose parental rights have been terminated by court order, either voluntarily or involuntarily, or any other person whose interest in the child derives from or through such person whose parental rights have been so terminated, including but not limited to grandparents, stepparents, former stepparents, blood relatives and family members, if the child subsequently has been legally adopted except where a final order of adoption is entered pursuant to § 63.1-231 or (ii) who has been convicted of a violation of subsection A of § 18.2-61, § 18.2-63 or subsection B of § 18.2-366 when the child who is the subject of the petition was conceived as a result of such violation.

§ 20-107.2. Court may decree as to custody and support of minor children

Upon entry of a decree providing (i) for the dissolution of a marriage, (ii) for a divorce, whether from the bond of matrimony or from bed and board, (iii) that neither party is entitled to a divorce, or (iv) for separate maintenance, the court may make such further decree as it shall deem expedient concerning the custody or visitation and support of the minor children of the parties as provided in Chapter 6.1 (§ 20-124.1 et seq.) of Title 20, including an order that either party provide health care coverage.

WASHINGTON

Senate Bill Report EHB 1773

As Reported By Senate Committee On:
Judiciary, April 2, 1999

Title: An act relating to visitation rights in nonparental actions for child custody.

Brief Description: Changing visitation rights in nonparental actions for child custody.

Background: Current statutes allow a nonparent to petition the court for visitation with a child when the parents have filed for dissolution or at any time. The court may order visitation with a nonparent if it is in the child's best interest. The court must dismiss a petition for visitation by a nonparent if the that the petitioner has a significant relationship with the child. If the court dismisses the petition, the court must order the petitioner to pay reasonable attorney fees and costs to the party who opposed the petition. Visitation with a grandparent is presumed to be in the child's best interest when a significant relationship exists between the grandparent and the child. In December 1998, the state Supreme Court held that the visitation statutes were unconstitutional because they "impermissibly interfere with a parent's fundamental interest in the care, custody, and companionship of the child." The court stated that the best interest of the child standard, without any threshold finding that the child would be harmed if visitation were discontinued, was insufficient to overrule a parent's fundament right.

Summary of Bill: The third-party visitation statutes are amended. A nonparent who is related to the child through blood, marriage, or adoption may petition for visitation with the child at anytime when a dissolution, legal separation or modification of parenting plan proceeding has been parent or parents or may intervene in a pending dissolution, legal separation or modification of parent plan proceeding. The nonparent must demonstrate by clear, cogent, and convincing evidence that: (a) a significant relationship exists between the nonparent and the (b) denial of visitation would result in a substantial likelihood of harm to the child's well-being; and (c) visitation is in the child's best interest. If the court grants visitation to the nonparent, the time awarded must be divided between the primary residential parent and the nonprimary residential parent in an amount proportionate to the time awarded them in the parenting plan, unless the court finds that it would not be in the best interest of the child in maintaining contact with both parents.

When determining the child's best interest, the court may consider the following: the strength of the relationship between the child and the petitioner; the relationship between the petitioner and the parents; the nature and reason for the parent's objection to visitation; the effect visitation would have on the relationship between the child and the child's parents; the residential timesharing arrangements; the good faith of the petitioner; any criminal history or history of abuse by the petitioner; and any other factor the court finds relevant.

Testimony For: The Washington Supreme Court recently struck down all nonparental actions for visitation. Without this bill, nonparents such as grandparents cannot obtain visitation with their grandchildren. The bill sets forth a three prong test in keeping with the Supreme Court case and will allow grandparents a chance to obtain court ordered visitation with their grandchildren. Children feel cut off from their family when they are not allowed to see their grandparents. Following a divorce, a grandchild's relationship with his or her grandparents may become even more important in the child's life.

TROXEL v. GRANVILLE (99-138)

137 Wash. 2d 1, 969 P.2d 21, affirmed.

Opinion of O'Connor, J.

NOTICE: This opinion is subject to formal revision before publication in the preliminary print of the United States Reports. Readers are requested to notify the Reporter of Decisions, Supreme Court of the United States, Washington, D.C. 20543, of any typographical or other formal errors, in order that corrections may be made before the preliminary print goes to press.

SUPREME COURT OF THE UNITED STATES
No. 99—138
JENIFER TROXEL, et vir, PETITIONERS v.
TOMMIE GRANVILLE
ON WRIT OF CERTIORARI TO THE SUPREME COURT
OF WASHINGTON

[June 5, 2000]

Justice O'Connor announced the judgment of the Court and delivered an opinion, in which The Chief Justice, Justice Ginsburg, and Justice Breyer join.

Section 26.10.160(3) of the Revised Code of Washington permits "[a]ny person" to petition a superior court for visitation rights "at any time," and authorizes that court to grant such visitation rights whenever "visitation may serve the best interest of the child." Petitioners Jenifer and Gary Troxel petitioned a Washington Superior Court for the right to visit their grandchildren, Isabelle and Natalie Troxel. Respondent Tommie Granville, the mother of Isabelle and Natalie, opposed the petition. The case ultimately reached the Washington Supreme Court, which held that §26.10.160(3) unconstitutionally interferes with the fundamental right of parents to rear their children.

I

Tommie Granville and Brad Troxel shared a relationship that ended in June 1991. The two never married, but they had two daughters, Isabelle and Natalie. Jenifer and Gary Troxel are Brad's parents, and thus the paternal grandparents of Isabelle and Natalie. After Tommie and Brad separated in 1991, Brad lived with his parents and regularly brought his daughters to his parents' home for weekend visitation. Brad committed suicide in May 1993. Although the Troxels at first continued to see Isabelle and Natalie on a regular basis after their son's death, Tommie Granville informed the Troxels in October 1993 that she wished to limit their visitation with her daughters to one short visit per month. In re Smith, 137 Wash. 2d 1, 6, 969 P.2d 21, 23—24 (1998); In re Troxel, 87 Wash. App. 131, 133, 940 P.2d 698, 698—699 (1997).

In December 1993, the Troxels commenced the present action by filing, in the Washington Superior Court for Skagit County, a petition to obtain visitation rights with Isabelle and Natalie. The Troxels filed their petition under two Washington statutes, Wash. Rev. Code §§26.09.240 and 26.10.160(3) (1994). Only the latter statute is at issue in this case. Section 26.10.160(3) provides: "Any person may petition the court for visitation rights at any time including, but not limited to, custody proceedings. The court may order visitation rights for any person when visitation may serve the best interest of the child whether or not there has been any change of circumstances." At trial, the Troxels requested two weekends of overnight visitation per month and two weeks of visitation each summer. Granville did not oppose visitation altogether, but instead asked the court to order one day of visitation per month with no overnight stay. 87 Wash. App., at 133—134, 940 P.2d, at 699. In 1995, the Superior Court issued an oral ruling and entered a visitation decree ordering visitation one weekend per month, one week during the summer, and four hours on both of the petitioning grandparents' birthdays. 137 Wash. 2d, at 6, 969 P.2d, at 23; App. to Pet. for Cert. 76a—78a.

Granville appealed, during which time she married Kelly Wynn. Before addressing the merits of Granville's appeal, the Washington Court of Appeals remanded the case to the Superior Court for entry of written findings of fact and conclusions of law. 137 Wash.2d, at 6, 969 P.2d, at 23. On remand, the Superior Court found that visitation was in Isabelle and Natalie's best interests:

"The Petitioners [the Troxels] are part of a large, central, loving family, all located in this area, and the Petitioners can provide opportunities for the children in the areas of cousins and music. 'The court took into consideration all factors regarding the best interest of the children and considered all the testimony before it. The children would be benefitted from spending quality time with the Petitioners, provided that that time is balanced with time with the childrens' [sic] nuclear family. The court finds that the childrens' [sic] best interests are served by spending time with their mother and stepfather's other six children." App. 70 a.Approximately nine months after the Superior Court entered its order on remand, Granville's husband formally adopted Isabelle and Natalie. Id., at 60a—67a.

The Washington Court of Appeals reversed the lower court's visitation order and dismissed the Troxels' petition for visitation, holding that nonparents lack standing to seek visitation under §26.10.160(3) unless a custody action is pending. In the Court of Appeals' view, that limitation on nonparental visitation actions was "consistent with the constitutional restrictions on state interference with parents' fundamental liberty interest in the care, custody, and management of their children." 87 Wash. App., at 135, 940 P.2d, at 700 (internal quotation marks omitted). Having resolved the case on the statutory ground, however, the Court of Appeals did not expressly pass on Granville's constitutional challenge to the visitation statute. Id., at 138, 940 P.2d, at 701. The Washington Supreme Court granted the Troxels' petition for review and, after consolidating their case with two other visitation cases, affirmed. The court disagreed with the Court of Appeals' decision on the statutory issue and found that the plain language of §26.10.160(3) gave the Troxels standing to seek visitation, irrespective of whether a custody action was pending. 137 Wash. 2d, at 12, 969 P.2d, at 26—27. The Washington Supreme Court nevertheless agreed with the Court of Appeals' ultimate conclusion that the Troxels could not obtain visitation of Isabelle and Natalie pursuant to §26.10.160(3). The court rested its decision on the Federal Constitution, holding that §26.10.160(3) unconstitutionally infringes on the fundamental right of parents to rear their children. In the court's view, there were at least two problems with the nonparental visitation statute. First, according to the Washington Supreme Court, the Constitution permits a State to interfere with the right of parents to rear their children only to prevent harm or potential harm to a child. Section 26.10.160(3) fails that standard because it requires no threshold showing of harm. Id., at 15—20, 969 P.2d, at 28—30. Second, by allowing " 'any person' to petition for forced visitation of a child at 'any time' with the only requirement being that the visitation serve the best interest of the child," the Washington visitation statute sweeps too broadly. Id., at 20, 969 P.2d, at 30. "It is not within the province of the state to make significant decisions concerning the custody of children merely because it could make a 'better' decision." Ibid., 969 P.2d, at 31. The Washington Supreme Court held that "[p]arents have a right to limit visitation of their children with third persons," and that between parents and judges, "the parents should be the ones to choose whether to expose their children to certain people or ideas." Id., at 21, 969 P.2d, at 31. Four justices dissented from the Washington Supreme Court's holding on the constitutionality of the statute. Id., at 23—43, 969 P.2d, at 32—42. We granted certiorari, 527 U.S. 1069 (1999), and now affirm the judgment.

II

The demographic changes of the past century make it difficult to speak of an average American family. The composition of families varies greatly from household to household. While many children may have two married parents and grandparents who visit regularly, many other children are raised in single-parent households. In 1996, children living with only one parent accounted for 28 percent of all children under age 18 in the United States. U.S. Dept. of Commerce, Bureau of Census, Current Population

Reports, 1997 Population Profile of the United States 27 (1998). Understandably, in these single-parent households, persons outside the nuclear family are called upon with increasing frequency to assist in the everyday tasks of child rearing. In many cases, grandparents play an important role. For example, in 1998, approximately 4 million children—or 5.6 percent of all children under age 18—lived in the household of their grandparents. U.S. Dept. of Commerce, Bureau of Census, Current Population Reports, Marital Status and Living Arrangements: March 1998 (Update), p. i. (1998).The nationwide enactment of nonparental visitation statutes is assuredly due, in some part, to the States' recognition of these changing realities of the American family. Because grandparents and other relatives undertake duties of a parental nature in many households, States have sought to ensure the welfare of the children therein by protecting the relationships those children form with such third parties. The States' nonparental visitation statutes are further supported by a recognition, which varies from State to State, that children should have the opportunity to benefit from relationships with statutorily specified persons–for example, their grandparents. The extension of statutory rights in this area to persons other than a child's parents, however, comes with an obvious cost. For example, the State's recognition of an independent third-party interest in a child can place a substantial burden on the traditional parent-child relationship. Contrary to Justice Stevens' accusation, our description of state nonparental visitation statutes in these terms, of course, is not meant to suggest that "children are so much chattel." Post, at 10 (dissenting opinion). Rather, our terminology is intended to highlight the fact that these statutes can present questions of constitutional import. In this case, we are presented with just such a question. Specifically, we are asked to decide whether §26.10.160(3), as applied to Tommie Granville and her family, violates the Federal Constitution. The Fourteenth Amendment provides that no State shall "deprive any person of life, liberty, or property, without due process of law." We have long recognized that the Amendment's Due Process Clause, like its Fifth Amendment counterpart, "guarantees more than fair process." Washington v. Glucksberg, 521 U.S. 702, 719 (1997). The Clause also includes a substantive component that "provides heightened protection against government interference with certain fundamental rights and liberty interests." Id., at 720; see also *Reno v. Flores*, 507 U.S. 292, 301—302 (1993).

The liberty interest at issue in this case—the interest of parents in the care, custody, and control of their children—is perhaps the oldest of the fundamental liberty interests recognized by this Court. More than 75 years ago, in *Meyer* v. *Nebraska*, 262 U.S. 390, 399, 401 (1923), we held that the "liberty" protected by the Due Process Clause includes the right of parents to "establish a home and bring up children" and "to control the education of their own." Two years later, in *Pierce* v. *Society of Sisters*, 268 U.S. 510, 534—535 (1925), we again held that the "liberty of parents and guardians" includes the right "to direct the upbringing and education of children under their control." We explained in *Pierce* that "[t]he child is not the mere creature of the State; those who nurture him and direct his destiny have the right, coupled with the high duty, to recognize and prepare him for additional obligations." Id., at 535. We returned to the subject in *Prince* v. *Massachusetts*, 321 U.S. 158 (1944), and again confirmed that there is a constitutional dimension to the right of parents to direct the upbringing of their children. "It is cardinal with us that the custody, care and nurture of the child reside first in the parents, whose primary function and freedom include preparation for obligations the state can neither supply nor hinder." Id., at 166. In subsequent cases also, we have recognized the fundamental right of parents to make decisions concerning the care, custody, and control of their children. See, e.g., *Stanley* v. *Illinois*, 405 U.S. 645, 651 (1972) ("It is plain that the interest of a parent in the companionship, care, custody, and management of his or her children 'come[s] to this Court with a momentum for respect lacking when appeal is made to liberties which derive merely from shifting economic arrangements' " (citation omitted)); *Wisconsin* v. *Yoder*, 406 U.S. 205, 232 (1972) ("The history and culture of Western civilization reflect a strong tradition of parental concern for the nurture and upbringing of their children. This primary role of the parents in the upbringing of their children is now established beyond debate as an enduring American tradition"); *Quilloin* v. *Walcott*, 434 U.S. 246, 255 (1978) ("We have recognized on numerous occasions that the relationship between parent and child is constitutionally protected"); *Parham* v. *J. R.*, 442 U.S. 584, 602 (1979) ("Our jurisprudence historically has reflected Western civilization concepts of the family as a unit with broad parental authority over minor children. Our cases have consistently followed that course"); *Santosky* v. *Kramer*, 455 U.S. 745, 753 (1982) (discussing "[t]he fundamental liberty interest of natural parents in the care, custody, and management of their child"); Glucksberg, supra, at 720 ("In a long line of cases, we have held that, in addition to the specific freedoms protected by the Bill of Rights, the 'liberty' specially protected by the Due Process Clause includes the righ[t] . . . to direct the education and upbringing of one's children" (citing *Meyer* and *Pierce*)). In light of this extensive precedent, it cannot now be doubted that the Due Process Clause of the Fourteenth Amendment protects the fundamental right of parents to make decisions concerning the care, custody, and control of their children. Section 26.10.160(3), as applied to Granville and her family in this case, unconstitutionally infringes on that fundamental parental right. The Washington nonparental visitation statute is breathtakingly broad. According to the statute's text, "[a]ny person may petition the court for "visitation may serve the best interest of the child." §26.10.160(3) (emphases added). That language effectively permits any third party seeking visitation to subject any decision by a parent concerning visitation of the parent's children to state-court review. Once the visitation petition has been filed in court and the matter is placed before a judge, a parent's decision that visitation would not be in the child's best interest is accorded no deference. Section 26.10.160(3) contains no requirement that a court accord the parent's decision any presumption of validity or any weight whatsoever. Instead, the Washington statute places the best-interest determination solely in the hands of the judge. Should the judge disagree with the parent's estimation of the child's best interests, the judge's view necessarily prevails. Thus, in practical effect, in the State of Washington a court can disregard and overturn any decision by a fit custodial parent concerning visitation whenever a third party affected by the decision files a visitation petition, based solely on the judge's determination of the child's best interests. The Washington Supreme Court had the opportunity to give §26.10.160(3) a narrower reading, but it declined to do so. See, e.g., 137 Wash.2d, at 5, 969 P.2d, at 23 ("[The statute] allow[s] any person, at any time, to petition for visitation without regard to relationship to the child, without regard to changed circumstances, and without regard to harm"); id., at 20, 969 P.2d, at 30 ("[The statute] allow[s] 'any person' to petition for forced visitation of a child at 'any time' with the only requirement being that the visitation serve the best interest of the child"). Turning to the facts of this case, the record reveals that the Superior Court's order was based on precisely the type of mere disagreement we have just described and nothing more. The Superior Court's order was not founded on any special factors that might justify the State's interference with Granville's fundamental right to make decisions concerning the rearing of her two daughters. To be sure, this case involves a visitation petition filed by grandparents soon after the death of their son—the father of Isabelle and Natalie—but the combination of several factors here compels our conclusion that §26.10.160(3), as applied, exceeded the bounds of the Due Process Clause.

First, the Troxels did not allege, and no court has found, that Granville was an unfit parent. That aspect of the case is important, for there is a presumption that fit parents act in the best interests of their children. As this Court explained in Parham: "[O]ur constitutional system long ago rejected any notion that a child is the mere creature of the State and, on the contrary, asserted that parents generally have the right, coupled with the high duty, to recognize and prepare [their children] for additional obligations. . . . The law's concept of the family rests on a presumption that parents possess what a child lacks in maturity, experience, and capacity for judgment required for making life's difficult decisions. More important, historically it has recognized that natural bonds of affection lead parents to act in the best interests of their children." 442 U.S., at 602 (alteration in original) (internal quotation marks and citations omitted). Accordingly, so long as a parent adequately cares for his or her children (i.e., is fit), there will normally be no reason for the State to inject itself into the private realm of the family to further question the ability of that parent to make the best decisions concerning the rearing of that parent's children. See, e.g., Flores, 507 U.S., at 304. The problem here is not that the Washington Superior Court intervened, but that when it did so, it gave no special weight at all to Granville's determination of her daughters' best interests. More importantly, it appears that the Superior Court applied exactly the opposite presumption. In reciting its oral ruling after the conclusion of closing arguments, the Superior Court judge explained:

"The burden is to show that it is in the best interest of the children to have some visitation and some quality time with their grandparents. I think in most situations a commonsensical approach [is that] it is normally in the best interest of the children to spend quality time with the grandparent, unless the grandparent, [sic] there are some issues or problems involved wherein the grandparents, their lifestyles are going to impact adversely upon the children. That certainly isn't the case here from what I can Super. Ct., Dec. 14, 19, 1994), p.213 (hereinafter Verbatim Report).

The judge's comments suggest that he presumed the grandparents' request should be granted unless the children would be "impact[ed] adversely." In effect, the judge placed on Granville, the fit custodial parent, the burden of disproving that visitation would be in the best interest of her daughters. The judge reiterated moments later: "I think [visitation with the Troxels] would be in the best interest of the children and I haven't been shown it is not in [the] best interest of the children." Id., at 214.

The decisional framework employed by the Superior Court directly contravened the traditional presumption that a fit parent will act in the best interest of his or her child. See Parham, supra, at 602. In that respect, the court's presumption failed to provide any protection for Granville's fundamental constitutional right to make decisions concerning the rearing of her own daughters. Cf., e.g., Cal. Fam. Code Ann. §3104(e) (West 1994) (rebuttable presumption that grandparent visitation is not in); Me. Rev. Stat. Ann., Tit. 19A, §1803(3)(1998) (court may award grandparent visitation if in best interest of child and "would not significantly interfere with any parent-child relationship or with the parent's rightful authority over the child"); Minn. Stat. §257.022(2)(a)(2) (1998) (court may award grandparent visitation if in best interest of child and "such visitation would not interfere with the parent-child relationship"); Neb. Rev. Stat. §43—1802(2) (1998) (court must find "by clear and convincing evidence" that grandparent visitation "will not adversely interfere with the parent-child relationship"); R. I. Gen. Laws §15—5—24.3(a)(2)(v) (Supp.1999) (grandparent must rebut, by clear and convincing evidence, presumption that parent's decision to refuse grandparent visitation was reasonable); Utah Code Ann. §30—5—2(2)(e) (1998) (same); Hoff v. Berg, 595 N. W. 2d 285, 291—292 (N. D. 1999) (holding North Dakota grandparent visitation statute unconstitutional because State has no "compelling interest in presuming visitation rights of grandparents to an unmarried minor are in the child's best interests and forcing parents to accede to court-ordered grandparental visitation unless the parents are first able to prove such visitation is not in the best interests of their minor child"). In an ideal world, parents might always seek to cultivate the bonds between grandparents and their grandchildren. Needless to say, however, our world is far from perfect, and in it the decision whether such an intergenerational relationship would be beneficial in any specific case is for the parent to make in the first instance. And, if a fit parent's decision of the kind at issue here becomes subject to judicial review, the court must accord at least some special weight to the parent's own determination. Finally, we note that there is no allegation that Granville ever sought to cut off visitation entirely. Rather, the present dispute originated when Granville informed the Troxels that she would prefer to restrict their visitation with Isabelle and Natalie to one short visit per month and special holidays. See 87 Wash. App., at 133, 940 P.2d, at 699; Verbatim Report 12. In the Superior Court proceedings Granville did not oppose visitation but instead asked that the duration of any visitation order be shorter than that requested by the Troxels. While the Troxels requested two weekends per month and two full weeks in the summer, Granville asked the Superior Court to order only one day of visitation per month (with no overnight stay) and participation in the Granville family's holiday celebrations. See 87 Wash. App., at 133, 940 P.2d, at 699; Verbatim Report 9 ("Right off the bat we'd like to say that our position is that grandparent visitation is in the best interest of the children. It is a matter of how much and how it is going to be structured") (opening statement by Granville's attorney). The Superior Court gave no weight to Granville's having assented to visitation even before the filing of any visitation petition or subsequent court intervention. The court instead rejected Granville's proposal and settled on a middle ground, ordering one weekend of visitation per month, one week in the summer, and time on both of the petitioning grandparents' birthdays. See 87 Wash. App., at 133—134, 940 P.2d, at 699; Verbatim Report 216—221. Significantly, many other States expressly provide by statute that courts may not award visitation unless a parent has denied (or unreasonably denied) visitation to the concerned third party. See, e.g., Miss. Code Ann. §93—16—3(2)(a) (1994) (court must find that "the parent or custodian of the child unreasonably denied the grandparent visitation rights with the child"); Ore. Rev. Stat. §109.121(1)(a)(B) (1997) (court may award visitation if the "custodian of the child has denied the grandparent reasonable opportunity to visit the child"); R. I. Gen. Laws §15—5—24.3(a)(2)(iii)—(iv) (Supp. 1999) (court must find that parents prevented grandparent from visiting grandchild and that "there is no other way the petitioner is able to visit his or her grandchild without court intervention"). Considered together with the Superior Court's reasons for awarding visitation to the Troxels, the combination of these factors demonstrates that the visitation order in this case was an unconstitutional infringement on Granville's fundamental right to make decisions concerning the care, custody, and control of her two daughters. The Washington Superior Court failed to weight. In fact, the Superior Court made only two formal findings in support of its visitation order. First, the Troxels "are part of a large, central, loving family, all located in this area, and the [Troxels] can provide opportunities for the children in the areas of cousins and music." App. 70a. Second, "[t]he children would be benefitted from spending quality time with the [Troxels], provided that that time is balanced with time with the childrens' [sic] nuclear family." Ibid. These slender findings, in combination with the court's announced presumption in favor of grandparent visitation and its failure to accord significant weight to Granville's already having offered meaningful visitation to the Troxels, show that this case involves nothing more than a simple disagreement between the Washington Superior Court and Granville concerning her children's best interests. The Superior Court's announced reason for ordering one week of visitation in the summer demonstrates our conclusion well: "I look back on some personal experiences We always spen[t] as kids a week with one set of grandparents and another set of grandparents, [and] it happened to work out in our family that [it] turned out to be an enjoyable experience. Maybe that can, in this family, if that is how it works out." Verbatim Report 220—221. As we have explained, the Due Process Clause does not permit a State to infringe on the fundamental right of parents to make childrearing decisions simply because a state judge believes a "better" decision could be made. Neither the Washington nonparental visitation statute generally—which places no limits on either the persons who may petition for visitation or the circumstances in which such a petition may be granted—nor the Superior Court in this specific case required anything more. Accordingly, we hold that §26.10.160(3), as applied in this case, is unconstitutional.

Because we rest our decision on the sweeping breadth of §26.10.160(3) and the application of that broad, unlimited power in this case, we do not consider the primary constitutional question passed on by the Washington Supreme Court—whether the Due Process Clause requires all nonparental visitation statutes to include a showing of harm or potential harm to the child as a condition precedent to granting visitation. We do not, and need not, define today the precise scope of the parental due process right in the visitation context. In this respect, we agree with Justice Kennedy that the constitutionality of any standard for awarding visitation turns on the specific manner in which that standard is applied and that the constitutional protections in this area are best "elaborated with care." Post, at 9 (dissenting opinion). Because much state-court adjudication in this context occurs on a case-by-case basis, we would be hesitant to hold that specific nonparental visitation statutes violate the Due Process Clause as a per se matter.1 (1993) (interpreting best-interest standard in grandparent visitation statute normally to require court's consideration of certain factors); *Williams* v. *Williams*, 256 Va. 19, 501 S. E. 2d 417, 418 (1998) (interpreting Virginia nonparental visitation statute to require finding of harm as condition precedent to awarding visitation). Justice Stevens criticizes our reliance on what he characterizes as merely "a guess" about the Washington courts' interpretation of §26.10.160(3). Post, at 2. Justice Kennedy likewise states that "[m]ore specific guidance should await a case in which a State's highest court has considered all of the facts in the course of elaborating the protection afforded to parents by the laws of the State and by the Constitution itself." Post, at 10. We respectfully disagree. There is no need to hypothesize about how the Washington courts might apply §26.10.160(3) because the Washington Superior Court did apply the statute in this very case. Like the Washington Supreme Court, then, we are presented with an actual visitation order and the reasons why the Superior Court believed entry of the order was appropriate in this case. Faced with the Superior Court's application of §26.10.160(3) to Granville and her family, the Washington Supreme Court chose not to give the statute a narrower construction. Rather, that court gave §26.10.160(3) a literal and expansive interpretation. As we have explained, that broad construction plainly encompassed the Superior Court's application of the statute. See supra, at 8—9. There is thus no reason to remand the case for further proceedings in the Washington Supreme Court. As Justice Kennedy recognizes, the burden of litigating a domestic relations proceeding can itself be "so disruptive of the parent-child relationship that the constitutional right of a custodial parent to make certain basic determinations for the child's welfare becomes implicated." Post at 9. In this case, the litigation costs incurred by

Granville on her trip through the Washington court system and to this Court are without a doubt already substantial. As we have explained, it is apparent that the entry of the visitation order in this case violated the Constitution. We should say so now, without forcing the parties into additional litigation that would further burden Granville's parental right. We therefore hold that the application of §26.10.160(3) to Granville and her family violated her due process right to make decisions concerning the care, custody, and control of her daughters.

Accordingly, the judgment of the Washington Supreme Court is affirmed. It is so ordered.

WEST VIRGINIA

§48-2B-1. Legislative findings; intent

The Legislature finds that circumstances arise where it is appropriate for circuit courts of this state to order that grandparents of minor children may exercise visitation with their grandchildren. The Legislature further finds that in such situations, as in all situations involving children, the best interests of the child or children are the paramount consideration. It is the express intent of the Legislature that the provisions for grandparent visitation that are set forth in this article are exclusive.

Custody: No statutory factors

WISCONSIN

880.155(3m)(a)

(a) Except as provided in par. (b), the court may not grant visitation privileges to a grandparent or stepparent under this section if the grandparent or stepparent has been convicted under s. 940.01 of the first-degree intentional homicide, or under s. 940.05 of the 2nd-degree intentional homicide, of a parent of the child, and the conviction has not been reversed, set aside or vacated.

880.155(3m)(b) (b)

Paragraph (a) does not apply if the court determines by clear and convincing evidence that the visitation would be in the best interests of the child. The court shall consider the wishes of the child in making the determination.

880.155(4) (4)

The court may issue any necessary order to enforce a visitation order that is granted under this section upon a showing of good cause.

880.155(4m) (4m) 880.155(4m)(a)

If a grandparent or stepparent granted visitation privileges with respect to a child under this section is convicted under s. 940.01 of the first-degree intentional homicide, or under s. 940.05 of the 2nd-degree intentional homicide, of a parent of the child, and the conviction has not been reversed, set aside or vacated, the court shall modify the visitation order by denying visitation with the child upon petition, motion or order to show cause by a person having custody of the child, or upon the court's own motion, and upon notice to the grandparent or stepparent granted visitation privileges.

767.24(3)

(3) Custody to agency or relative.

767.24(3)(a)

(a) If the interest of any child demands it, and if the court finds that neither parent is able to care for the child adequately or that neither parent is fit and proper to have the care and custody of the child, the court may declare the child to be in need of protection or services and transfer legal custody of the child to a relative of the child, as defined in s. 48.02 (15), to a county department, as defined under s. 48.02 (2g), or to a licensed child welfare agency. If the court transfers legal custody of a child under this subsection, in its order the court shall notify the parents of any applicable grounds for termination of parental rights under s. 48.415.

WYOMING

Chapter 7. Grandparents' visitation rights

20-7-101. Establishing grandparents' visitation rights

(a) A grandparent may bring an original action against any person having custody of the grandparent's minor grandchild to establish reasonable visitation rights to the child. If the court finds, after a hearing, that visitation would be in the best interest of the child and that the rights of the child's parents are not substantially impaired, the court shall grant reasonable visitation rights to the grandparent. In any action under this section for which the court appoints a guardian ad litem, the grandparent shall be responsible for all fees and expenses associated with the appointment.

(c) No action to establish visitation rights may be brought by a grandparent under subsection (a) of this section if the minor grandchild has been adopted and neither adopting parent is a natural parent of the child.

(d) In any action or proceeding in which visitation rights have been granted to a grandparent under this section, the court may for good cause upon petition of the person having custody or who is the guardian of the child, revoke or amend the visitation rights granted to the grandparent.

20-7-102. Establishing primary caregivers' visitation rights

(a) With notice or reasonable efforts to provide notice to the non custodial parent, a person may bring an original action against any person having custody of the child to establish reasonable visitation rights to the child if the person bringing the original action has been the primary caregiver for the child for a period of not less than six (6) months within the previous eighteen (18) months. If the court finds, after a hearing, that visitation would be in the best interest of the child and that the rights of the child's parents are not substantially impaired, the court shall grant reasonable visitation rights to the primary caregiver. In any action under this section for which the court appoints a guardian ad litem, the person bringing the original action under this section shall be responsible for all fees and expenses associated with the appointment.

(b) No action to establish visitation rights under subsection (a) of this section may be brought by a person related to the child by blood or by a person acting as primary caregiver for the child prior to the adoption of the minor child when neither adopting parent is related by blood to the child.

In any action or proceeding in which visitation rights have been granted to a primary caregiver under this section, the court may for good cause upon petition of the person having custody or who is the guardian of the child, revoke or amend the visitation rights granted to the primary caregiver.

Notes

Chapter 1

1. Alfred R. Radcliffe-Brown, *Structure and Function in Primitive Society,* (Glencoe, Illinois: Free Press, 1952), p.123.

2. Émile Durkheim, *The Elementary Forms of the Religious Life* (New York: Free Press, 1968), p. 171.

3. Robert E. L. Roberts, Leslie N. Richards, and Vern L. Bengston, "International Solidarity in Families: Untangling the Ties That Bind," in *Families: Intergenerational and Generational Connections*, ed. Susan K. Pfeifer and Marvin B. Sussman (New York: Haworth Press, 1991), p. 13.

4. Will Durant, *Ceasar and Christ: A History of Roman Civilization from Its Beginnings to A.D. 337* (New York: Simon and Schuster, 1944), p. 58.

5. Israel Abrahams, *Jewish Life in the Middle Ages* (Philadelphia: Jewish Publication Society, 1993), p. 219.

6. Ibid.

7. William B. Helmreich, *The World of the Yeshiva: An Intimate Portrait of Orthodox Jewry* (New York: Free Press, 1982).

8. Irving Howe, *World of Our Fathers* (New York: Simon and Schuster, 1976), p. 8.

9. Roland Lardinois, "The World Order and the Family Institution in India," in *A History of the Family,* ed. André Burguière (Cambridge: Belknap Press of Harvard University Press, 1996), p. 593.

10. Lala Lajpat Rai, *Unhappy India,* 2d ed. (New York: AMS Press, 1972), p. 198.

11. Thierry Bianquis,"The Family in Arab Islam," in *A History of the Family,* ed. André Burguière (Cambridge: Belknap Press of Harvard University Press, 1996), p. 633.

12. Will Durant, *The Age of Faith: A History of Medieval Civilization— Christian, Islamic, and Judaic—From Constantine to Dante: A.D. 325–1300* (New York: MJF Books, 1950), p. 220.

13. Patrick Beillevaire, "The Family: Instruments and Model of the Japanese Nation," in *A History of the Family*, ed. André Burguière (Cambridge: Belknap Press of Harvard University Press, 1996), p. 242.

14. Nancy Foner, *Ages in Conflict: A Cross Cultural Perspective, on Inequality between Old and Young* (New York: Columbia University Press, 1984), p. 158.

15. Ibid., p. 35.

16. Philip Mayer, "Witches," in *Witchcraft and Sorcery, Selected Readings*, ed. Max Marwick (Baltimore, Md.: Penguin, 1970), p. 55.

17. Narayan Sastry, "The Importance of International Demographic Research for the United States," *Population Research and Policy Review* 19, no. 3 (June 2000): 100.

18. Altina L. Waller, *Feud: Hatfields, McCoys, and Social Change in Appalachia, 1860–1900* (Chapel Hill: University of North Carolina Press, 1988).

19. Bruce Catton, "Union Leadership and Discipline in the Civil War," *Marine Corps Gazette,* 40 (January 1965):18–25.

20. Wilhelm Reich, *The Mass Psychology of Fascism*, trans. Vincent R. Carfagno (New York: Farrar, Strauss and Giroux, 1970), p. 53.

21. Ibid.

22. Maxine Baca Zinn and D. Stanley Eitzen, "Economic Restructuring and Systems Inequality," in *Race, Class and Gender: An Anthology*, 3rd ed., ed. Margaret L. Anderson and Patricia Hill Collins (Belmont, Calif.: Wadsworth, 1998), p. 233.

23. William J.Goode, *World Revolution and Family Patterns* (New York: Free Press of Glencoe, 1963).

24. U.S. Bureau of the Census, *Statistical Abstracts of the United States, 1994,* 114th ed. (Washington, D.C.: United States Government Printing Office, 1994).

25. Historical Poverty Tables, Table 3: Poverty Status of People, by Age, Race, and Hispanic Origin: 1959–2000, U.S. Bureau of the Census Web Site, www.census.gov/hhes/poverty/histpov/hstpov3.html.

26. Gerhard Falk, *Hippocrates Assailed: The American Health Delivery System* (Lanham, Md.: University Press of America, 1999), p. 309.

27. Studs Terkel, *Hard Times: An Oral History of the Great Depression* (New York: Pantheon, 1970), pp.1–6.

28. Morgana Bruner and the Editors of *Time, The Time Almanac, 1999* (New York: Time-Life, 1998), pp. 885 and 797.

29. David Hackett Fischer, *Growing Old in America* (New York: Oxford University Press, 1978), p. 88.

30. Ursula A. Falk and Gerhard Falk, *Ageism, the Aged and Aging in America* (Springfield, Ill.: Charles C. Thomas, 1997), p. 91.

31. Administration on Aging, *Profile of Older Americans: 1997* (Washington, D.C.: Department of Health and Human Services, 1997).

32. Fischer, *Growing Old in America,* p. 119.

33. Jack Levin and William C. Levin, *Ageism: Prejudice and Discrimination against the Elderly* (Belmont, Calif.: Wadsworth, 1980), p. 78.

34. Ibid.

Chapter 2

1. U.S. National Center for Health Statistics, *Monthly Vital Statistics Report* 47, no. 25 (October 1999).

2. Paul Uhlenberg, "Grandparenthood over Time," in *Handbook on Grandparenthood*, ed. Maximiliane E. Szinovacz (Westport, Conn.: Greenwood Press, 2000), pp. 23–39.

3. Ralph Thomlinson, *Population Dynamics: Causes and Consequences of World Demographic Change* (New York: Random House, 1965), p. 116.

4. M. P. Atkinson and B. L. Glass, "Marital Age Heterogamy and Homogamy," *Journal of Marriage and the Family* 47, no. 3 (1985): 685–92.

5. U.S. National Center for Health Statistics, *Vital Statistics of the United States* (Washington, D.C.: U.S. Government Printing Office, 1999), p. 126.

6. Carole Haber and Brian Gratton, *Old Age and the Search for Security: An American Social History* (Bloomington: Indiana University Press, 1993), p. 43.

7. Maximiliane E. Szinovacz, "Living with Grandparents: Variations by Cohort, Race, and Family Structure," *International Journal of Sociology and Social Policy* 16, no. 2 (1996): 88–121.

8. Kyriakos Markides and Stanley Black, "Race, Ethnicity, and Aging: The Impact of Inequality," in *Handbook of Aging and the Social Sciences*, 4th ed., ed. Robert H. Binstock and Linda K. George (San Diego: Academic Press, 1996), pp. 153–170.

9. Vern L. Bengston and Robert A. Harootyan, eds., *Intergenerational Linkages: Hidden Connections in American Society* (New York: Springer, 1994).

10. Kenneth Roberto and John Stoes, "Grandchildren and Grandparents: Roles, Influence, and Relationships," *Intergenerational Journal of Aging and Human Development* 34 (1992): 227–39.

11. Andrew J. Cherlin and Frank F. Furstenberg Jr., *The New American Grandparent: A Place in the Family, A Life Apart* (New York: Basic Books, 1986), p. 37.

12. Merrill Silverstein and Jeffery D. Long, "Trajectories of Grandparents' Perceived Solidarity with Adult Grandchildren: A Growth Curve Analysis over 23 Years," *Journal of Marriage and the Family* 60, no. 4 (November 1998): 922.

13. Terry L. Mills, "When Grandchildren Grow Up: Role Transition and Family Solidarity among Baby Boomers' Grandchildren and Their Grandparents," *Journal of Aging Studies* 13, no. 2 (1999): 219.

14. Karen L. Fingerman, "The Good, the Bad, and the Worrisome: Emotional Complexities in Grandparents' Experiences with Individual Grandchildren," *Family Relations* 47, no. 4 (October 1998): 403.

15. Bernice Neugarten and Katherine Weinstein, "The Changing American Grandparent," *Journal of Marriage and the Family* 26, no. 2 (1964): 201.

16. Candida Peterson, "Grandfathers' and Grandmothers' Satisfaction with the Grandparenting Role: Seeking New Answers to New Questions," *International Journal of Aging and Human Development* 49, no. 1 (1999): 76.

17. Jeff Brazil, "You Talking to Me?" *American Demographics* 20, no. 12 (December 1998): 56.

18. "The Elderly As Caregivers," *Futurist* 33, no. 9 (November 1999): 13.

19. Thomas A. Lugaila, "Marital Status and Living Arrangements: March 1997," *Current Population Reports, Population Characteristics*, Series P-20, no. 514 (1998): 105.

20. Margaret P. Jendrick, "Grandparents Who Parent Their Grandchildren," *Gerontologist* 34, no. 4 (1994): 206.

21. Nancy M. Pinson et al., "Grandparents Raising Grandchildren," *Journal of Counseling and Development* 74, no. 6 (July/August 1996): 548.

22. Bonita F. Bowers and Barbara J. Myers, "Grandmothers Providing Care for Grandchildren: Consequences of Various Levels of Caregiving," *Family Relations* 48, no. 3 (July 1999): 303.

23. Ariel Kalil et al., "Effect of Grandmother Coresidence and Quality of Family Relationships on Depressive Symptoms in Adolescent Mothers," *Family Relations* 47, no. 4 (October 1998): 433.

24. Ibid., p. 440.

25. Nazli Baydar and Jeanne Brooks-Gunn, "Profiles of Grandmothers Who Help Care for Their Grandchildren in the United States," *Family Relations* 47, no. 4 (October 1998): 385.

26. Laura Landry Meyer, "Research into Action: Recommended Intervention Strategies for Grandparent Caregivers," *Family Relations* 47, no. 4 (October 1998): 387.

27. Deborah M. Whitley et al., "Strengths-Based Case Management: The Application to Grandparents Raising Grandchildren," *Journal of Contemporary Human Services* 80, no. 2 (March/April 1999): 110.

28. Roberta G. Sands and Robin S. Goldberg-Glen, "Factors Associated with Stress among Grandparents Raising Their Grandchildren," *Family Relations* 49, no. 1 (January 2000): 97.

29. Ann R. Pebley and Laura L. Rudkin, "Grandparents Caring for Grandchildren," *Journal of Family Issues* 20, no. 2 (March 1999): 218.

30. Cynthia Cannon Poindexter and Nathan L. Linsk, "Stories of Seven African-American Grandmothers," *Journal of Gerontological Social Work* 33, no. 1 (September 1999): 65.

31. Ibid., p. 63

32. Denise Burnette, "Social Relationships of Latino Grandparent Caregivers," *Gerontologist* 39, no. 1 (February 1999): 49.

33. Denise Burnette, *How to Best Reach and Assist Minority Grandparents Raising Their Grandchildren* (Washington, D.C.: American Association of Retired Persons, 1997), pp. 27–28.

34. Meredith Minkler and Esme Fuller-Thomson, "The Health of Grandparents Raising Grandchildren: Results of a National Study," *American Journal of Public Health* 89, no. 9 (September 1999): 1384.

35. Ibid., p. 1386.

36. Denise Burnette, "Custodial Grandparents in Latino Families: Patterns of Service Use and Predictors of Unmet Needs," *Social Work* 44, no. 1 (January 1999): 22.

37. John W. Wright, John B. Wright, and Virginia Norey, eds., *The New York Times 2000 Almanac* (New York: Penguin, 1999), p. 374.

38. U.S. House of Representatives, 102d Congress, Subcommittee on Human Services, Select Committee on Aging, *Grandparents: New Roles and Responsibilities*, Comm. Pub. No. 102–876 (Washington, D.C.: U.S. Government Printing Office, 1992), p. 187.

39. Vermont Statute tit. 15, sec. 1013(b).

40. Montana Code sec. 40-9-102.

41. House of Representatives, *Grandparents: New Roles and Responsibilities*, p. 187.

42. California Civil Code sec. 4600 (6) (West 1983 & Comm. Supp. 1990).

43. Richard S. Victor, Michael A. Robbins, and Scott Bassett, "Statutory Review of Third-Party Rights Regarding Custody, Visitation, and Support," *Family Law Quarterly* 25, no. 1 (spring 1991): 20.

44. "Supreme Court Strikes Down Grandparents' Visitation Rights," *Buffalo News*, June 7, 2000, p. A7.

45. Meredith Minkler, "Intergenerational Households Headed by Grandparents," *Journal of Aging Studies* 13, no. 2 (summer 1999): 199.

46. Leatha Lamison-White, *Poverty in the United States* (Washington, D.C.: Bureau of the Census, 1997), p. 160.

47. *Operations Handbook: Foster Grandparents Program* (Washington, D.C.: Federal Domestic Volunteer Agency, 1989).

48. Generations Together: An Intergenerational Studies Program Web site, www.gt.pitt.edu.

49. Arthur Kornhaber, *Contemporary Grandparenting* (Thousand Oaks, Calif.: Sage Publications, 1996), p. 196.

Chapter 3

1. Susan M. Kettmann, *The 12 Rules of Grandparenting: A New Look at Traditional Roles and How to Break Them* (New York: Checkmark Books, 2000), p. 19.

Chapter 5

1. George O. Hagestadt and Linda M. Burton, "Grandparenthood, Life Context and Family Development," *International Journal of Aging and Human Development* 43, no. 2 (December 1996): 135.

2. Jason L. Thomas, "The Grandparents Role: A Double Bind," *International Journal of Aging and Human Development* 31, no. 3 (November 1990): 169.

3. John W. Wright, John B. Wright, and Virginia Norey, eds., *The New York Times 2000 Almanac* (New York: Penguin, 1999), p. 296. See also Lynne M. Casper and Kenneth R. Bryson, *Co-resident Grandparents and Their Grandchildren: Grandparent-Maintained Families*, Population Working Paper #26 (Washington, D.C. U.S. Bureau of the Census, 1998).

4. John Aldous, "New View of Grandparents in Intergenerational Context," *Journal of Family Issues* 16, no. 1 (January 1995): 104–22.

5. Dorothy Chalfie, *Going It Alone: A Close Look at Grandparents Parenting Grandchildren* (Washington, D.C.: American Association of Retired Persons, 1994).

6. Jason DeParle, "As Welfare Rolls Shrink, Load on Relatives Grows," *New York Times*, July 28, 1998, Late New York Edition, p. F7.

7. More information about AIM is available online at www.takingaim.net.

8. Steven Crystal and Dorothy Shea, "Cumulative Advantage, Cumulative Disadvantage, and Inequality among Elderly People," *Gerontologist* 30, no. 4 (August 1990): 437.

9. Linda M. Burton, "Black Grandparents Rearing Children of Drug-Addicted Parents: Stressors, Outcomes, and Social Service Needs," *Gerontologist* 32, no. 6 (December 1992): 744–51.

10. Margie Johnson, Susan Goad, and Britt Canada, "Attitudes toward Nursing As Experienced by Nursing and Non-Nursing College Males," *Journal of Nursing Education* 23, no. 9 (November 1984): 387.

11. Meredith Minkler and Kathleen M. Roe, "Grandparents and Surrogate Parents," *Generations* 20, no. 1 (spring 1996): 34.

12. Meredith Minkler and Kathleen M. Roe, "Community Intervention to Support Grandparent Caregivers," *Gerontologist* 33, no. 6 (December 1993): 807–11.

13. Margaret P. Jendrick, "Grandparents Who Parent Their Grandchildren: Circumstances and Decisions," *Gerontologist* 34, no. 2 (April 1994): 206–16.

14. Paul L. Dressel and Sandra K. Barnhill, "Reframing Gerontological Thought and Practice: The Case of Grandmothers with Daughters in Prison," *Gerontologist* 34, no. 5 (October 1994): 685–91.

15. AARP Webplace, AARP Grandparent Information Center, www.aarp.org/confacts/programs/gic.html.

16. Renee S. Woodworth, "You're Not Alone—You're One in a Million," *Child Welfare* 75, no. 5 (September/October 1996): 620.

17. Ibid., p. 624.

18. Ibid., p. 629.

19. New York Public Health Law, sec. 2504.

20. New York Education Law, sec. 3212.

21. California Family Code, sec. 6550.

22. District of Columbia Code, sec. 16-4704.

23. *Troxel* v. *Granville*, 530 U.S. 57 (2000).

24. Ohio Revised Code, sec. 2151.01.

25. New York Social Services Law, sec. 384-b.

26. New York Domestic Relations Law, sec. 111.

27. Thomas S. Szasz, *The Myth of Mental Illness: Foundations of a Theory of Personal Conduct* (New York: Hoeber-Harper, 1961), p. 237.

28. Social Security Act, sec. 402(a)(1)(A), as amended by sec. 103(a) of Public Law No. 104-193.

29. 45 Code of Federal Regulations, sec. 205.10.

30. 42 Code of Federal Regulations, sec. 36.602.

31. Marcia D. Brown-Standridge and Caroline Walters Floyd, "Healing Bittersweet Legacies: Revisiting Contextual Family Therapy for Grandparents Raising Grandchildren in Crisis," *Journal of Marital and Family Therapy* 26, no. 2 (Arpil 2000): 185.

32. Ibid.

Chapter 6

1. Andrew Greeley, *Ethnicity in the United States: A Preliminary Reconnaissance* (New York: John Wiley and Sons, 1974), p.178.

2. Ibid.

3. Ibid.

4. Michèle Lamont, *The Cultural Territories of Race: Black and White Boundaries* (Chicago: University of Chicago Press, 1999), p. 384.

5. Irving Howe, *World of Our Fathers* (New York: Simon & Schuster, 1976), p. 244.

6. Ruth Landes and Mark Zborowski, "The Context of Marriage: Family Life As a Field of Emotions," in *Comparative Perspectives on Marriage and the Family*, ed. H. Kent Geiger (Boston: Little, Brown, 1968), p. 77.

7. Fred Kaplan, "Alleged Slur Can't Help As Mrs. Clinton Struggles to Win Over Jewish Voters," *Boston Globe*, July 18, 2000, p. A3.

8. Marvin S. Hill, "The Rise and Maturation of the Early Mormon Kingdom of God," in *Ethnic Families in America: Patterns and Variations*, 3rd ed., ed. Charles H. Mindel, Robert W. Habenstein, and Roosevelt Wright Jr. (New York: Elsevier, 1988), p. 381.

9. Ibid.

10. Timothy H. Brubaker and Carol M. Michael, "Amish Families in Later Life," in *Ethnic Dimensions of Aging*, ed. Donald E. Gelfand and Charles M. Barresi (New York: Springer, 1987), p. 109.

11. William M. Kephart and William W. Zellner, *Extraordinary Groups: An Examination of Unconventional Life-Styles*, 5th ed. (New York: St. Martin's Press, 1994), p. 35.

12. Ibid., p. 112.

13. U.S. Bureau of the Census, *Statistical Abstract of the United States: The National Data Book* (Washington, D.C.: U.S. Government Printing Office, 1992). Available online at www.census.gov/Press-Release/www/2002/cbo2cn59.html.

14. Matilda White Riley, "The Family in an Aging Society: A Matrix of Social Relationships," *Journal of Family Issues* 4, no. 3 (September 1983): 439.

15. Arthur Kornhaber and Kenneth L. Woodward, *Grandparents/Grandchildren: The Vital Connection* (New Brunswick, N.J.: Transaction Press, 1985), pp. 152–59.

16. Charlene Ramirez-Barranti, "The Grandparent/Grandchild Relationship: Family Resources in an Era of Voluntary Bonds," *Family Relations* 34, no. 3 (July 1985): 343.

17. M. G. Wong, "The Chinese American Families," in *Ethnic Families in America*, p. 230.

18. Charlotte Ikels, *Aging and Adaptation: Chinese in Hong Kong and the United States* (Hamden, Conn.: Archon Books, 1983), p. 226.

19. Wong, "The Chinese American Families," p. 231

20. Vicky Chiu-Wan Tan and Daniel E. Detzner, "Grandparents As a Family Resource in Chinese-American Families: Perceptions of the Middle Generation," in *Resiliency in Native American and Immigrant Families*, ed. Hamilton I. McCubbin et al. (Thousand Oaks, Calif.: Sage Publications, 1998), p. 243.

21. Leo Grebler, Joan W. Moore, and Ralph Guzman, *The Mexican-Amercan People, The Nation's Second Largest Minority* (New York: Free Press, 1970), p. 359.

22. Timothy H. Brubaker, ed., *Family Relationships in Later Life* (Beverly Hills, Sage Publications, 1983), p. 196.

23. Ibid.

24. David Alvirez and Frank D. Bean, "The Mexican American Family," in *Ethnic Families in America*, p. 279.

25. Diana Kendall, *Sociology in Our Times*, 3rd ed. (Belmont, Calif.; Thompson Learning, 2001), p. 321.

26. R. J. Taylor, "Aging and Supportive Relationships," in *The Black American Elderly: Research on Physical and Psychosocial Health*, ed. James S. Jackson (New York: Springer, 1988), p. 259.

27. George O. Hagestadt, "The Aging Society As a Context for Family Life," *Daedalus* 115, no. 1 (winter 1986): 119.

28. Kendall, *Sociology in Our Times*, p. 472.

29. C. P. M. Knipsheer, "Temporal Embeddedness and Aging within the Multigenerational Family: The Case of Grandparenting," in *Emergent Theories of Aging*, ed. James E. Birren and Vern L. Bengston (New York: Springer, 1988), p. 420.

30. T. W. Pullam, "The Eventual Frequencies of Kin in a Stable Population," *Demography* 19 (November 1982): 549.

31. Linda M. Burton and Vern L. Bengston, "Black Grandmothers: Issues of Timing and Meaning of Roles," in *Grandparenthood: Research and Policy Perspectives*, ed. Vern L. Bengston and Joan F. Robertson (Beverly Hills: Sage Publications, 1985), p. 61.

32. Charles H. Mindel, Roosevelt Wright Jr., and Ruth Starrett, "Informal and Formal Social and Health Service Use by Black and White Elderly: A Comparative Cost Approach," *Gerontologist* 26, no. 3 (June 1986): 279.

33. Kendall, *Sociology in Our Times*, p. 472.

34. Andrew J. Cherlin and Frank F. Furstenberg Jr., *The New American Grandparent: A Place in the Family, A Life Apart* (New York: Basic Books, 1986), p. 156.

35. Ibid., p. 164.

36. William Kornblum, in collaboration with Carolyn Smith, *Sociology in a Changing World*, 5th ed. (Fort Worth: Harcourt College Publishers, 2000), p. 427.

37. Sandra L. McGuire, "Reduce Ageism in Kids by Screening What They Read," *Childhood Education* 69 (summer 1993): 204–10.

38. Meredith Tupper, "The Representation of Elderly Persons in Primetime Television Advertisement" (master's thesis, University of South Florida, 1995).

39. More information about these programs is available online at www.seniorcorps.org.

Chapter 7

1. Robert N. Butler, *Why Survive? Being Old in America* (New York: Harper & Row, 1975), p. 13.

2. Edmond Grant, ed. *The Motion Picture Guide* (New York: Cine Books, 1996), p. 310.

3. Ibid.

4. Ibid.

5. Ibid., p. 104.

6. Ibid., p. 122.

7. Edmond Grant, ed., *The 1999 Motion Picture Guide* (New York: Cine Books, 1999).

8. Ibid. p. 199.

9. *Variety Film Reviews*, 24 vols. (New York: Garland Publishing, 1997), 12..

10. Ibid.

11. Ibid., 10.

12. Ibid., 9.

13. Ibid., 6.

14. Kenneth Munden, *American Film Institute Catalogue* (New York: R. R. Bowker, 1971), p. 430.

15. George Gerbner, "Learning Productive Aging As a Social Role: The Lessons of Television," in *Achieving a Productive Aging Society*, ed. Scott A. Bass, Francis G. Caro, and Yung-Ping Chen (Westport, Conn.: Auburn House, 1993), p. 207.

16. Robert N. Butler, Myrna I. Lewis, and Tray Sunderland, *Aging and Mental Health: Positive Psychosocial and Biomedical Approaches*, 4th ed. (New York: Merrill, 1991), p. 30.

17. Meredith Tupper, "The Representation of Elderly Persons in Prime-Time Television Advertising" (master's thesis, University of South Florida, 1995).

18. Ken Dychtwald and Joe Flower, *Age Wave: The Challenges and Opportunities of an Aging America* (Los Angeles: J. P. Tarcher, 1989), p. 268.

19. John J. Burnett, "Examining the Media Habits of the Affluent Elderly," *Journal of Advertising Research* 31, no. 5 (October–November 1991): 33.

20. Richard A. Davis and James A. Davis, *TV's Image of the Elderly: A Practical Guide for Change* (Lexington, Mass.: Lexington Books, 1985), p. 47.

21. John Bell, "In Search of a Discourse on Aging: The Elderly on Television," *Gerontologist* 12, no. 3 (June 1992): 305.

22. Gene D. Cohen, "Journalistic Elder Abuse: It's Time to Get Rid of Fictions, Get Down to Fact," *Gerontologist* 34, no. 3 (June 1994): 399.

23. Maria D. Vesperi, "Perspectives on Aging in Print Journalism," in *Changing Perceptions of Aging and the Aged*, ed. Dena Shenck and W. Andrew Achenbaum (New York: Springer, 1994), p. 163.

24. Michael Hilt, "Descriptive Analysis of News Magazines' Coverage of John Glenn's Return to Space," *Educational Gerontology* 26, no. 2 (March 2000): 161.

25. Charles Dickens, *Martin Chizzlewit* (New York: Browne, Hablot, Knight, 1882).

26. Marcel Proust, *Remembrance of Things Past* (New York: Random House, 1934).

27. Maurice Maeterlinck, *The Intruder,* in *An Anthology of Belgian Theatre*, ed. Bettina Knapp (Troy, N.Y.: Whitston Publishing, 1981).

28. Samuel Hopkins Adams, *Grandfather Stories* (New York: Random House, 1955).

29. Glenway Westcott, *The Grandmothers: A Family Portrait* (New York: Random House, 1927).

30. Conrad Richter, *The Grandfathers* (New York: Alfred Knopf, 1964).

31. Albert Ramsdell Gurney, *The Dining Room* (New York: Dramatic Play Service, 1982).

32. John Greenfield and Juliette Yakov, *Short Story Index 1994–1998* (New York: T. H. Wilson, 1999).

33. Johanna Spyri, *Heidi* (Mahwah, N.J.: Troll, 1988).

34. Valerie Flournoy, *The Patchwork Quilt* (New York: Dial Books for Young Readers, 1985).

35. Helen V. Griffith, *Grandaddy's Place* (New York: Greenwillow Books, 1987).

36. Amy Schwartz, *Oma and Bobo* (New York: Bradbury Press, 1987).

37. James Stevenson, *What's Under My Bed?* (New York: Greenwillow Books, 1983).

38. Eve Bunting, *The Wednesday Surprise* (New York: Clarion, 1989).

39. Eloise Greenfield, *Grandpa's Face* (New York: Philomel Books, 1988).

40. Holly Keller, *The Best Present* (New York: Greenwillow Books, 1989).

41. Evan Levine, *Not the Piano, Mrs. Medley!* (New York: Orchard Books, 1991).

42. Patricia MacLachlan, *Three Names* (New York: HarperCollins, 1991).

43. Patricia MacLachlan, *Journey* (New York: Delacorte, 1991).

44. Patricia Polacco, *Thunder Cake* (New York: Philomel Books, 1990).

45. M. E. Kerr, *Gentlehands* (New York: Harper & Row, 1978).

46. Cynthia Voigt, *Homecoming* (New York: Atheneum, 1981).

47. Bruce Brooks, *Everywhere* (New York: Harper & Row, 1990).

48. Dennis Hasley, *Shadows* (New York: Farrar, 1991).

49. Joseph Richman, "The Foolish and Wisdom of Age: Attitudes Toward the Elderly As Reflected in Jokes," *Gerontologist* 17, no. 3 (June 1977): 210.

50. D. Dwayne Smith, "The Portrayal of Elders in Magazine Cartoons," *Gerontologist* 19, no. 4 (December 1979): 401–12.

Chapter 8

1. Vern L. Bengston and Neal A. Cutler, "Generations and Intergenerational Relations," in *Handbook of Aging and the Social Sciences*, ed. Robert Binstock and Ethel Shanas (New York: Van Nostrand Reinhold, 1976), p. 174.

2. Glen H. Elder Jr., *Children of the Great Depression: Social Change in Life Experience* (Chicago: University of Chicago Press, 1974), p. 257.

3. Dean Hoge and Isadore Bender, "Factors Influencing Value Changes among College Graduates in Adult Life," *Journal of Personality and Social Psychology* 29, no. 4 (April 1974): 572.

4. Samuel Payne, David Summers, and Thomas R. Stewart, "Value Differences across Three Generations," *Sociometry* 36, no. 1 (March 1973): 20–30.

5. Nicolai D. Kondratieff, "The Long Waves in Economic Life," *Review of Economic Statistics* 17, no. 4 (November 1935): 105.

6. Milton Rokeach, *The Nature of Human Values* (New York: Free Press, 1973).

7. Gail Wilson, "Women's Work: The Role of Grandparents in Inter-generational Transfers," *Sociological Review* 35, no. 4 (1987): 703.

8. Louis Moss and Harvey H. Goldstein, *The Recall Method in Social Surveys* (London: University of London Press, 1979), p. 229.

9. Charles Bell, *Middle Class Families: Social and Geographical Mobility* (London: Routledge & Kegan Paul, 1968), p. 59.

10. M. Anne Hill and June O'Neill, "Family Endowment and the Achievement of Young Children with Special Reference to the Underclass," *Journal of Human Resources* 29, no. 4 (1994): 1064.

11. Kenneth A. Coleman, "The Value of Productive Activities of Older Americans," in *Older and Active: How Americans Over 55 Are Contributing to Society*, ed. Scott A. Bass (New Haven, Conn.: Yale University Press, 1995), pp. 169–203.

12. Ibid., p. 31.

13. Neal A. Cutler and Steven J. Devlin, "A Framework for Understanding Financial Responsibilities among Generations," *Generations* 20, no. 1 (spring 1996): 24.

14. Liora S. Findler, "The Role of Grandparents in the Social Support System of Mothers of Children with a Physical Disability," *Families in Society: The Journal of Contemporary Human Services* 81, no. 4 (July/August 2000): 370.

15. Colleen Leahy Johnson, *Ex Familia: Grandparents, Parents, and Children Adjust to Divorce* (New Brunswick, N.J.: Rutgers University Press, 1988), p. 92.

16. Joan Marie Kalter, "You're Forbidden to Visit Your Grandchildren," *New Choices for Retirement Living* 32, no. 9 (November 1992): 38.

17. Arthur Kornhaber, *Contemporary Grandparenting* (Thousand Oaks, Calif.: Sage Publications, 1996).

18. Betty G. Fishman and Leo Fishman, *The American Economy* (Princeton, N.J.: Van Nostrand, 1962), p. 398.

19. Jodie T. Allen, "The American Dream Tax," *U.S. News & World Report*, June 26, 2000, p. 22.

20. Charles Horton Cooley, *Human Nature and the Social Order* (1902; reprint, New York: Schocken Books, 1954), pp. 168–211

21. Ursula Adler Falk and Gerhard Falk, *Ageism, the Aged, and Aging in America* (Springfield, Ill.: Charles C. Thomas, 1997), p. 98.

Bibliography

Abrahams, Israel. *Jewish Life in the Middle Ages*. Philadelphia: Jewish Publication Society, 1993.

Adams, Samuel Hopkins. *Grandfather Stories*. New York: Random House, 1955.

Administration on Aging. *Profile of Older Americans: 1997*. Washington, D.C.: Department of Health and Human Services, 1997.

Aldous, John. "New View of Grandparents in Intergenerational Context." *Journal of Family Issues* 16, no. 1 (January 1995): 104–22.

Allen, Jodie T. "The American Dream Tax." *U.S. News & World Report*, June 26, 2000, p. 22.

Alvirez, David, and Frank D. Bean. "The Mexican American Family." In *Ethnic Families in America: Patterns and Variations*, edited by Charles H. Mindel and Robert W. Habenstein. New York: Elsevier, 1976.

Atkinson, M. P., and B. L. Glass. "Marital Age Heterogamy and Homogamy." *Journal of Marriage and the Family* 47, no. 3 (1985): 685–92.

Baydar, Nazli, and Jeanne Brooks-Gunn. "Profiles of Grandmothers Who Help Care for Their Grandchildren in the United States." *Family Relations* 47, no. 4 (October 1998): 385.

Beillevaire, "The Family: Instruments and Model of the Japanese Nation." In *A History of the Family*, edited by André Burguière. Cambridge: Belknap Press of Harvard University Press, 1996.

Bell, Colin. *Middle Class Families: Social and Geographical Mobility*. London: Routledge & Kegan Paul, 1968.

Bell, John. "In Search of a Discourse on Aging: The Elderly on Television." *Gerontologist* 12, no. 3 (June 1992): 305.

Bengston, Vern L., and Neal A. Cutler. "Generations and Intergenerational Relations." In *Handbook of Aging and the Social Sciences*, edited by Robert Binstock and Ethel Shanas. New York: Van Nostrand Reinhold, 1976.

Bengston, Vern L., and Robert A. Harootyan, eds. *Intergenerational Linkages: Hidden Connections in American Society.* New York: Springer, 1994.

Bianquis, Thierry. "The Family in Arab Islam." In *A History of the Family,* edited by André Burguière. Cambridge: Belknap Press of Harvard University Press, 1996.

Bowers, Bonita F., and Barbara J. Myers. "Grandmothers Providing Care for Grandchildren: Consequences of Various Levels of Caregiving." *Family Relations* 47, no. 4 (October 1998): 303.

Brazil, Jeff. "You Talking to Me?" *American Demographics* 20, no. 12 (December 1998): 56.

Brooks, Bruce. *Everywhere.* New York: Harper & Row, 1990.

Brown-Standridge, Marcia D., and Caroline Walters Floyd. "Healing Bittersweet Legacies: Revisiting Contextual Family Therapy for Grandparents Raising Grandchildren in Crisis." *Journal of Marital and Family Therapy* 26, no. 2 (April 2000): 185.

Brubaker, Timothy H., ed. *Family Relationships in Later Life.* Beverly Hills: Sage Publications, 1983.

Brubaker, Timothy H., and Carol M. Michael. "Amish Families in Later Life." In *Ethnic Dimensions of Aging,* edited by Donald E. Gelfand and Charles M. Barresi. New York: Springer, 1987.

Bruner, Morgana, and the Editors of *Time. The Time Almanac,* 1999. New York: Time-Life, 1998.

Bunting, Eve. *The Wednesday Surprise.* New York: Clarion, 1989.

Burnett, John J. "Examining the Media Habits of the Affluent Elderly." *Journal of Advertising Research* 31, no. 5 (October–November 1991): 33.

Burnette, Denise. "Custodial Grandparents in Latino Families: Patterns of Service Use and Predictors of Unmet Needs." *Social Work* 44, no. 1 (January 1999): 22.

———. *How to Best Reach and Assist Minority Grandparents Raising Their Grandchildren.* Washington, D.C.: American Association of Retired Persons, 1997.

———. "Physical and Emotional Well-Being of Custodial Grandparents in Latino Families." *American Journal of Orthopsychiatry* 69, no. 3 (July 1999): 305.

———. "Social Relationships of Latino Grandparent Caregivers." *Gerontologist* 39, no. 1 (February 1999): 49.

Burton, Linda M. "Black Grandparents Rearing Children of Drug-Addicted Parents: Stressors, Outcomes, and Social Service Needs." *Gerontologist* 32, no. 6 (December 1992): 744–51.

Burton, Linda M., and Vern L. Bengston. "Black Grandmothers: Issues of

Timing and Meaning of Roles." In *Grandparenthood: Research and Policy Perspectives*, edited by Vern L. Bengston and Joan F. Robertson. Beverly Hills: Sage Publications, 1985.

Butler, Robert N. *Why Survive? Being Old in America*. New York: Harper & Row, 1975.

Butler, Robert N., Myrna I. Lewis, and Tray Sunderland. *Aging and Mental Health: Positive Psychosocial and Biomedical Approaches*. 4th ed. New York: Merrill, 1991.

Catton, Bruce. "Union Leadership and Discipline in the Civil War." *Marine Corps Gazette* 40 (January 1965): 18–25.

Chalfie, Dorothy. *Going It Alone: A Close Look at Grandparents Parenting Grandchildren*. Washington, D.C.: American Association of Retired Persons, 1994.

Cherlin, Andrew J., and Frank F. Furstenberg Jr. *The New American Grandparent: A Place in the Family, A Life Apart*. New York: Basic Books, 1986.

Chiu-Wan Tan, Vicky, and Daniel E. Detzner. "Grandparents As a Family Resource in Chinese-American Families: Perceptions of the Middle Generation." In *Resiliency in Native American and Immigrant Families*, edited by Hamilton I. McCubbin, Elizabeth A. Thompson, Julie E. Fromer, and Anne I. Thompson. Thousand Oaks, Calif.: Sage Publications, 1998.

Cohen, Gene D. "Journalistic Elder Abuse: It's Time to Get Rid of Fictions, Get Down to Fact," *Gerontologist* 34, no. 3 (June 1994): 399.

Coleman, Kenneth A. "The Value of Productive Activities of Older Americans." In *Older and Active: How Americans Over 55 Are Contributing to Society*, edited by Scott A. Bass. New Haven, Conn.: Yale University Press, 1995.

Cooley, Charles Horton. *Human Nature and the Social Order.* 1902. Reprint, New York: Schocken Books, 1954.

Crystal, Steven, and Dorothy Shea. "Cumulative Advantage, Cumulative Disadvantage, and Inequality among Elderly People." *Gerontologist* 30, no. 4 (August 1990): 437.

Cutler, Neal A., and Steven J. Devlin. "A Framework for Understanding Financial Responsibilities among Generations." *Generations* 20, no 1 (spring 1996): 24.

Davis, Richard A., and James A. Davis. *TV's Image of the Elderly: A Practical Guide for Change*. Lexington, Mass.: Lexington Books, 1985.

Dickens, Charles. *Martin Chizzlewit.* New York: Browne, Hablot, Knight, 1882.

Dressel, Paul L., and Sandra K. Barnhill. "Reframing Gerontological Thought and Practice: The Case of Grandmothers with Daughters in Prison." *Gerontologist* 34, no. 5 (October 1994): 685–91.

Durant, Will. *The Age of Faith: A History of Medieval Civilization—Christian, Islamic, and Judaic—From Constantine to Dante: A.D. 325–1300.* New York: MJF Books, 1950.

———. *Caesar and Christ: A History of Roman Civilization from Its Beginnings to A.D. 337.* New York: Simon & Schuster, 1944.

Dychtwald, Ken, and Joe Flower. *Age Wave: The Challenges and Opportunities of an Aging America.* Los Angeles: J. P. Tarcher, 1989.

Elder, Glen H., Jr. *Children of the Great Depression: Social Change in Life Experience.* Chicago: University of Chicago Press, 1974.

"The Elderly As Caregivers." *Futurist* 33, no. 9 (November 1999): 13.

Falk, Gerhard. *Hippocrates Assailed: The American Health Delivery System.* Lanham, Md.: University Press of America, 1999.

Falk, Ursula A., and Gerhard Falk. *Ageism, the Aged, and Aging in America.* Springfield, Ill.: Charles C. Thomas, 1997.

Findler, Liora S. "The Role of Grandparents in the Social Support System of Mothers of Children with a Physical Disability." *Families in Society: The Journal of Contemporary Human Services* 81, no. 4 (July/August 2000): 370.

Fingerman, Karen L. "The Good, the Bad, and the Worrisome: Emotional Complexities in Grandparents' Experiences with Individual Grandchildren." *Family Relations* 47, no. 4 (October 1998): 403.

Fishman, Betty G., and Leo Fishman. *The American Economy.* Princeton, N.J.: Van Nostrand, 1962.

Fischer, David Hackett. *Growing Old in America.* New York: Oxford University Press, 1978.

Flournoy, Valerie. *The Patchwork Quilt.* New York: Dial Books for Young Readers, 1985.

Foner, Nancy. *Ages in Conflict: A Cross-Cultural Perspective on Inequality between Old and Young.* New York: Columbia University Press, 1984.

Gerbner, George. "Learning Productive Aging As a Social Role: The Lessons of Television." In *Achieving a Productive Aging Society,* edited by Scott A. Bass, Francis G. Caro, and Yung-Ping Chen. Westport, Conn.: Auburn House, 1993.

Goode, William J. *World Revolution and Family Patterns.* New York: Free Press of Glencoe, 1963.

Grant, Edmond, ed. *The Motion Picture Guide.* New York: Cine Books, 1996.

———. *The 1999 Motion Picture Guide.* New York: Cine Books, 1999.

Grebler, Leo, Joan W. Moore, and Ralph Guzman. *The Mexican-American People, The Nation's Second Largest Minority.* New York: Free Press, 1970.

Greeley, Andrew. *Ethnicity in the United States: A Preliminary Reconnaissance.*

New York: John Wiley and Sons, 1974.

Greenfield, Eloise. *Grandpa's Face.* New York: Philomel Books, 1988.

Griffith, Helen V. *Grandaddy's Place.* New York: Greenwillow Books, 1987.

Gurney, Albert Ramsdell. *The Dining Room.* New York: Dramatic Play Service, 1982.

Haber, Carole, and Brian Gratton. *Old Age and the Search for Security: An American Social History.* Bloomington: Indiana University Press, 1993.

Hagestadt, George O. "The Aging Society As a Context for Family Life." *Daedalus* 115, no. 1 (winter 1986): 119.

Hagestadt, George O., and Linda M. Burton. "Grandparenthood, Life Context and Family Development." *International Journal of Aging and Human Development* 43, no. 2 (December 1996): 135.

Hasley, Dennis. *Shadows.* New York: Farrar, 1991.

Helmreich, William B. *The World of the Yeshiva: An Intimate Portrait of Orthodox Jewry.* New York: Free Press, 1982.

Hill, M. Anne, and June O'Neill. "Family Endowment and the Achievement of Young Children with Special Reference to the Underclass." *Journal of Human Resources* 29, no. 4 (1994): 1064.

Hill, Marvin S. "The Rise and Maturation of the Early Mormon Kingdom of God." In *Utah: A Cooperative History*, edited by David Miller. Provo, Utah: Brigham Young University Press, 1976.

Hilt, Michael. "Descriptive Analysis of News Magazines' Coverage of John Glenn's Return to Space." *Educational Gerontology* 26, no. 2 (March 2000): 161.

Hoge, Dean, and Isadore Bender. "Factors Influencing Value Changes among College Graduates in Adult Life." *Journal of Personality and Social Psychology* 29, no. 4 (April 1974): 472–585.

Howe, Irving. *World of Our Fathers.* New York: Simon & Schuster, 1976.

Ikels, Charlotte. *Aging and Adaptation: Chinese in Hong Kong and the United States.* Hamden, Conn.: Archon Books, 1983.

Jendrick, Margaret P. "Grandparents Who Parent Their Grandchildren." *Gerontologist* 34, no. 2 (1994): 206–16

Johnson, Colleen Leahy. *Ex Familia: Grandparents, Parents, and Children Adjust to Divorce.* New Brunswick, N.J.: Rutgers University Press, 1988.

Johnson, Margie, Susan Goad, and Britt Canada. "Attitudes toward Nursing as Experienced by Nursing and Non-Nursing College Males." *Journal of Nursing Education* 23, no. 9 (November 1984): 387.

Kalter, Joan Marie. "You're Forbidden to Visit Your Grandchildren." *New Choices for Retirement Living* 32, no. 9 (November 1992): 38.

Kaplan, Fred. "Alleged Slur Can't Help As Mrs. Clinton Struggles to Win Over Jewish Voters." *Boston Globe*, July 18, 2000, p. A3.

Keller, Holly. *The Best Present.* New York: Greenwillow Books, 1989.

Kendall, Diana. *Sociology in Our Times.* 3rd ed. Belmont, Calif.: Thompson Learning, 2001.

Kephart, William M., and William M. Zellner. *Extraordinary Groups: An Examination of Unconventional Life-Styles.* 5th ed. New York: St. Martin's Press, 1994.

Kerr, M. E. *Gentlehands.* New York: Harper & Row, 1978.

Kettmann, Susan M. *The 12 Rules of Grandparenting: A New Look at Traditional Roles and How to Break Them.* New York: Checkmark Books, 2000.

Knipsheer, C. P. M. "Temporal Embeddedness and Aging within the Multigenerational Family: The Case of Grandparenting." In *Emergent Theories of Aging,* edited by James E. Birren and Vern L. Bengston. New York: Springer, 1988.

Kondratieff, Nicolai D. "The Long Waves in Economic Life." *Review of Economic Statistics* 17, no. 4 (November 1935): 105.

Kornblum, William, in collaboration with Carolyn Smith. *Sociology in a Changing World.* 5th ed. Fort Worth: Harcourt College Publishers, 2000.

Kornhaber, Arthur. *Contemporary Grandparenting.* Thousand Oaks, Calif.: Sage Publications, 1996.

Kornhaber, Arthur, and Kenneth L. Woodward. *Grandparents/Grandchildren: The Vital Connection.* New Brunswick, N.J.: Transaction Press, 1985.

Lajpat Rai, Lala. *Unhappy India.* 2d ed. New York: AMS Press, 1972.

Lamison-White, Leatha. *Poverty in the United States.* Washington, D.C.: Bureau of the Census, 1997.

Lamont, Michèle. *The Cultural Territories of Race; Black and White Boundaries.* Chicago: University of Chicago Press, 1999.

Landes, Ruth, and Mark Zborowski. "The Context of Marriage: Family Life As a Field of Emotions." In *Comparative Perspectives on Marriage and the Family,* edited by H. Kent Geiger. Boston: Little, Brown, 1968.

Lardinois, Roland. "The World Order and the Family Institution in India." In *A History of the Family,* edited by André Burguière. Cambridge: Belknap Press of Harvard University Press, 1996.

Levin, Jack, and William C. Levin. *Ageism, Prejudice and Discrimination against the Elderly.* Belmont, Calif.: Wadsworth, 1980.

Levine, Evan. *Not the Piano, Mrs. Medley!* New York: Orchard Books, 1991.

Lugaila, Thomas A. "Marital Status and Living Arrangements: March 1997." *Current Population Reports, Population Characteristics,* Series P-20, no. 514 (1998).

MacLachlan, Patricia. *Journey.* New York: Delacorte, 1991.

———. *Three Names.* New York: HarperCollins, 1991.

Maeterlinck, Maurice. *The Intruder.* In *An Anthology of Belgian Theatre*, edited by Bettina Knapp. Troy, N.Y.: Whitston Publishing, 1981.

Markides, Kyriakos, and Stanley Black. "Race, Ethnicity, and Aging: The Impact of Inequality." In *Handbook of Aging and the Social Sciences*, 4th ed., edited by Robert H. Binstock and Linda K. George. San Diego: Academic Press, 1996.

Mayer, Philip. "Witches." In W*itchcraft and Sorcery; Selected Readings*, edited by Max Marwick. Baltimore, Md.: Penguin, 1970.

Meyer, Laura Landry. "Research into Action: Recommended Intervention Strategies for Grandparent Caregivers." *Family Relations* 47, no. 4 (October 1998): 387.

Mills, Terry L. "When Grandchildren Grow Up: Role Transition and Family Solidarity among Baby Boomers." *Journal of Aging Studies* 13, no. 2 (1999): 219–239.

Mindel, Charles H., Roosevelt Wright Jr., and Ruth Starrett. "Informal and Formal Social and Health Service Use by Black and White Elderly: A Comparative Cost Approach." *Gerontologist* 26, no. 3 (June 1986): 230.

Minkler, Meredith. "Intergenerational Households Headed by Grandparents." *Journal of Aging Studies* 13, no. 2 (summer 1999): 199.

Minkler, Meredith, and Esme Fuller-Thomson. "The Health of Grandparents Raising Grandchildren: Results of a National Study." *American Journal of Public Health* 89, no. 9 (September 1999): 1384.

Minkler, Meredith, and Kathleen M. Roe. "Community Intervention to Support Grandparent Caregivers." *Gerontologist* 33, no. 2 (December 1993): 807–11.

———. "Grandparents and Surrogate Parents." *Generations* 20, no. 1 (spring 1996): 34.

Moss, Louis, and Harvey H. Goldstein. *The Recall Method in Social Surveys.* London: University of London Press, 1979.

Munden, Kenneth. *American Film Institute Catalogue.* New York: R. R. Bowker, 1971.

Neugarten, Bernice, and Katherine Weinstein. "The Changing American Grandparent." *Journal of Marriage and the Family* 26, no. 2 (1964): 201.

Operations Handbook: Foster Grandparents Program. Washington, D.C.: Federal Volunteer Agency, 1989.

Payne, Samuel, David Summers, and Thomas R. Stewart. "Value Differences across Three Generations." *Sociolmetry* 36, no. 1 (March 1973): 20–30.

Pebley, Ann R., and Laura L. Rudkin. "Grandparents Caring for Grandchildren." *Journal of Family Issues* 20, no. 2 (March 1999): 218.

Peterson, Candida. "Grandfathers' and Grandmothers' Satisfaction with the Grandparenting Role: Seeking New Answers to New Questions." *International Journal of Aging and Human Development* 49, no. 1 (1999): 76.

Pinson, Nancy M., Edward S. Fabian, N. K. Schlossberg, and Mary Pyle. "Grandparents Raising Grandchildren." *Journal of Counseling and Development* 74, no. 6 (July/August 1996): 548.

Poindexter, Cynthia Cannon, and Nathan L. Linsk. "Stories of Seven African-American Grandmothers." *Journal of Gerontological Social Work* 33, no. 1 (September 1999): 63.

Polacco, Patricia. *Thunder Cake*. New York: Philomel Books, 1990.

Proust, Marcel. *Remembrance of Things Past*. New York: Random House, 1934.

Pullam, T. W. "The Eventual Frequencies of Kin in a Stable Population." *Demography* 19 (November 1982): 549.

Radcliffe-Brown, Alfred R. *Structure and Function in Primitive Society, Essays and Addresses*. London: Cohen & West, 1952.

Ramirez-Barranti, Charlene. "The Grandparent/Grandchild Relationship: Family Resources in an Era of Voluntary Bonds." *Family Relations* 34, no. 3 (July 1985): 343.

Reich, Wilhelm. *Mass Psychology of Fascism*. Translated by Vincent R. Carfagno. New York: Farrar, Strauss & Giroux, 1970.

Richman, Joseph. "The Foolish and Wisdom of Age: Attitudes Toward the Elderly As Reflected in Jokes." *Gerontologist* 17, no. 3 (June 1977): 210.

Richter, Conrad. *The Grandfathers*. New York: Alfred Knopf, 1964.

Riley, Matilda White. "The Family in an Aging Society: A Matrix of Social Relationships." *Journal of Family Issues* 4, no. 3 (September 1983): 439.

Roberto, Kenneth, and John Stoes. "Grandchildren and Grandparents: Roles, Influence, and Relationships." *Intergenerational Journal of Aging and Human Development* 34 (1992): 227–39.

Roberts, Robert E. L., Leslie N. Richards, and Vern L. Benston. "Intergenerational Solidarity in Families: Untangling the Ties That Bind." In *Families: Intergenerational and Generational Connections*, edited by Susan K. Pfeifer and Marvin B. Sussman. New York: Haworth Press, 1991.

Rokeach, Milton. *The Nature of Human Values*. New York: Free Press, 1973.

Sands, Roberta G., and Robin S. Goldberg-Glen. "Factors Associated with Stress among Grandparents Raising Their Grandchildren." *Family Relations* 49, no. 1 (January 2000): 97.

Schwartz, Amy. *Oma and Bobo*. New York: Bradbury Press, 1987.

Silverstein, Merrill, and Jeffery D. Long. "Trajectories of Grandparents' Perceived Solidarity with Adult Grandchildren: A Growth Curve Analysis over 23 Years." *Journal of Marriage and the Family* 60, no. 4 (November 1998): 922.

Smith, D. Dwayne. "The Portrayal of Elders in Magazine Cartoons." *Gerontologist* 19, no. 4 (December 1979): 37.

Spyri, Johanna. *Heidi.* Mahwah, N.J.: Troll, 1988.

Stevenson, James. *What's Under My Bed?* New York: Greenwillow Books, 1983.

"Supreme Court Strikes Down Grandparents' Visitation Rights." *Buffalo News,* June 7, 2000, p. A7.

Szasz, Thomas S. *The Myth of Mental Illness: Foundations of a Theory of Personal Conduct.* New York: Hoeber-Harper, 1961.

Szinovacz, Maximiliane E. "Living with Grandparents: Variations by Cohort, Race, and Family Structure." *International Journal of Sociology and Social Policy* 16, no. 2 (1996): 88–121.

Taylor, R. J. "Aging and Supportive Relationships." In *The Black American Elderly: Research on Physical and Psychosocial Health,* edited by James S. Jackson. New York: Springer, 1988.

Terkel, Studs. *Hard Times: An Oral History of the Great Depression.* New York: Pantheon, 1970.

Thomas, Jason L. "The Grandparents Role: A Double Bind." *International Journal of Aging and Human Development* 31, no. 3 (November 1990): 169.

Thomlinson, Ralph. *Population Dynamics: Causes and Consequences of World Demographic Change.* New York: Random House, 1965.

Tupper, Meredith. "The Representation of Elderly Persons in Prime-Time Television Advertising." Master's thesis, University of South Florida, 1995.

Uhlenberg, Paul. "Grandparenthood over Time." In *Handbook on Grandparenthood,* edited by Maximiliane E. Szinovacz. Westport, Conn.: Greenwood Press, 2000.

U.S. Bureau of the Census. *Statistical Abstract of the United States: The National Data Book.* Washington, D.C.: U.S. Government Printing Office, 1992.

———. *Statistical Abstracts of the United States, 1994.* 114th ed. Washington, D.C.: U.S. Government Printing Office, 1994.

U.S. House of Representatives, 102d Congress, Subcommittee on Human Services, Select Committee on Aging. *Grandparents: New Roles and Responsibilities,* Comm. Pub. No. 102–876. Washington, D.C.: U.S. Government Printing Office, 1992.

U.S. National Center for Health Statistics. *Monthly Vital Statistics Report* 47, no. 25 (October 1999).

———. *Vital Statistics of the United States.* Washington, D.C.: U.S. Government Printing Office, 1999.

Vesperi, Maria D. "Perspectives on Aging in Print Journalism." In *Changing Perceptions of Aging and the Aged,* edited by Dena Shenck and W. Andrew Achenbaum. New York: Springer, 1994.

Victor, Richard S., Michael A. Robbins, and Scott Bassett. "Statutory Review of
    Third-Party Rights Regarding Custody, Visitation, and Support." *Family
    Law Quarterly* 25, no. 1 (spring 1999): 20.
Voigt, Cynthia. *Homecoming.* New York: Atheneum, 1981.
Waller, Altina L. *Feud: Hatfields, McCoys, and Social Change in Appalachia,
    1860–1900.* Chapel Hill: University of North Carolina Press, 1988.
Westcott, Glenway. *The Grandmothers: A Family Portrait.* New York: Random
    House, 1927.
Whitley, Deborah M., Kim R. White, Susan J. Kelley, and B. Beatrice Yorke.
    "Strengths-Based case Management: The Application to Grandparents
    Raising Grandchildren." *Journal of Contemporary Human Services* 80, no.
    2 (March/April 1999): 110.
Wilson, Gail. "Women's Work: The Role of Grandparents in Inter-generational
    Transfers." *Sociological Review* 35, no. 4 (1987): 703.
Wong, M. G. "The Chinese American Families." In *Ethnic Families in America:
    Patterns and Variations*, 3rd. ed., edited by Charles H. Mindel, Robert W.
    Habenstein, and Roosevelt Wright Jr. New York: Elsevier, 1988.
Woodworth, Renee S. "You're Not Alone—You're One in a Million." *Child Wel-
    fare* 75, no. 5 (September/October 1996): 620.
Wright, John W., John B. Wright, and Virginia Norey, eds. *The New York Times
    2000 Almanac.* New York: Penguin, 1999.
Zinn, Maxine Baca, and D. Stanley Eitzen. "Economic Restructuring and Sys-
    tems Inequality." In *Race, Class, and Gender: An Anthology*, 2d. ed., edited
    by Margaret L. Andersen and Patricia Hill Collins. Belmont, Calif.:
    Wadsworth, 1998.

Index